America's National Heritage Areas

A GUIDE TO THE NATION'S NEW KIND OF NATIONAL PARK

ROBERT MANNING

Globe Pequot

Guilford, Connecticut

Globe Pequot

An imprint of Globe Pequot, the trade division of The Rowman & Littlefield
Publishing Group, Inc.
4501 Forbes Blvd., Ste. 200
Lanham, MD 20706
www.rowman.com

Distributed by NATIONAL BOOK NETWORK

Front cover photos: (top left) Journey Through Hallowed Ground National
Heritage Area; (top right) Kenai Mountains-Turnagain Arm National Heritage
Area; (lower left) Champlain Valley National Heritage Partnership; (lower right)
Mormon Pioneer National Heritage Area

Back cover photos: (left) Mountains to Sound Greenway National Heritage Area;
(center) Journey Through Hallowed Ground National Heritage Area; (right)
Maritime Washington National Heritage Area

British Library Cataloguing in Publication Information Available

Library of Congress Cataloging-in-Publication Data Available

978-1-4930-6066-5 (paper)
978-1-4930-6067-2 (electronic)

♾️™ The paper used in this publication meets the minimum requirements of
American National Standard for Information Sciences—Permanence of Paper for
Printed Library Materials, ANSI/NISO Z39.48-1992.

America's National Heritage Areas

Civil War sites such as Shiloh Battlefield are well represented in the national heritage areas (Tennessee Civil War National Heritage Area).

Many national heritage areas offer outstanding opportunities for hiking and other forms of outdoor recreation (Blue Ridge National Heritage Area).

NOTE TO READERS

The names of National Heritage Areas (NHAs) can take several forms. Most begin with a place name that signals where they're located (e.g., Baltimore) or the name of the primary topic they address (e.g., Crossroads of the American Revolution). This name is then followed by "National Heritage Area." In the examples above, the full name of these NHAs is Baltimore National Heritage Area and Crossroads of the American Revolution National Heritage Area.

However, it's sometimes a little more complicated. For example, two NHAs begin with the name of a person who was instrumental in establishing and supporting them; an example is Maurice D. Hinchey Hudson River Valley National Heritage Area. And some NHAs use variations on the term "National Heritage Area." For instance, the Illinois and Michigan Canal is the primary focus of an NHA in Illinois, but its official title is Illinois and Michigan Canal National Heritage Corridor, referencing its long, linear geography that follows the canal over its 100-mile length. While these variations can be a little confusing, try not to let them distract you. You'll find the official name of each NHA in the Table of Contents, on the map of all NHAs on pages x and xi, and on the title page of each of the chapters that describe them.

To address these variations in names and to reduce the redundancy of using the full, official names of NHAs each time they're noted, the text in this book uses two conventions. First, all NHAs are referred to as "NHA"s, even when their official name might be National Heritage Corridor or some other construction. Second, the official name of each NHA is used the first time it's mentioned, but it's shortened to the operative descriptive name of the area after that. For example, Baltimore National Heritage Area becomes "Baltimore," and Maurice D. Hinchey Hudson River Valley National Heritage Area becomes "Hudson River Valley."

Independence National Historical Park and the Liberty Bell help tell the story of American freedom and democracy (Schuykill River Greenways National Heritage Area).

CONTENTS

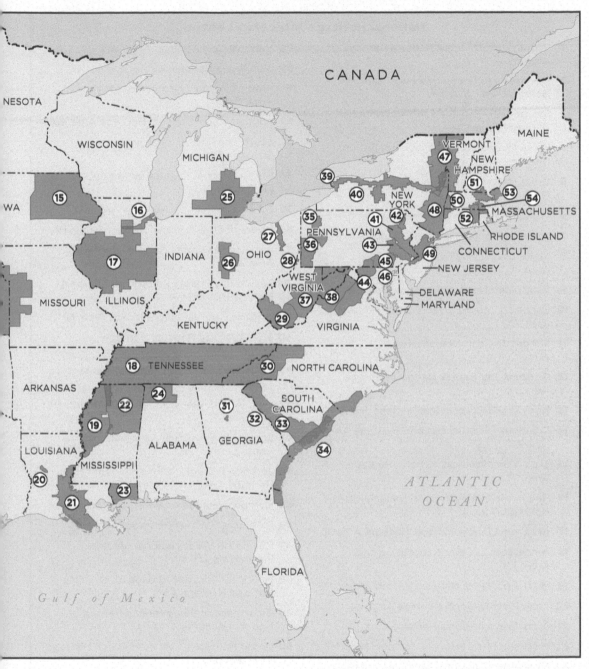

America's National Heritage Areas
See Map Legend on page xii.

National Heritage Sites Map Legend

1 Maritime Washington National Heritage Area, WA

2 Mountains to Sound Greenway National Heritage Area, WA

3 Sacramento-San Joaquin Delta National Heritage Area, CA

4 Kenai Mountains–Turhagain Arm National Heritage Area, AK

5 Great Basin National Heritage Area, NV & UT

6 Yuma Crossing National Heritage Area, AZ

7 Mormon Pioneer National Heritage Area, UT

8 Santa Cruz Valley National Heritage Area, AZ

9 South Park National Heritage Area, CO

10 Cache La Poudre River National Heritage Area, CO

11 Sangre de Cristo National Heritage Area, CO

12 Northern Rio Grande National Heritage Area, NM

13 Northern Plains National Heritage Area, ND

14 Freedom's Frontier National Heritage Area, KS & MO

15 Silos & Smokestacks National Heritage Area, IA

16 Illinois and Michigan Canal National Heritage Area, IL

17 Abraham Lincoln National Heritage Area, IL

18 Tennessee Civil War National Heritage Area, TN

19 Mississippi Delta National Heritage Area, MS

20 Cane River National Heritage Area, LA

21 Atchafalaya National Heritage Area, LA

22 Mississippi Hills National Heritage Area, MS

23 Mississippi Gulf Coast National Heritage Area, MS

24 Muscle Shoals National Heritage Area, AL

25 MotorCities National Heritage Area, MI

26 National Aviation Heritage Area, OH

27 Canalway National Heritage Area, OH

28 Wheeling National Heritage Area, WV

29 National Coal Heritage Area, WV

30 Blue Ridge National Heritage Area, NC

31 Arabia Mountain National Heritage Area, GA

32 Augusta Canal National Heritage Area, GA

33 South Carolina National Heritage Corridor, SC

34 Gullah Geechee Cultural Heritage Corridor, FL, GA, SC, NC

35 Oil Region National Heritage Area, PA

36 Rivers of Steel National Heritage Area, PA

37 Appalachian Forest National Heritage Area, WV

38 Shenandoah Valley Battlefields National Historic District, VA

39 Niagara Falls National Heritage Area, NY

40 Erie Canalway National Heritage Corridor, NY

41 Delaware and Lehigh National Heritage Corridor, PA

42 Lackawanna Valley National Heritage Area, PA

43 Schuylkill River Greenways National Heritage Area, PA

44 Journey Through Hallowed Ground National Heritage Area, VA, WV, PA, MD

45 Susquehanna National Heritage Area, PA

46 Baltimore National Heritage Area, MD

47 Champlain Valley National Heritage Partnership, NY & VT

48 Maurice D. Hinchey Hudson River Valley National Heritage Area, NY

49 Crossroads of the American Revolution National Heritage Area, NJ

50 Upper Housatonic Valley National Heritage Area, MA & CT

51 Freedom's Way National Heritage Area, MA & NH

52 The Last Green Valley National Heritage Corridor, MA & CT

53 Essex National Heritage Area, MA

54 John H. Chafee Blackstone River Valley National Heritage Corridor, MA & RI

PART I:
NATIONAL
HERITAGE AREAS

Some readers will be familiar with National Heritage Areas (NHAs), but most probably won't, and that's too bad. This book is designed to help remedy that situation by offering readers a guide to America's large and growing system of NHAs; most of the book is devoted to descriptions of the nation's NHAs, including the remarkable natural and cultural history they protect and the educational and recreational opportunities they offer. But first, let's take a little time to learn more about NHAs. While they're a lot like their better known cousins, national parks, they're also different in important ways. So what are NHAs? How do they work? And why are they important? Part I of this book answers these and related questions. It also outlines how you can find, enjoy, and appreciate much of America's natural and cultural history in the NHAs and how to use this guidebook.

A New Kind of National Park

Welcome to America's National Heritage Areas! NHAs are relatively new places and they're not yet well known among the public; count yourself fortunate to have discovered them now, before so many others ultimately will. NHAs are much like national parks, except they're different. Does that sound like Yogi Berra? President Ronald Reagan said it better; at the dedication of the first NHA in 1984, he presciently noted to those in attendance that they were helping to establish "a new kind of national park." Fast forward to today and there's now a system 55 NHAs scattered around the nation. NHAs are typically large areas—sometimes even vast expanses—that reflect the sense of place of these distinctive regions, including their natural and cultural history, educational offerings, and outstanding collections of visitor attractions and recreation opportunities.

While NHAs aren't really national parks, they're close cousins. Jon Jarvis, recent Director of the National Park Service (NPS), echoed this idea when he spoke of NHAs as "part of the family." In official bureaucratic language NHAs are "related areas" of the NPS which describes them as "linked in importance and purpose to places managed directly by the National Park Service by preserving important segments of the nation's natural and cultural heritage." NHAs receive some (limited) funds from the NPS and, perhaps more importantly, a ready supply of technical assistance and related guidance. Both national parks and NHAs can only be established by Congress. Moreover, national parks and NHAs share a strong sense of purpose;

1

The lovely and historic Santa Cruz Valley includes dramatic expanses of grasslands in southern Arizona (Santa Cruz Valley National Heritage Area).

their conservation, education, and recreation related objectives echo one another.

But the methods employed by NHAs to achieve these objectives are different—very different—than those used in conventional national parks. National parks are generally large areas of public land owned and managed by the NPS. NHAs take a more inclusive, partnership-based approach; they offer non-profit organizations, private enterprise, interested citizens, and all levels of government the opportunity to help define, celebrate, conserve, and share the natural, historic, cultural, scenic, and recreational resources that have been vital in shaping the identity and destiny of the regions within their borders. Perhaps NHAs might best be described as "parknerships." Moreover, NHAs are composed primarily of private lands; they're "living landscapes" where residents live, work, and play.

NHAs are much like the national parks found in many other countries, particularly in Europe where the population density is high compared to the US, and it's especially challenging to find large areas of public lands. Instead, these national parks include a mix of public and private lands, even including whole communities. Jon Jarvis, former Director of the US NPS, once said that "America invented the idea of national parks, the idea went around the world, and it came back different." The US can benefit from the experience of other countries in establishing these new kinds of national parks.

Before establishment, Congress must be convinced that NHAs are (or can become) cohesive, distinctive, and nationally important landscapes organized around history, environment, industry, geography, and/or other themes. In other words, NHAs must be recognizable "places." This assurance often

Baltimore's visitor-friendly Inner Harbor is one the nation's first urban redevelopment projects and is a powerful draw for both residents and visitors; national heritage areas include a mix of public and private lands (Baltimore National Heritage Area).

requires a feasibility study that may lead to establishment of an NHA by Congress. Once established, NHAs must conserve the resources that are important to their identity while balancing community needs for sustainable economic development that commonly focuses on heritage-based education, recreation, and tourism. This program of work must be guided by a management plan. NHAs are usually managed (actually, the word "coordinated" is often preferred) by a local partner organization, usually a local non-profit, that is entrusted with planning and management responsibility. Many NHAs include units of the National Park System, but private land is generally not acquired by the federal government for the purposes of NHAs.

An Expanded Democratic Ideal

NHAs are an important manifestation of the evolution of national parks and the underlying character of their democratic ideal. Yellowstone became America's first national park (and the world's inaugural national park as well) in 1872, the first time a nation set aside a large area of its land "for the benefit and enjoyment of the people" (as stated in the enlightened legislation that established the park). In this way, Yellowstone and subsequent national parks are foundational manifestations of the American concept of democracy.

Because there was no NPS until 1916, the US Army managed Yellowstone and other early national parks with little or no input from the public. Even after establishment of the NPS, the agency closely managed the national parks in a manner that's defined primarily by the language of the agency's 1916 Organic Act that set forth its management objectives; these objectives require that the parks be preserved, but that they also be available for public enjoyment and appreciation. However, starting in the middle part of the 20th century, some new units of the National Park System began to adopt a more aggressively democratic and partnership-based approach to park management, especially where new parks were created in places that were predominately private rather than public lands, places like Cape Cod National Seashore. In addition to the area's public parks and beaches, this unit of the National Park System includes several towns that help protect the region's ecological, historical, and scenic integrity through participation in a regional advisory council, development of local land use regulations, economic incentives, and other means. More recently, NHAs have further advanced the notion of democracy in park management by enabling local citizens groups to help identify the resources and values that define their communities, and to help craft a grassroots program of planning, management, and coordination designed to ensure protection of the integrity of these resources and community values.

A Large Landscape-Scale Approach to Conservation

NHAs and their bottom-up, partnership-based approach to parks have other important characteristics and qualities that recommend them to the future of effective conservation and sustainable heritage-based tourism. For example, they advance the cause of a large landscape-scale approach to conservation. Modern ecological knowledge, such as the wide geographic range needed by many prominent wildlife species, highlights the need for coordinated environmental management across large regional environments, land management agencies, and public and private landowners. Wildlife in Yellowstone National Park—grizzly bears, wolves, and bison, for example—tend to wander in and out of the park and are vulnerable when outside the park. This suggests that most conventional national parks are far too small and insular to be fully effective. The same integrated and coordinated regional approach is required to tell coherent historical and cultural stories as well. It's challenging, for example, to effectively tell the story of the American Civil War by focusing on just a few isolated historic sites. However, obstacles of limited public land ownership, along with multiple and often conflicting objectives of landowners, too often frustrate effective NPS natural and cultural conservation programs.

NHAs can help solve this problem by building partnerships among public and private landowners in large regions of the country. Moreover, this can diminish the need for very large public land ownership, drastically reducing the costs of effective conservation. Management of NHAs typically requires relatively little federal funding (perhaps a few hundred thousand dollars annually); moreover, this funding must usually be matched by non-federal dollars, and federal funding is usually designed to sunset for NHAs after an initial period of about 10 years. In these ways, NHAs are seen as a means to extend the reach of the conservation objectives of national parks in a coordinated and remarkably efficient and effective manner.

In keeping with their potential to conserve natural and cultural resources at a landscape scale, most NHAs are large—even very large. For example, Tennessee Civil War NHA is more than 42,000 square miles, larger than five of the New England states combined. Northern Rio Grande National Heritage Area includes 10,000 square miles of north central New Mexico and is nearly three times the size of Yellowstone National Park. Even in the east, where most national parks tend to be relatively small, some NHAs are large; for example, Champlain Valley National Heritage Partnership is nearly 9,000 square miles. This size encourages and facilitates planning and management that encompasses much of the geographic scope of natural and cultural landscapes; in such large areas, it's more feasible to protect natural features and processes (e.g., the habitat of wide-ranging wildlife species) and to tell coherent stories of American history (e.g., the Civil War). The size advantage of NHAs is amplified by the fact that many are directly adjacent to one another. Examples include Sangre de Christo and Northern Rio Grande (Colorado and New Mexico), Great Basin and Mormon Pioneer (Nevada

Many National Heritage Areas are very large; Susquehanna National Heritage Area pictured here is eight times the size of Yellowstone National Park.

and Utah), and large clusters of NHAs in the Southeast and Northeast/New England.

NHAs have advanced programs that magnify this large-scale approach to conservation even further. For example, Operation Pollination is a large-scale effort across multiple NHAs and their partners to reverse the decline of pollinators such as bees, butterflies, and bats; these pollinators are vital to flowering plants, but have been endangered by pesticides, invasive species, and habitat loss. Participating NHAs and their partners sign a pledge to support pollinators by planting a pollinator garden, holding educational programs, and raising awareness about this issue. Nearly all NHAs also belong to the Alliance of National Heritage Areas that shares information on effective conservation and community-led sustainable heritage-based tourism programs through workshops, publications, and annual conferences.

A Coordinated System of National Parks and National Heritage Areas

Of course, conservation of natural and cultural history can be accomplished through both conventional national parks and NHAs, as well as innovative combinations of these approaches. For example, in large landscape conservation efforts, conventional national parks—environmentally and culturally sensitive lands that are managed by the NPS—may be needed as the core of large, integrated landscapes, and sizable buffer areas of mixed ownership properties—in the form of NHAs—add to the probability of successful conservation management. Conservation of the large region of the Great Basin geographic province that constitutes much of the American West and Southwest takes this form; Great Basin National Park in Nevada is the core area of nearly 80,000 acres owned and closely managed by the NPS, and this is complimented by the vast—more than 10 million-acre—Great Basin National Heritage Area that links the park to surrounding national forests, tribal lands, and numerous small communities in the states of Nevada and Utah. Other examples include the NPS site, Cane River Creole National Historical Park, and Cane River NHA, and the NPS site, Blackstone River Valley National Historical Park, and John H. Chafee Blackstone River Valley National Heritage Corridor.

In an analogous way, the telling of coherent and meaningful stories of history and culture is more effective when it can draw directly on the large regional contexts from

Great Basin National Park is the core of the much larger Great Basin National Heritage Area.

which these stories emanate. For example, in the case of the Illinois & Michigan Canal NHA described at the beginning of this chapter, this history-changing nearly 100-mile engineering project, a grand manifestation of America's 19th-century Industrial Revolution, can best be interpreted and appreciated in its entirety, as opposed to an isolated historic site and/or museum. This strategy requires and is enriched by a mosaic of public, private, and non-profit lands and organizations, the kinds of places found in America's NHAs.

Balancing Conservation, Education, and Recreation

National parks have strong conservation, education, and recreation-related objectives. As defined by the Organic Act of 1916 that established the NPS, national parks are to "conserve the scenery and the natural historic objects and the wildlife therein," but also to "provide for the enjoyment of the same" through education and recreation. Balancing these sometimes conflicting objectives of conservation and use can be challenging. NHAs have similar objectives,

but balance conservation and use through sustainable programs of heritage-based education, recreation, and tourism. Some of the funds for these programs come from NPS grants to NHAs, and NPS review of these grants helps ensure that they contribute to conservation. Moreover, successful programs of heritage-based tourism raise funds for NHAs and their partners that can be invested in conservation-related initiatives. Based on this model, NHAs develop and maintain visitor attractions such as parks, historic sites, museums, festivals, living history programs, trails, scenic drives, and much more.

Education and the Power of Place

Many Americans know that the national parks have famously been called "America's best idea," a reference to writer and conservationist Wallace Stegner's essay arguing that national parks are such an important manifestation of American democracy. More recently, the national parks are also being called "America's classroom," referencing the ways in which the parks are increasingly being used to teach students at all levels about the nation's natural and cultural history. American schools and colleges are revolutionizing their curricula to include high-impact practices—real life case studies, internships, field and work trips, summer jobs—that focus on student engagement with real places and problems.

The educational programs of the NPS have been an important component of its mission from its very beginning. NPS rangers in their signature "flat hats" are the traditional public face of the parks, telling stories around the campfire, taking visitors on nature walks, and generally "interpreting"

This reenactment of the Civil War battle at Gettysburg is an example of the "power of place" as an education tool (Journey Through Hallowed Ground National Heritage Area).

the natural and cultural history of the parks to its wide-eyed visitors. The national parks are the envy of many teachers for their power to engage. NHAs are powerful extensions of this educational mission, using their nationally significant cultural landscapes and natural and cultural history—their power of place—to educate both residents and visitors about the role these places play in America's history and future.

NHAs extend the educational role of the national parks in both formal and informal contexts. The experience and expertise of NHAs in building partnerships—with schools, historic sites, museums, national parks, and more—add to this power of place. Moreover, the remarkable diversity of the system of NHAs (read more about this below) and their lived-in landscapes magnify their potential to connect and engage with such a wide variety of people and places.

Community Pride and Wellbeing

NHAs are a source of pride for those who live within them. These are places that have distinctive natural and cultural histories that make significant contributions to the larger American story; Congress has recognized these places as important to the nation. Moreover, the people who live near and care about these places have had the wisdom and foresight to protect this heritage and the generosity to share it with others, and this should add to community pride. The array of attractions in NHAs—history, culture, education, recreation—should contribute to the quality of life for those who live there. And, of course, the sustainable programs of heritage-based tourism that are an integral part of all NHAs contribute to the economic wellbeing of the community and its residents.

Efficiency and Effectiveness

It was noted earlier that NHAs have a reputation for being an efficient and effective way of protecting the natural and cultural history of the regions they help manage, of offering an array of educational and recreational attractions, and of developing thriving heritage-based tourism programs. And the numbers back this up. The latest figures report the activities of NHAs for 2020 and they're impressive. The 55 NHAs received a modest $20.9 million from the federal government (these funds are allocated by the NPS) and leveraged this with $88.5 million in funds and in-kind services from a variety of other sources. They engaged with more than 8,000 formal and informal partners and benefited from the work of more than 23,000 volunteers, an estimated $10.1 million value. Nearly 247 historic sites and more than 8,600 acres of cultural landscapes were preserved and maintained. Nearly 150 recreation projects were undertaken, more than 500 miles of trails were maintained, 64 miles of new trails were developed, and NHAs made recreation grants to partners totaling nearly $600,000. All NHAs are periodically evaluated to help ensure their efficiency and effectiveness.

Contributions to Diversity

By definition, NHAs are grassroots efforts to define and protect the cultural heritage of distinctive regions, and this has led to a focus on diversity, equity, and inclusion. The Alliance of National Heritage Areas (noted above) defines diversity as "meaningful representation of different groups in cultural heritage development, included but not limited to race, age, gender identity, sexual orientation, physical/mental ability, ethnicity, geography, and perspective." Equity is defined as "policies and practices that help communities gain access to opportunity, networks, and resources toward reaching their full cultural heritage potential." And inclusion is defined as "authentic engagement of diverse groups in cultural heritage development, providing all community members with a genuine sense of belonging."

The success of this commitment to diversity is evident in the bold new array of cultural landscapes found in so many NHAs—the heritage associated with the use of the nation's vast coal and oil deposits; the steel, railroad, aircraft, and automobile industries; development of the blues, rock and roll, and other new forms of music; the evolution of American agriculture; the birth of the American Industrial Revolution, and the emergence of Gullah Geechee, Cajun, and Creole cultures. And this is why NHAs celebrate such a wide array of American

National heritage areas celebrate American history but are careful to address the conflicts and issues that have troubled the nation as well; National Coal Heritage Area in West Virginia, for example, tells the story of how and why miners organized strikes for better working conditions.

triumphs such as the Declaration of Independence, the Hudson River School painters, the Appalachian Trail, the literature of William Faulkner and Louisa May Alcott, and the philosophy of Henry David Thoreau, but also commemorate the tragedy of slavery, the Trail of Tears, the brutal murder of Emmett Till, the Japanese internment camps of World War II, and the sometimes violent struggle for fairness by the United Automobile Workers and the United Farm Workers. This approach helps ensure conservation of a rich diversity of natural and cultural landscapes and candid dialogue on difficult, even painful topics. NHAs complement the traditional focus of many national parks that are more representative of what has been called the "great men, great events" approach.

The "new kind of national park" represented by NHAs has also helped bring parks to a greater diversity of people, especially those who live in urban areas. Since NHAs don't require large tracts of public land, it's easier to establish them in areas where most land is already in private ownership. NHAs are living landscapes—places where people live, work, and play—and are more conducive to urban and urban-proximate areas.

From National Parks to National Heritage Areas

Visitors to NHAs may sometimes assume they're in national parks. As noted above, national parks and NHAs share foundational objectives. NHAs often look a lot like national parks and act like them too (though the non-governmental status of nearly all NHA management entities allows them to be more innovative and agile). They help conserve nationally important cultural landscapes and offer a host of associated visitor attractions. Like national parks, many have visitor centers (or sometimes share visitor centers with the NPS). Examples include the lovely National Park Service Regional Visitor Center in Salem, Massachusetts, that serves the region's NPS sites and the larger Essex NHA, Appalachian Forest NHA's Appalachian Forest Discovery Center in the

Many national heritage areas bring parks to the people in the nation's population centers (Maritime Washington National Heritage Area).

historic Darden Mill, and the Blackstone Valley Heritage Corridor Visitor Center at Blackstone River Valley NHA. Most NHAs offer visitor "passports" and stamps that can be obtained at attraction sites (many national park and NHA visitors enjoy collecting these stamps in their passports), some NHAs have "rangers" who offer interpretive programs to visitors, just like national parks, and some even have junior rangers programs which are traditional favorites of younger visitors to the national parks. In a very pragmatic way, President Reagan was right when he welcomed establishment of the first NHA as "a new kind of national park."

Some observers think NHAs are a revolution in the definition and management of parks, even a new paradigm, but others believe they're more of an evolution. However, there's little doubt that there's a global trend toward the model of parks represented by NHAs, parks that include a wider range of participants, encompass a broader scale of size and topics, and address lived-in landscapes. They go by different names in the various regions of the world—"greenline" parks, reserves, preserves, and NHAs are probably the most well-known in Europe and the United States. None of this obviates the need for national parks as they've been conventionally defined in the United States; in fact, national parks and NHAs nicely complement one another. Visit the NHAs and see for yourself.

A Growing System of National Heritage Areas

The first NHA was established in 1984, and at this writing, there are 55 NHAs (though one is currently inactive). This number will

Journey Through Hallowed Ground National Heritage Area began with a grassroots movement to protect Manassas Battlefield.

increase as several regions are currently awaiting designation, and more are certain to apply. As noted earlier, both national parks and NHAs are established by Congress, but this process is often driven by public involvement. Establishment of many national parks was influenced by citizens who devoted much time, energy, and love to this cause. Examples include John Muir's determined efforts to establish Yosemite National Park and Marjorie Stoneman Douglas's work in the cause of Everglades National Park.

NHAs have magnified this grassroots approach. For example, in the early 1990s, a theme park was proposed near Virginia's Civil War Manassas Battlefield where Confederate forces won a solid victory over the Union at great expense to both armies. Historians and concerned citizens worried that a theme park would desecrate this important

historic site, a part of the National Park System. Organizations of citizens, including the National Trust for Historic Preservation, the Civil War Trust, the Piedmont Environmental Council, and Scenic America joined forces in an effort to protect the area around Manassas Battlefield and many of the other significant sites that make up the especially rich cultural landscapes of the larger region. Through these efforts, Journey Through Hallowed Ground NHA was established in 2008. This 180-mile-long, up to 75-mile-wide swath of land through four states, from Gettysburg in the north to Monticello in the south, tells a holistic story of many of our nation's early leaders and the conflicts the country has faced.

Abraham Lincoln NHA is another good example. Here, a group of local citizens in central Illinois came together in 1998 to form the non-profit group, Looking for Lincoln Heritage Coalition, to discover, document, and tell the story of their most famous resident who helped guide our nation through some of its most difficult years. After 10 years of hard but rewarding work, Abraham Lincoln NHA was established by Congress. This is a big NHA, 43 counties in central Illinois, where Lincoln lived from his early 20s, raising his family and pursuing his passion for law and politics. This NHA uniquely tells Lincoln's compelling story by adding the context and backdrop of his life, including the people and places that shaped him in matters of unity, equality, race, and democracy; central Illinois is where he developed the courage and wisdom to lead the nation through the Civil War years.

Similarly, in 1990, a group of local citizens hiked from Snoqualmie Pass in Washington's Cascade Mountains to the shores of Puget Sound to highlight their vision for preserving this scenic corridor in the face of booming regional development. Soon after, the Mountains to Sound Greenway Trust, a non-profit organization, was formed to help make this dream come true. Over the next three decades, the Greenway Trust led a coalition of non-profit, business, and government leaders who worked together to conserve public lands, restore native habitat, and connect an expansive network of trails across what is now known as Mountains to Sound Greenway NHA. The Greenway is an iconic 1.5-million-acre cultural landscape that spans three watersheds and extends nearly 100 miles from Seattle and Puget Sound on the west, across the Cascade Mountains, and on to Ellensburg and Central Washington in the east. With hard work and broad support from local people (including the area's Native American tribes), and the area's Congressional delegation, Mountains to Sound Greenway NHA was established by Congress in 2019. Collectively, the NHAs are a new kind of national park system that's driven more directly by the people who live, work, and play there—tens of millions of them—in these nationally important regions.

Discovering America in the National Heritage Areas

Like the National Park System, the growing system of National Heritage Areas is remarkably diverse. NHAs are found throughout much of the nation, from urban areas to the wilds of Alaska. Moreover, they include many of the most iconic examples of our nation's natural and cultural history; these are the places that Americans themselves have identified and are working hard to protect and share, places that are representative of our natural environment, our history and culture, and our sweeping system of recreation

Alaska's Kenai Mountains include glaciers and the nation's largest icefield (Kenai Mountains-Turnagain Arm National Heritage Area).

opportunities. Searching for America? Find it in the National Heritage Areas.

Geography

NHAs are scattered across the nation and the system of NHAs continues to grow. A large number of NHAs are clustered in the Northeast and Southeast, but those in the Midwest and West tend to be larger. Some NHAs are in or around large urban areas. For example, Baltimore NHA includes much of the city with an emphasis on its historic and active port, Fort McHenry and the birth of the Star-Spangled Banner, as well as the contributions of the area's African American population to the city's rich history and culture. Other NHAs with strong urban connections include Chicago (Illinois and Michigan Canal NHA), Seattle (Maritime Washington NHA), Atlanta (Arabia Mountain NHA), and Detroit (MotorCities NHA). Other NHAs are rural; examples include The Last Green Valley NHA and Upper Housitonic Valley NHA in quiet corners of New England, the three NHAs in Mississippi, and Northern Plains NHA in North Dakota. Some are farther out on the rural end of the spectrum: drive "the loneliest road in America" at Great Basin NHA and enjoy the solitude this NHA offers with its 16,000 square miles (larger than many states) and fewer than 25,000 residents. Still not rural enough? Visit the many wilderness areas found within the system of NHAs, including Alaska's Kenai Mountains-Turnagain Arm NHA.

Nature

There are many ways to describe the natural diversity found in America's system of

American's coastlines are well represented in the system of national heritage areas (Maritime Washington National Heritage Area).

NHAs. Consider, for example, major natural features—mountains, valleys, rivers, seashores—that help define the national landscape. Several NHAs include portions of the country's major mountain ranges. South Park NHA, for example, lies in the geographic center of Colorado and features a high-elevation grassland basin surrounded by the dramatic peaks of the Rocky Mountains, several rising to more than 14,000 feet. Other mountain ranges represented in the NHAs include the Appalachians (Appalachian

Rhododendron decorate the hillsides in spring at Blue Ridge National Heritage Area.

Forest NHA), Adirondacks (Champlain Valley NHA), Blue Ridge Mountains (Blue Ridge NHA), Cascades (Mountains to Sound Greenway NHA), and the Sangre de Christos (Northern Rio Grande NHA). At some NHAs you'll find impressive glaciers and icefields mixed in with the mountains; at Alaska's Kenai Mountains-Turnagain Arm NHA, for example, visitors can hike to the edge of the Harding Icefield, an astonishing 700 square miles of ice, the largest such natural phenomenon in the nation.

Major American rivers in the NHAs include the Mississippi, Colorado, Rio Grande, Susquehanna, Tennessee, and Missouri. At Mississippi Delta NHA, visitors can explore the river's signature natural feature, the massive Mississippi River Delta— 200 miles long and nearly 90 miles wide, an area of nearly 7,000 square miles. Yuma Crossing NHA sits hard on the banks of the Colorado River; this legendary waterway is 1,400 miles long, drains much of the American Southwest, carved the Grand Canyon, and now provides water and power to millions of people in seven southwestern states.

NHAs highlight a host of other natural features. Examples include the dramatic desert lands of Santa Cruz Valley NHA and the lovely and historic valley at aptly named The Last Green Valley NHA, an 1,100-square-mile island of green in densely populated Connecticut and Massachusetts. Some of the last remaining expanses of America's Great Plains can be found at North Dakota's Northern Plains NHA and Iowa's Silos and Smokestacks NHA. Dramatic coastlines are featured at Maritime Washington NHA (a staggering 3,000 miles of Pacific Ocean coast), and South Carolina NHA, marked by

an expanse of the region's coastal salt marshes, estuaries, natural harbors, and islands.

The system of NHAs is highly biodiverse and includes habitat for an enormous variety of plants and animals. Iconic examples include thousand-year-old cypress trees and majestic oaks draped in Spanish moss at Atchafalaya NHA, ancient bristlecone pines at Great Basin NHA, a 20,000-acre preserve of restored tall grass prairie (including a resident herd of bison) at Illinois and Michigan Canal NHA, old-growth rainforests at Maritime Washington NHA, and vast forests of giant saguaro cactuses at Santa Cruz Valley NHA. Alpine meadows light up with spring and summer wildflowers in the mountains of Olympic National Park, part of Maritime Washington NHA, and hillsides are covered in flowering rhododendron and mountain laurel at Blue Ridge NHA. Interesting and iconic animals also populate NHAs; examples include mountain lions (Northern Rio Grande NHA), alligators (Atchafalaya NHA), golden eagles (Cache la Poudre River NHA), elk (Blue Ridge NHA), grizzly bears (Kenai Mountains-Turnagain Arm NHA), and wild salmon (Mountains to Sound Greenway NHA).

History

Of course, the nation's rich history complements its natural resources. One way to think about American history is to divide it into important periods, and most are well-represented in the nation's system of NHAs. Of course, all NHAs had thousands of years of prehistory and many offer insights to the people who lived there during this period. Many groups of Native Americans are represented in NHAs; there are 18 federally

The Taos Pueblo in Northern Rio Grande National Heritage Area allows contemporary Native Americans to tell their story.

recognized tribes at Maritime Washington NHA alone. Shell middens at Susquehanna NHA and burial mounds at Mississippi Hills NHA, Silos and Smokestacks NHA, and Muscle Shoals NHA are silent messengers of native people from the prehistoric past. Present-day Native Americans tell their own fascinating stories at the magical pueblos in Northern Rio Grande NHA and on reservations in other NHAs.

Unfortunately, native peoples were treated very poorly by European-American settlers and the US government, both of which assumed ownership of native lands and broke treaties that had been negotiated in good faith. The Indian Removal Act of 1862 banished tribes of Native American people to western reservations; the infamous Trail of Tears, the forced relocation of the Cherokee from the Appalachian Mountains

to a reservation in what would become the State of Oklahoma, is acknowledged at Blue Ridge NHA and several others. The Bismarck-Mandan Railroad Bridge across the Upper Missouri River in Northern Plains NHA signifies the taking of Indian land for construction of an intercontinental railroad; this significant place is now an International Site of Conscience.

Recorded history begins with Spanish, French, and other explorers in North America and this is recognized in several NHAs, including Mississippi Gulf Coast and Santa Cruz Valley. Early American settlement began in the first part of the 17th century and is represented by the group of Puritans who landed on the shores of "New England," and this story is told *in situ* at Essex NHA. Early American settlement continued along the coast and expanded inland to the

Appalachian Mountains and is well represented at Blue Ridge NHA. Great Smoky Mountains National Park is a part of this NHA and the park's Cades Cove area features a recreated early American settlement. Later, the period of American expansion moved farther west and this story is told at Silos and Smokestacks NHA and Northern Plains NHA. The Homestead Act of 1862 promised 160 acres of land and a better life, attracting immigrants from Europe and other parts of the world to America's frontier territories. This period is marked by the historic Lewis and Clark Expedition that spent the winter of 1803 at what is now Northern Plains NHA; here the expedition added Sacagawea, a 16-year-old Shoshone girl, as a liaison to Native American tribes.

The American Revolution was fought from 1775-1783 and this story is richly told and illustrated at many NHAs, marking the very places where this history occurred. Elements of the Revolution include the

The bitter winter encampment of General George Washington's Continental Army in 1779-80 is one of many pivotal American Revolutionary War sites in the national heritage areas (Crossroads of the American Revolution National Heritage Area).

Declaration of Independence, the US Constitution, Independence Hall, the Liberty Bell, "the shot heard round the world," the bitterly cold winter encampment of General George Washington's Continental Army at Valley Forge, and the war's many important battlefields; all are well represented in the NHAs. Crossroads of the American Revolution NHA in New Jersey is perhaps the best example. New Jersey stood at the juncture of the British stronghold of New York and the new nation's capital of Philadelphia; General George Washington and his Continental Army spent more time in New Jersey—more than 800 days—than any other state during the seven years of the war. Other NHAs contribute to interpreting the American Revolution including Freedom's Way, Hudson River Valley, Schuylkill River, Champlain Valley, and Upper Housatonic Valley.

The story of America's Industrial Revolution in the early-to-mid 19th century is also well told in the NHAs. A vital element of the Industrial Revolution was the power needed to fuel emerging industries. Water power was instrumental in this process, and the region of the Blackstone River Valley NHA is widely acknowledged as the place where America's Industrial Revolution began. Here, at Old Slater Mill, the quickly flowing water of the river was harnessed to spin cotton, and America was changed economically and socially forever.

Of course, other sources of fuel were needed as well and these stories are told in several other NHAs. Vast deposits of coal were found in the hills of Pennsylvania and West Virginia and "King Coal" powered much of America, heating homes, fueling trains, and running industry; National Coal

NHA and several others use the historic mines that pepper these regions to educate America about the importance of the manifold and extensive uses of coal. Oil was also vital to the evolution of industry. The first commercial oil well was developed in the mid-19th-century in what is now Oil Region NHA; the well consisted of a pipe driven into the ground, a hand pump, and a bathtub to collect the oil. This area is now known as the "valley that changed the world." Not only did "black gold" emerge from this initial primitive oil well, but in a sense, so did Standard Oil and other industrial giants.

Iron and steel were also instrumental elements of the Industrial Revolution. Iron, mined in several areas that are now NHAs, was combined with emerging technologies and the fire of coal and oil, to create "Big Steel" in Pittsburg and other areas, facilitating construction of the Brooklyn Bridge, the Empire State Building, railroad engines, massive ships, and eventually automobiles and airplanes. Rivers of Steel NHA showcases development of this industry.

The Slater Mill complex at John H. Chafee Blackstone River Valley National Heritage Corridor is widely recognized as the start of the American Industrial Revolution.

Nineteenth-century canals are early manifestations of America's Industrial Revolution (Erie Canalway National Heritage Corridor).

Construction of canals for the efficient transport of raw materials to industry and finished products to consumers played a vital role in the Industrial Revolution as well, and the NHAs offer many such sites. For example, in 1817, the New York legislature voted to construct the Erie and Champlain Canals; eight years later, the canal system opened, allowing boats to travel from the Atlantic Ocean to the upper Great Lakes. This 500-mile system of canals is an engineering marvel and a triumph of human labor, and it's the heart of Erie Canalway NHA. Other 19th-century canals are preserved at several NHAs. (Lots of these canals offer rides on historic canal boats—read on.)

The period of the Civil War from 1861 to 1865 and the associated Reconstruction and Jim Crow years immediately following were wrenching; learn about these periods in several units of the NHA system. Tennessee Civil War NHA and Shenandoah Valley Battlefields NHA are the primary actors. Tennessee was a pivotal state, President Lincoln calling it "the keystone of the Southern arch." Civil War battlefield sites are numerous in the state, both in number and importance. Historians count nearly 3,000 military engagements here, including the infamous battles at Shiloh, Stones River, Fort Donelson, Chickamauga/Chattanooga, and Franklin. The Shenandoah Valley was also a strategic location between north and south and saw lots of action, including General "Stonewall" Jackson's brilliant maneuvering to keep Union forces occupied and away from the vulnerable Confederate capital of Richmond, Virginia, General Robert E. Lee's Gettysburg Campaign in 1862 (the "high-water mark" of the Confederate Army), and General Phillip Sheridan's Shenandoah Campaign in 1864, driving Confederate troops from the Shenandoah Valley.

At the turn of the 20th century, the nation was engaged in a Conservation Movement and there was growing concern over dwindling natural resources and the wasteful ways in which they were being consumed. In response to this concern, many areas of the country were set aside as parks and forest reserves. Vermont's George Perkins Marsh (celebrated at Champlain Valley NHA) was instrumental in laying the intellectual foundation of the Conservation Movement, and Niagara Falls State Park (a key feature of Niagara Falls NHA) was the nation's first state park, designed by influential landscape architect Frederick Law Olmsted. John James Audubon and John and William Bartram were three of America's most famous naturalists and contributed to this national movement as illustrated at Schuylkill River Greenways NHA. John Muir effectively advocated for establishment of Yosemite National Park and is generally acknowledged as the father of the national parks: his story is told at his historic home in Sacramento-San Juaquin Delta NHA. And

Vermont's George Perkins Marsh was a prophet of America's 19th-century Conservation Movement (Champlain Valley National Heritage Partnership).

Henry David Thoreau's powerful writings on the relationship between man and nature are celebrated at his famous cabin at Walden Pond in Freedom's Way NHA.

Though the Civil War won the emancipation of slaves, racial discrimination has continued to plague the nation, leading to the Civil Rights Movement of the second half of the 20th century and continuing today. Signature events included the brutal murder of Emmett Till (Mississippi Delta NHA), integration of the University of Mississippi by James Meredith in 1962, and integration of Little Rock Central High School by nine brave African American children as reflected in the famous Supreme Court case, *Brown v. Board of Education*. These and related accounts are described at Freedom's Frontier NHA and several others.

Federally enforced integration of Arkansas's Little Rock Central High School in 1957 was an outgrowth of the famous Supreme Court ruling *Brown v. Board of Education* (Freedom's Frontier National Heritage Area).

The contemporary Environmental Movement is also addressed in a number of NHAs; this is a period in which environmental pollution and related issues were first seen to threaten human health and welfare. The massive oil spill of the Exxon *Valdez* in 1989 at Kenai Mountains-Turnagain Arm NHA is a signature event. Schuylkill River Greenways NHA and Blackstone River Valley NHA are working hard to clean up waters polluted by the Industrial Revolution. Restoration of coal mines and other industrial brownfields is underway at Lackawanna NHA and Rivers of Steel NHA. Niagara Falls NHA's innovative public shuttle bus system is a convenience to visitors, but also reduces carbon emissions. Water conservation programs are underway at Sacramento-San Joaquin Delta NHA, and Yuma Crossing NHA is restoring natural wetlands along the banks of the Colorado River.

Culture

Distinctive cultures and the way they've been synthesized and blended to form new and creative expressions of language, music, art, food, and crafts are at the heart of several NHAs. In south-central Louisiana, Cajun culture has emerged from the descendants of the area's early French Canadians, African and Caribbean Creoles, Spanish, Native Americans, and European Americans, and a new language emerged. Sometimes called "Louisiana French," this blended and colorful language is spoken by many residents at Atchafalaya NHA. The phrase *Laissez les bons temps rouler* means "Let the good times roll," summing up the region's approach to much of life. Similarly, at Gullah Geechee Cultural Heritage Corridor along the lowlands of the nation's southeastern coast, former African and Caribbean slaves, along with European immigrants, crafted a distinct language—Gullah—a simplified form of communication developed among people who spoke many languages. Gullah is still spoken by about 5,000 descendants of these early Americans. This new culture has also presented itself in creative forms of music, arts and crafts, architecture, and spirituality.

National heritage areas such as Gullah Geechee, Atchafalaya, and Cane River feature local foods that represent unique blends of multiple cultures.

Bluegrass music—influenced by ballad singing, gospel, blues, the Anglo-Irish fiddle, old-time, and sacred music—evolved in the isolated hills and valleys of what is now Blue Ridge NHA in North Carolina and is played throughout the region for the benefit of both residents and visitors. This NHA has also been recognized for the quality and innovation of its crafts that have been elevated to arts.

Since their establishment in 1851, the villages of the Rio Culebra in Sangre de Christo NHA have been representative of early Hispano American settlement. The vernacular architecture of the villages is distinctive. The original settlers of the Culebra Villages brought with them a form of land settlement and irrigation that was based on principles of equity, shared scarcity, and cooperation in which water was viewed as a resource rather than a commodity.

At Santa Cruz Valley NHA in southern Arizona, human history is especially long and diverse. An ancient Native American presence can be traced back 12,000 years, and portions of the landscape have been continuously farmed over the last 4,000 years. The people who live here today represent several cultures, including Native Americans, descendants of Spanish ancestors who colonized the Valley in the late 17th century, Mexican families who settled here before it was part of the United States, and more recent generations of pioneers searching for the American dream. A local agriculture based on this long and diverse cultural history has emerged and is at the heart of greater Tucson's designation by the United Nations as the first "City of Gastronomy." The NHA's farms feature heirloom Sonoran Desert-adapted fruit orchards and vegetable gardens.

Other examples of cultural diversity and distinctiveness include the Shakers (Freedom's Way NHA), the Amish (Susquehanna

Blues is a singular American musical innovation; find a "juke" in Mississippi Delta National Heritage Area and enjoy the show.

NHA), the birth of the blues in Mississippi Delta NHA, and the "musical melting pot" and nationally important recording studios at Muscle Shoals NHA.

Many NHAs honor their heritage of immigrants from diverse parts of the world. Men and women from all over Europe came to America to work in New England textile mills (e.g., Blackstone River Valley NHA), to farm fertile lands (e.g., Silos and Smokestacks NHA and Northern Plains NHA), and to work in the coal mines of Pennsylvania and West Virginia (Lackawanna Valley NHA and National Coal NHA) and Pittsburg's steel mills (Rivers of Steel NHA). Asians immigrated to California to help build railroads and farm the great Delta region (Sacramento-San Joaquin Delta NHA). Mexican and other Spanish-speaking people came to southern California to farm the fertile lands irrigated by the Colorado River (Yuma Crossing NHA). All were in search of freedom and a better life and have contributed to the rich multicultural fabric of America.

Of course, an important way of teaching and learning about the past (and maybe the

The massive National Museum of the US Air Force is one of many educational sites featured in America's system of 55 national heritage areas (National Aviation Heritage Area).

future!) is through museums, and nearly all NHAs offer this type of attraction. Some are world class; the Peal Museum at Baltimore NHA, the Detroit Historical Museum at MotorCities NHA, the National Museum of the United States Air Force at National Aviation NHA, and the Arizona-Sonoran Desert Museum at Santa Cruz Valley NHA are good examples. Many others are more specialized, but highly entertaining and informative; examples include the North Dakota Heritage Center and State Museum at Northern Plains NHA, Henry Ford Museum of American Innovation at MotorCities NHA, the Shelburne Museum at Champlain Valley NHA, Old Sturbridge Village at The Last Green Valley NHA, Negro Leagues Baseball Museum at Freedom's Frontier NHA, Delta Blues Museum at Mississippi Delta NHA, Hancock Shaker Village at Upper Housatonic Valley NHA, Washington State Ski and Snowboard Museum at Mountains to Sound NHA, and Living History Farms at Silos and Smokestacks NHA. Notice the diversity?

Nearly all NHAs include historic and often charming towns that make great places to learn about the area's history and enjoy opportunities to visit museums, take walking tours of historic downtowns and village greens, and find visitor-friendly facilities and services. For example, Natchitoches, perhaps the first settlement in the vast lands of the Lousiana Purchase, is a lovely, historic town in Cane River NHA. Hudson River Valley NHA includes a long string of historic towns, some of which feature the homes of prominent American families such as the Rockefellers, Vanderbilts, and Roosevelts; many of these homes and gardens are open to the public. NHAs that feature historic canals are often lined with colorful "canal towns" that sprouted up along the route. And scenic byways that run through so many NHAs connect historic and interesting villages. Alaska's Kenai Mountains-Turnagain Arm NHA includes a series of "trail friendly" towns that support hikers. A few NHAs that were once isolated include the remains of interesting "company towns"; built by mining and textile companies, these communities often included homes, schools, stores, churches, and recreation facilities for workers, resulting in unusual and interesting social dynamics. For example, the rural, agrarian character of much of West Virginia was transformed by the coal and railroad industries and many new company towns were constructed for workers. However, the towns rapidly introduced great cultural diversity associated with the inflow of immigrants from Europe and elsewhere, the stores run by these companies were sometimes exploitive, and there were occasional violent conflicts between labor and industry. Some NHAs feature ghost towns that offer glimpses into the past; examples include Mormon Pioneer NHA and Santa Cruz Valley NHA.

Ghost towns offer silent stories of early America in several national heritage areas (Great Basin National Heritage Area).

Many NHAs feature the economic heritage that has marked their distinctive past and that will help guide their future as they continue to build a program of sustainable heritage-based tourism. As noted above, prominent examples include regions that have large deposits of coal and oil, have been centers of iron and steel making, and rivers that have supported mills and textiles. But there are many other forms of economic development. Examples include quarrying granite and other valuable stone (Arabia Mountain NHA), shipbuilding and seafaring (Essex NHA and Baltimore NHA), agriculture (Upper Housatonic Valley NHA, Sacramento-San Joaquin Delta NHA, The Last Green Valley NHA, Yuma Crossing NHA, Silos and Smokestacks NHA), ranching and sheep herding (Cache la Poudre NHA, Great Basin NHA, South

Park NHA), fishing (Maritime Washington NHA), logging (Appalachian Forest NHA, Mountains to Sound NHA), automobiles (MotorCities NHA), and aviation (National Aviation NHA). In many cases, this economic activity is continuing, at least in some form; but in all cases, these NHAs are working to conserve their heritage by preserving and/or creatively adapting and reusing historic structures, conducting oral history projects, and offering engaging public education programs. For example, Wheeling NHA's Wheeling Artisan Center is housed in three renovated downtown historic buildings.

Many NHAs engage residents and visitors with some of America's most persistent and pressing societal issues. For example, the heritage of slavery and the contemporary issues of racial discrimination and inequality are explored in an honest, open, and sophisticated manner at Freedom's Frontier NHA; educational programs challenge visitors to wrestle with the meaning of "freedom" in the American context. Internment of Japanese citizens during World War II is explored at Topaz, an internment camp at Great Basin NHA. The inherent tension between labor and industry is examined from both sides at National Coal NHA and MotorCities NHA. Mistreatment of Native Americans and African Americans is acknowledged at Sites of Conscience at Northern Plains NHA and South Carolina NHA. And contemporary environmental issues such as water conservation and problems associated with large dams and reservoirs are illustrated in the ways Yuma Crossing NHA, Sacramento-San Joaquin Delta NHA, and Maritime Washington NHA are managed today.

Recreation

Of course, many visitors to NHAs are interested in recreation opportunities, and NHAs offer a bounty in both quantity and quality. In fact, development of sustainable

National Parks such as Canyonlands offer the very best of America's outdoor recreation opportunities (Mormon Pioneer National Heritage Area).

heritage-based tourism is an important objective of all NHAs; this contributes to community pride and the local economy, helping to fund conservation, education, and recreation programs. Many NHAs include major national parks such as Great Smoky Mountains (Blue Ridge NHA), Great Basin (Great Basin NHA), Bryce Canyon, Zion, Canyonlands, and Capitol Reef (Mormon Pioneer NHA), New River Gorge (National Coal NHA), Cuyahoga Valley (Ohio and Erie Canalway NHA), Great Sand Dunes (Sangre de Christo NHA), Saguaro (Santa Cruz Valley NHA), Shenandoah (Shenandoah Valley Battlefields NHA), and Kenai Fjords (Kenai Mountains-Turnagain Arm NHA). All of these parks are nationally important landscapes and offer some of the finest scenic driving, hiking, camping, boating, fishing, and wildlife viewing in the nation. Many other units of the National Park System—historic and cultural sites—are also found in NHAs and often include trails for hiking and biking and other recreation opportunities. Most NHAs have developed walking tours through historic districts and gardens and driving tours.

NHAs include many other nationally distinctive recreation opportunities. Examples include National Scenic Byways and All American Roads that offer some of the nation's most strikingly beautiful and educational driving opportunities. Baltimore NHA features the Star Spangled Banner Byway, a 106-mile drive that interprets the siege of Baltimore and Fort McHenry by the British during the War of 1812. Portions of several National Historic and Scenic Trails are found in many NHAs. For example, Shenandoah Valley Battlefields NHA

and Upper Housatonic River NHA both include portions of the 2,200-mile Appalachian National Scenic Trail; consider following the white blazes and walking a few miles on this internationally famous long-distance trail. Other examples include the Iditarod National Historic Trail in Kenai Mountains-Turnagain Arm NHA, and the Natchez Trace National Scenic Trail in Mississippi Hills NHA. Other NHAs include National Wild and Scenic Rivers. For example, National Coal NHA in the Appalachian Mountains includes the Bluestone National Scenic River; the river flows through an ancient and rugged gorge and the area is ecologically diverse and offers great hiking.

Other types of adventures in NHAs include rides on historic railroads (e.g., Great Basin NHA, Lackawanna Valley NHA, Ohio and Erie Canalway NHA, Sangre de Christo NHA) and canal boats (e.g., Augusta Canal NHA, Illinois and Michigan Canal NHA, Delaware and Lehigh NHA, and Ohio and

Many national heritage areas offer visitors rides on canal boats, historic trains, antique cars, electric trolleys, replica airplanes, coal mine cars, and other conveyances (Maid of the Mist tour boat, Niagara Falls National Heritage Area).

The River Walk in the historic city of Natchitoches is a popular tourist attraction (Cane River National Heritage Area).

Erie Canalway NHA). Lackawana Valley NHA and Blue Ridge NHA offer visitors adventurous tours into coal mines. Tour boats offer rides at a number of NHAs including Baltimore NHA's lively and tourist-friendly Inner Harbor, an up-close-and-personal tour of Niagara Falls on the famous Maid of the Mist (Niagara Falls NHA), and a 90-minute tour of Pittsburg's three rivers on the 94-foot riverboat, Explorer (Rivers of Steel NHA). National Aviation NHA offers visitors a thrilling ride on lookalike Wright "B" Flyers, the Wright brothers' first production airplane.

Many NHAs help celebrate their heritage with festivals and other events. For example, The Last Green Valley NHA works with its partners to sponsor Spring Outdoors, Walktober, and the Harvest Tour, featuring local farms, orchards, vintners, brewers, and restaurants. National Aviation NHA is the site of an annual airshow and MotorCities NHA helps sponsor the annual Michigan Auto Heritage Day. The Hudson River Valley Ramble is held each September at Hudson River Valley NHA and offers historic home tours and walks in the region's parks and grand gardens.

Is shopping a form of recreation? If so you're in luck. As noted above, many NHAs have a long history of local arts and crafts that can serve as remembrances of your visits to America's NHAs. These purchases contribute to heritage-based tourism and help maintain local arts and crafts traditions.

Using this Guidebook

This book is designed as a guide to America's National Heritage Areas. The present chapter offers an introduction to NHAs—what they are and the types of attractions they offer. The remaining chapters of the book describe each of the 54 active NHAs. Each chapter begins with where the NHA is located, a one-sentence description of the NHA, and a short list of some of the area's iconic visitor attractions. The first half of each chapter then describes the NHA in more detail—its history and prominent natural and cultural resources are emphasized. The second half of each chapter briefly describes some of the area's most important attractions—visitor centers, historic sites, museums, national and state parks, trails, scenic drives, and much more. While the book is designed primarily for visitors to the NHAs, it might make good reading for residents of these areas as well; the people who live, work, and play in these living landscapes can be proud of their natural and cultural heritage and may not have taken full advantage of some these areas' attractions.

Instead of reading the book from front to back, most readers will want to be more selective. Look at the map on page x and xi to see the distribution of NHAs; which are located near you and how can you conveniently combine visits to more than one NHA? Scan the Table of Contents to get a sense of which NHAs you might find most interesting and enjoyable based on their descriptive names. Then read the short chapters describing the NHAs that capture your imagination to find out much more about their natural and cultural history and the attractions they offer. Next, go to the two websites noted at the end of each chapter to learn even more; one of these official websites has been developed by the NPS and the other by the organization that manages the NHA. Finally, decide which NHAs you'll visit to learn more about them firsthand, to see how they've helped shape America's natural and cultural history, and to take advantage of the rich set of education and recreation opportunities they offer.

Lincoln Home National Historic Site features the Springfield home where Lincoln lived before becoming the 16th president of the United States and offers insights to him as a spouse, parent, and neighbor.

Lincoln traveled a full day from his Springfield home to argue some of his cases at the Mount Pulaski Courthouse.

PART II:
THE NATIONAL HERITAGE AREA SYSTEM

The National Heritage Area system includes 55 diverse areas scattered across America's great and grand cultural landscape. (Note that one of these NHAs is currently inactive and is not included in the book.) The following sesctions describe each of these NHAs. Sections begin with a brief summary: the state(s) in which they're located, a one-sentence description of the NHA, and the names of a few sample attractions. The first half of each section describes the natural and cultural history of the NHA and the second half describes some of the area's important attractions. Sections end with the addresses of two official websites for each NHA, one by the National Park Service and one by the NHA's managing entity. Each section is illustrated with a few representative photographs. The 54 NHAs appear in alphabetical order, and a map of their geographic location is shown on pages x and xi.

Abraham Lincoln National Heritage Area

State: Illinois

Description: This large NHA in central Illinois uniquely tells the story of Abraham Lincoln by filling in the context and backdrop of his life, including the people and places that shaped him in matters of unity, equality, race, and democracy, and where he developed the courage and wisdom to lead the nation through the Civil War years.

Sample Attractions:
- Lincoln Home National Historic Site
- Abraham Lincoln Presidential Library and Museum
- Lincoln Tomb State Historic Site
- Looking for Lincoln Story Trail

The National Park Service often describes National Heritage Areas as "lived-in landscapes" and notes that NHAs are designed to connect sites that together tell a unique and important story about America's natural and/or cultural history. Moreover, the initiative for doing this should come from the ground up. And that's just what's happened in central Illinois when a group of local citizens came together to form the non-profit group Looking for Lincoln Heritage Coalition (Looking for Lincoln) in 1998 to discover, document, and tell the story of their most famous resident who helped guide our nation through some it most difficult years. After 10 years of hard but rewarding work, Abraham Lincoln National Heritage Area

(Abraham Lincoln) was established by Congress and Looking for Lincoln was designated as the organization to guide the NHA, with the help of the National Park Service and many other governmental, private, and non-profit organizations.

This is a big NHA, a 43-county swath of central Illinois from the Indiana border to the Mississippi River—the place where Lincoln lived beginning in his early 20s, raising his family and pursuing his passion for law and politics. Abraham Lincoln uniquely tells this story by filling in the context and backdrop of Lincoln's life, including the people and places that shaped him in matters of unity, equality, race, and democracy, and where he developed the courage and wisdom to lead the nation through the Civil War years. Many of the large and small communities of the region contribute to the Lincoln legacy with artifacts, anecdotes, buildings, and the larger landscape. This is the only NHA named for an American president.

A prime example of Illinois's role in Lincoln's development are his famous debates with Stephen A. Douglas in 1858. Lincoln was challenging the incumbent state senator, and the two conducted a series of seven three-hour debates throughout the state, one in each of the state's Congressional districts; all of these sites are in the NHA and the locations now feature plaques and statuary of Lincoln and Douglas. Illinois was a "free state" and all of these debates included the issue of slavery in the United States, including its potential expansion to the nation's western territories. Thousands of people attended some of the debates, especially those near the border with other states, and the events received much attention in major national newspapers. Lincoln argued that Douglas was in favor of nationalizing slavery. Transcripts of the debates were ultimately published in book form and, even though Lincoln lost the race for state senate, he rose to national attention and won the nomination for president at the Chicago Republican National Convention in 1860.

Attractions

Given the thirty years that Lincoln resided in central Illinois, the NHA includes many sites that were important to his upbringing, his family, his early career as a lawyer and politician, his campaign for the presidency, and other facets of his life. Enjoy this large portion of Illinois and the role it played in the life of one of America's greatest presidents.

Lincoln Home National Historic Site

This unit of the National Park System includes the Springfield home where Lincoln lived from 1844-1861 before becoming the 16th president of the United States. The site also includes a visitor center and the four-block area surrounding this early home; other historic homes are here, some of them open to the public. While the Lincoln home helps tell the story of his presidency, it also offers insights of him as a spouse, parent, and neighbor.

Lincoln Log Cabin State Historic Site

This 86-acre site includes a reproduction of the 19th-century home of Thomas and Sarah Lincoln, Abraham Lincoln's father and stepmother. Though Abraham Lincoln didn't live here, he often came to the site while he was practicing law in Springfield. A living history farm has been developed on the property and offers visitors insights into life in rural 19th-century Illinois.

Abraham Lincoln Presidential Library and Museum

Visit this site to follow Lincoln's life from his visits to his parent's rustic Indiana cabin to the White House. Learn about key moments in his life, the human tragedy of slavery, and the Civil War. This engaging facility creatively combines scholarship and showmanship to recreate the life of this important president.

Lincoln Tomb State Historic Site

This historic site is the final resting place of Lincoln, his wife, Mary, and three of their four sons (the other son is buried in Arlington National Cemetery). It's a large structure that includes a 72-foot square foundation with large projections on the north and south sides, double sets of stairs that lead to a terrace, a 117-foot obelisk, four bronze sculpture groups, a bronze sculpture of Lincoln, a rotunda, and hallways that lead to the burial chamber. It's a National Historic Landmark and is on the National List of Historic Places.

Lincoln Heritage Museum

Located at Lincoln College, this impressive museum includes rare and original historic pieces relating to Lincoln and the Civil War. The museum includes self-guided tours and immersive audio-visual displays.

Talking Houses of Pittsfield

Lincoln visited the community of Pittsfield on several occasions between 1838 and 1858; he became friends with several residents through politics and legal business. The homes of these friends and colleagues have

Lincoln Tomb State Historic Site is the final resting of place of Lincoln, his wife, Mary, and three of their four sons.

wayside exhibits that tell the story of Lincoln's relationships with these people.

Mount Pulaski Courthouse State Historic Site

This handsome brick courthouse was constructed in the town of Mount Pulaski in 1848 and is one of only two remaining courthouses in the Eighth Circuit of Illinois where Lincoln practiced law. Lincoln lived in Springfield and it took him a full day to reach the courthouse by horse and buggy. Visitors are given guided tours of the recreated courtroom.

Old State Capital State Historic Site

This historic state building was constructed from 1837 to 1840 on the central square of Springfield. It included chambers of both political parties of the General Assembly (Lincoln served his final term as state senator here), offices for the governor of the State and his staff, and a chamber for the Illinois Supreme Court (where Lincoln argued cases). Lincoln announced his candidacy for president here (as did Barack Obama). After his assassination, Lincoln's body lay in state here before he was buried in Springfield's Oak Ridge Cemetery.

Looking for Lincoln Story Trail

There are lots of important Lincoln-related communities and sites throughout Abraham Lincoln and the Looking for Lincoln Story Trail conveniently ties many of them together in this automobile route. Towns and sites include several of the attractions noted above. As an added bonus, part of this route is along famous Route 66, the "Main Street of America." Looking for Lincoln has developed over 200 exhibits (called "signboards," "waysides," and "text rails") in more than 50 communities throughout the NHA that are all part of the larger Looking for Lincoln Story Trail. Each exhibit includes a unique medallion that visitors can rub with paper and a crayon, making a collection.

For more information about Abraham Lincoln and to help plan your visit, see the area's official website (lookingfor lincoln.org) and the website of the National Park Service (nps.gov/places /abraham-lincoln-national-heritage -area.htm).

Appalachian Forest National Heritage Area

States: Maryland and West Virginia
Description: This lovely region of the ancient Appalachian Mountains traces the evolution of the interrelationships between forests and people; the region's forests provide a home for residents, a livelihood for some, a distinctive and vital culture, opportunities for recreation, and beauty for all to share.

Sample Attractions:
- Appalachian Forest Discovery Center
- Monongahela National Forest
- National Scenic Byways
- Cass Scenic Railroad State Park

The science of ecology documents the interrelationships among the natural world, but a more expansive view suggests that such reciprocal relationships extend to humans and nature as well: people and culture affect nature in many ways (e.g., people harvest trees, establish nature reserves) and the reverse is true as well (e.g., nature nurtures people and shapes communities in response to inherent natural conditions). Appalachian Forest National Heritage Area (Appalachian Forest) is a living example of these interrelationships.

The vast forests of this region grow in the Appalachian Mountains, one of the oldest mountain chains in the world, estimated to have formed nearly 500 million years ago by massive upheavals caused by the movement of tectonic plates. These mountains were once as high as the Rockies and Alps, but erosion has reduced them to their current maximum elevations of around 6,000 feet. Their north-south orientation presents natural barriers to east-west travel and for this reason, the Appalachians are sometimes referred to as the "eastern Continental Divide." The forests that grow here are especially diverse, affected by a wide range of elevations, their span from northern to southern climates, and plentiful rain. This is one of the most biologically diverse temperate regions

The Monongahela National Forest is a centerpiece of Appalachian Forest NHA.

in the world; indeed, the area includes more than 150 species of trees alone.

These extensive and diverse forests have shaped the people, culture, and history of the region. The often rugged and remote environment of the Appalachian Mountains isolated the settlers who lived here and in response they developed a culture that focused on independence and self-reliance, using the land and its forests for shelter, food, fuels, clothing, and tools, much as the preceding Native Americans had. Small valleys tucked between the mountains supported family farms. Forest products were important and included wood for building material and fuel as well as a host of other forest-related products such as ginseng and maple syrup. The isolation of the people and communities led to a distinctive culture that included folklore, oral histories, artistic creativity, and unique cultural expressions such as crafts, music, and dance; these expressions of culture were influenced by people of diverse nationalities over successive waves of settlement. This is an authentic and living heritage that's been shaped by the local mountains and forests.

Forests have played a leading role in the human and natural drama of this region. Trees were harvested on a small scale to clear land and support local farms and settlements. But later, forests were "mined" in the late 19th and early 20th centuries to help power America's expansion and the Industrial Revolution. Later, much of the forests regrew, forest reserves were established, and science-based sustainable forest management practices were developed and applied. This is an evolving story in which forests are now managed in diverse ways that range from "working forests" that provide a variety of forest products to wilderness areas where trees are allowed to recover and forests support their natural functions, including habitat for native plants and animals. This is an evolving story that traces the historic and current interrelationships between forests and people and ponders their future. The region's forests still provide a home for residents, a livelihood for some, a distinctive and vital culture, opportunities for recreation, and beauty for all to share.

Beginning in 2001, local stakeholder groups galvanized an effort to conserve and celebrate the natural and cultural heritage of the Appalachian Mountains with a special focus on the region's forests. The group conducted a feasibility study for establishing a National Heritage Area in the mountains of West Virginia and Maryland, and this led to establishment of Appalachian Forest by Congress in 2019. The NHA includes 16 counties in West Virginia and two in western Maryland that occupy the ridge of the Allegheny Mountains, a rugged range of the larger Appalachian Mountain chain. The NHA is managed by the non-profit organization Appalachian Forest Heritage Area, Inc. that works with many partner organizations, including the National Park Service.

Attractions

This large NHA offers a wide range of attractions including historic sites and museums that tell the story of the mountains, forests, people, and communities of this region. Moreover, lots of public lands (more than a million acres), including national forests and wildlife refuges, units of the National Park System, and state parks allow for hiking, biking, fishing, horseback riding, camping, climbing, river rafting, and snow sports. And the area's scenic byways offer hundreds of miles of scenic driving and welcoming towns and villages.

Canaan Valley National Wildlife Refuge offers many opportunities for outdoor recreation including birding, hiking, and fishing.

Appalachian Forest Discovery Center

The Discovery Center in the historic Darden Mill in Elkins, West Virginia, serves as the welcome center for visitors to Appalachian Forest. The center includes engaging exhibits and knowledgeable staff and is a good place to begin a visit.

C&O Canal National Historical Park

The C&O Canal is a harbinger of America's Industrial Revolution. Begun in 1828, the 185-mile canal runs along the Potomac River from Georgetown in Washington, DC, to Cumberland in western Maryland. Avoiding the rapids of the river, the canal transported goods including coal, lumber, and agricultural products between the eastern United States and the Midwest. The towpath of the canal has been restored into a delightful walking and biking trail and offers historic canal boat tours.

Monongahela National Forest

This large, diverse, and nationally known forest offers visitors scenic driving and lots of hiking, fishing, and other outdoor recreation opportunities. It's a "working forest" where timber is harvested on a sustainable basis and is famous for the nationally important controversy over the policy of clearcutting large areas of trees. Be sure to ask a ranger to discuss this issue.

Canaan Valley National Wildlife Refuge

This national wildlife refuge in West Virginia is a lovely, large, high elevation valley that's great for spotting wildlife, scenic driving, hiking, biking, and fishing. It features a 31-mile network of roads and trails

Driving Tours

Appalachian Forest has developed several driving tours that feature the area's themes; examples include the Civil War and mountain music and dance. Details are found on the Appalachian Forest website (see below).

Cass Scenic Railroad State Park

This West Virginia State Park takes visitors back in time to when steam-driven locomotives were a part of everyday life. The park's 11 miles of heritage railroad tracks and an authentic logging company town make this state park especially popular. Take a steam train ride to Bald Knob for great views.

For great views of Appalachian Forest NHA, take a steam train ride to Bald Knob.

Potomac Heritage National Scenic Trail Network

This National Scenic Trail is unlike most others in that it's a network of more than 700 miles of trails in Maryland, Pennsylvania, Virginia, and Washington, DC. (Most other national scenic trails are very long, continuous trails such as the Appalachian National Scenic Trail.) Much of the Potomac Heritage National Scenic Trail Network features outstanding natural, historic, and cultural sites. This system of trails is not yet complete.

National Scenic Byways
Several National Scenic Byways and other scenic roads crisscross the NHA offering beautiful views and opportunities to explore interesting NHA-related themes. Examples include Staunton-Parkerburg Turnpike National Scenic Byway (gateway to the Shenandoah Valley), Highland Scenic Highway (great views into surrounding valleys), the National Road All-American Road (a 620-mile road that connects the Potomac and Ohio Rivers), and the Midland Trail (a 180-mile route through the midsection of West Virginia).

For more information about Appalachian Forest and to help plan your visit, see the area's official website (appalachianforestnha.org) and the website of the National Park Service (nps.gov/places/appalachian-forest-national-heritage-area.htm).

Arabia Mountain National Heritage Area
State: Georgia
Description: This urban proximate NHA (just 40 miles from bustling Atlanta) features two dramatic granite mountains and lots of green space; the area provided stone for many prominent buildings, but is now used primarily for recreation.
Sample Attractions:
• Panola Mountain State Park
• Davidson-Arabia Nature Preserve
• Flat Rock Archives and Cemetery
• Historic Downtown Lithonia

Arabia Mountain National Heritage Area (Arabia Mountain) presents an interesting juxtaposition with nearby Atlanta. This 40,000-acre NHA is dominated by two dramatic granite mountains and lots of surrounding green space, but is found just 40 miles east of bustling Atlanta, one of the fastest growing places in the United States. To be more accurate, the mountains are actually monadnocks, isolated hills of bedrock that rise dramatically above the surrounding plains. These are formed when erosion-resistant rock is exposed due the erosion of overlaying softer rock. Arabia Mountain shows off two such formations, Arabia Mountain and Panola Mountain. (Nearby and more famous Stone Mountain, with its large controversial carving of four Confederate soldiers and heavily developed tourist attractions, is also a monadnock, but is not part of the NHA.)

Formation, erosion, and exposure of these mountains started approximately 400 million years ago, but there's been a lot of human history in more recent times. Native Americans, specifically the Creek and Cherokee Nations, lived here for thousands of years, using the area for trading and hunting. Evidence suggests that the area's South River was an important trading route among these people. After the Native Americans ceded land to the federal government in the 1820s, Europeans and enslaved Africans settled in the area and developed an agriculturally based lifestyle and economy as exemplified in Arabia Mountain by Lyon Farm and Parker House. More recently, the stone quarry industry dominated much of the land, mining and shaping the region's distinctive granite building materials. Quarries on and around Arabia Mountain supplied stone that was used for buildings throughout much of early America. The stone found at Arabia Mountain is called Tidal Grey or Lithonia granite (Lithonia means "town of stone" in Greek) and has high structural density and features a distinctive swirl pattern that makes it valuable as a building material. Many famous buildings around much of the eastern United States are constructed of this material; examples include the US Naval Academy, West Point, US Congressional offices in Washington, DC, the Brooklyn Bridge, and several state capitols. Initially, the quarries on and around Arabia Mountain were dug by hand, but starting in 1880, workers used drills, dynamite, and air compressors to "raise a ledge" or sever large blocks of stone, allowing more control over the size of the pieces that were quarried. Local railroads shipped the stone throughout the nation.

Other dimensions of the human history of Arabia Mountain include Flat Rock Community, the area's oldest black community, formed by a group of emancipated slaves from nearby farms, and a group of Trappist monks who founded the Monastery of the Holy Spirit in 1944, a site that includes 2,000 acres of green space.

Arabia Mountain NHA is now protected as part of the Davidson-Arabia Mountain Nature Preserve, and Panola Mountain is the central feature of Panola Mountain State Park, recognized as a National Natural Landmark. Both areas offer enormous fields of exposed granite, showy wildflowers in the spring (including diamorpha that rolls out its bright red carpet), seasonal pools of rain water called vernal pools, colorful leaves in the fall, and stunning 360-degree views year

Arabia Mountain and nearby Panola Mountain offer great hiking options to Atlanta residents and visitors.

round. The unique topography and geology of these mountains has given rise to some very unusual (and rare) plants and animals.

Arabia Mountain was established in 2006. Local lore suggests that the name "Arabia" was coined by granite quarry workers who noted that the area is "hot as Arabia" in summer. The area is managed by Arabia Mountain Heritage Alliance, and as the name suggests, includes many partner organizations.

Attractions

This diverse NHA helps preserve the area's unusual and striking monadnocks, as well as its important history as home to Native Americans, a productive agricultural area, a place and people shaped by slavery, a site of industrial granite production, and a contemporary nature preserve and park. Because of its location just outside Atlanta, Arabia Mountain is also a respite and recreation area for residents of this booming city and visitors to the area.

Panola Mountain State Park

Just 15 minutes from Atlanta, this state park is part of the core of Arabia Mountain, show-casing dramatic Panola Mountain, one of the area's prominent monadnocks. The park offers a wide range of outdoor recreation opportunities, including a campsite in a tree! Vaughters' Barn is an iconic manifestation of the region's agricultural heritage.

Davidson-Arabia Nature Preserve

This 2,550-acre preserve includes the NHA's namesake mountain/monadnock and its surrounding wetlands, pine and oak forests, multiple streams, two lakes, and rare plant species. Facilities and services include a network of hiking trails, a long hiking/bik-ing trail, and a nature center. The landscape includes remnants of the once thriving gran-ite industry. Especially popular is the Arabia Mountain Top Trail, a 1.3-mile (round trip) hike to the summit of Arabia Mountain and its 360-degree views. Visitors should be care-ful to "stay on the gray" so as not to disturb the area's vernal pools.

Atlanta Wild Animal Rescue Effort (AWARE)

This facility rehabilitates Georgia's injured and orphaned wild animals and educates the community about living in harmony with native wildlife. The facility offers tours to visitors.

Monastery of the Holy Spirit

In 1944, twenty-one Trappist monks left Gethsemani Abbey in Kentucky and embarked on a journey similar to those in early Christianity. Their travels led them to the wilderness of rural Georgia where they founded the Monastery of the Holy Spirit where the monks lead a monastic way of life. Visitors are welcome to explore the site and grounds to learn more about the monas-tic lifestyle. Interesting features include the facility's architecture, an impressive bonsai exhibit, and a shop that includes items made by resident monks.

Flat Rock Archives and Cemetery

This historic site showcases an early African American community founded by emanci-pated slaves. The site helps tell the story of this place and its people from enslavement to emancipation to the present day. It consists of an historic home, barn, smokehouse, cem-etery, and outhouse in a rural landscape. The archives include a range of historic mate-rial, including genealogical records, newspa-per articles, photographs, maps, rare books, church and school records, and tangible arti-facts related to African American history in the rural South.

Arabia Mountain Path

This 30-plus-mile paved path connects 21 interesting sites throughout the NHA, from historic downtown Lithonia to the Mon-astery of the Holy Spirit and is suitable for hikers and bikers.

Historic Downtown Lithonia

Lithonia was once a thriving granite indus-try town that is now on the National Reg-ister of Historic Places. This bustling quarry town has retained its historic character and includes an early African American school, two historic churches founded in the 1860s, and local shops

Arabia Mountain is a distinctive monadnock, an isolated hill of bedrock exposed due to erosion of overlaying softer rock.

Lyon Farm
The Lyon Homestead offers insights into the lives of Georgia's white farmers as well as the enslaved people who created resilient communities following emancipation (see Flat Rock Archives above). Joseph Lyon built a log cabin on the site in the 1820s. The largely self-sustaining farm included apples, cotton, muscadines, pears, lemons, sorghum, and bees.

Vaughters Farm
This farm was a productive dairy facility in DeKalb County and features rolling hills, grassy meadows, and a handsome barn. Now a part of Panola Mountain State Park and protected from urban sprawl spilling out of Atlanta, the site includes a 1.25-mile loop trail.

Paddling
The South River, once home to Native Americans and historic farmers, is an important component of Arabia Mountain. Paddling this peaceful river is an enjoyable way to appreciate this historic landscape.

> For more information about Arabia Mountain and to help plan your visit, see the area's official website (arabia alliance.org) and the website of the National Park Service (nps.gov/places /arabia-mountain-national-heritage -area.htm).

Atchafalaya National Heritage Area
State: Louisiana
Description: This large NHA includes the natural wonders of the 140-mile-long Atchafalaya River and America's largest freshwater swamp, along with Cajun culture and its distinctive language, cuisine, and music.
Sample Attractions:
- Jean Lafitte National Historical Park and Preserve
- Seven National Wildlife Refuges
- Water Heritage Trail
- Wetland Boat and Swamp Tours

Atchafalaya NHA includes a diverse natural wonder that is defined by America's largest freshwater swamp.

Atchafalaya is a Native American (Choctaw) word for "long river," and it's an apt name. The Atchafalaya River runs through its namesake National Heritage Area for 140 miles, stretching across 14 parishes in south-central Louisiana from the Baton Rouge area to the Gulf of Mexico. When asked how to pronounce the name of the river and NHA, locals suggest the following phonetic spelling and saying the word with cadence: "uh-CHA-ful-LIE-uh." (Some residents suggest speaking the word like it's a sneeze.) And the local slogan of the area is "Coming Atcha." You might get the idea that the people who live here like to enjoy life, and you'd be right; and they want to share it with you in Atchafalaya National Heritage Area (Atchafalaya).

Like all NHAs, this is both a place and a concept. The place includes a diverse natural wonder that is defined by the river and America's largest freshwater swamp (bigger even than the Everglades). Other components of the natural environment include upland forests, a large land-building delta as the river flows into the Gulf of Mexico,

twisting bayous and backwater lakes, graceful live oaks draped in Spanish moss, cypress trees that are more than 1,000 years old, beautiful scenery, fields of sugar cane and cotton, and abundant wildlife (including alligators, bears, and more than 240 species of birds). Add in the rich blend of history and people, home to the widely recognized and celebrated Cajun culture with its distinctive language, cuisine, and music and it all contributes to a concept—a diverse group of people who have learned to live together and with their environment over hundreds of years in sustainable, distinctive, and inseparable ways. As the locals like to say, there's "a story around every bend and music from every corner."

Louisiana's Cajun culture is deeply embedded in Atchafalaya. The word *Cajun* first appeared in the 19th century as a way to describe the Acadian people of Louisiana. The Acadians were descendants of French Canadians who were settling in southern Louisiana. They spoke a form of French (sometimes called "Louisiana French")

adapted to the area and that is still prevalent in parts of the NHA. It emerged in the 18th century from Acadian and French immigrants to the area as well as French and African Creoles who came to Louisiana from the West Indies. Elements of Spanish, Native American, African, and English combine to make a unique language that's spoken by the majority of Francophones in the state. To get you prepared for your visit, here's a quick vocabulary lesson that will come in handy:

Allons ("let's go")

Ca c'est bon ("That's good.")

Chefrette ("shrimp")

Une barbue ("catfish")

Cocodril ("alligator")

Courtbouillon (a rich, spicy tomato-based soup or stew made with fish fillets, onions, and sometimes mixed vegetables)

Fais do-do ("A Cajun dance party")

Frottior (A washboard or rubboard used as a musical instrument in zydeco and Cajun music)

Laissez les bons temps rouler ("Let the good times roll")

Distinctive foods and music are also staples of Cajun and Creole culture, reflecting 300 years of sharing among the people who live here. Gumbo, for example, melds African, European, and Native American cultures. The word is thought to be derived from *nkombo*, the Bantu word for okra, a staple of this soup/stew. Its origin is rooted in French

At Atchafalaya NHA visitors will find staples of Cajun and Creole culinary culture; gumbo, for example, melds African, European, and Native American cultures.

Cajun music traditionally relies on fiddles and accordions.

bouillabaisse, and its appeal is reinforced by the strong preference for soups by African people. Music also reflects a long and productive multicultural heritage. Originating in Nova Scotia, Cajun music uses one or two fiddles and an accordion that has Italian and German influences. Following African and Caribbean practices, zydeco musicians substitute a washboard for the fiddle. Other forms of music such as blues, boogie woogie, and rock and roll contributed to the well-known radio and television show, "Louisiana Hayride." Blues and gospel evolved from African-rooted antebellum traditions of spirituals, ring-shouts, and work hollers.

Atchafalaya was established in 2006 and is managed by the Louisiana Department of Culture, Recreation, and Tourism. The goals of the NHA are to enhance appreciation of its unique and authentic cultural identity, to interpret this culture to visitors, and to increase appreciation of the region's natural and cultural resources. Interpretive themes include the ways in which people have developed and acquired living skills tailored to the environment, a unique identity that is a blend of many cultures, and the ways in which the area's environment has influenced the people who live there.

Attractions

This large and diverse NHA offers an array of attractions, including its cultural diversity (language, food, music, crafts) and natural heritage. Learn about this place and people, and enjoy and appreciate them through driving tours and many forms of outdoor recreation in this beautiful and unique natural environment. Remember, it's America's foreign country.

Jean Lafitte National Historical Park and Preserve

Jean Lafitte and his brother, Pierre, were colorful characters—pirates and smugglers of French descent—who lived in the Louisiana area in the early 19th century, and the park that bears his name is a unit of the National Park System. The Prairie Acadian Cultural Center celebrates and illuminates the lives of the Acadians (Cajuns) who have lived in the this region of Louisiana for generations. The Wetlands Acadian Cultural Center examines the ways in which the region's watery environment has affected the people who live here.

Cypremort Point State Park

This state park offers unusual access to the Gulf of Mexico. The park includes a beach, and there's a boat launch just outside the park that's just a few miles from the Gulf; it's located in the heart of a Louisiana marsh and offers great wildlife viewing.

Lake Fausse Pointe State Park

This is a 6,000-acre park in the Atchafalaya Basin. At the edge of a large watery wilderness, the area supports lots of opportunities for fishing, boating, canoeing, hiking, and

Atchafalaya wetlands feature distinctive cypress trees, some more than 1,000 years old.

Many residents of the Atchafalaya region speak what is sometimes called "Louisiana French"; *cocodrils* is the local word for the alligators that inhabit the area's wetlands.

wildlife viewing, and it has a visitor center and boat rentals.

National Wildlife Refuges

There are a whopping seven national wildlife refuges in the NHA: Atchafalaya, Bayou, Grand Cole, Lake Ophelia, Mandalay, Bayou Teche, and Shell Keys. Here you'll find opportunities to see wildlife in their native habitat as well as to hike, canoe, and enjoy many other activities.

Water Heritage Trail

This driving route helps tell the story of this unique region of Louisiana. The trail includes more than 50 stops where you can learn about the natural and cultural environment of Atchafalaya. Use the NHA website (see below) to find an interactive map to help plan your route.

Biking

Cycling on the region's backroads is a good way to experience the NHA, and generally flat landscapes and a mild climate contribute to the enjoyment of this activity. The

Atchafalaya Basin Wilderness Trail is an iconic 55-mile route on a remote gravel trail.

Paddling

Paddling the river and wetlands is an intimate way to experience the NHA. Canoe or kayak under live oaks with trailing Spanish moss, paddle through cypress groves, see a variety of birds, and enjoy alligators as they move through the area. Consider the Bayou Teche/Lower Atchafalaya River Paddling Trail, Lake Fausse Pointe State Park and Canoe Trail, and the Grand Avoille Cove Paddling Trail.

Wetland Boat and Swamp Tours

Specially adapted power boats allow you to see a lot of the region in a short period of time. Check the NHA website (see below) for a list of tour boat operators.

Fishing

There are many opportunities for freshwater fishing in the Atchafalaya River and surrounding wetlands and saltwater fishing in the Gulf of Mexico. Recreational crawfishing using set nets or wire traps is a popular pastime and tied closely to cultural traditions.

Birding

The nearly 250 species of resident and migratory birds in Atchafalaya makes this a world-class birding area. The coastal area of Iberia Parish offers especially diverse and rich habitat—wetlands, seed, and soil. Consider walking the Iberia Parish Birding Trail.

> For more information about Atchafalaya and to help plan your visit, see the area's official website (atchafalaya.org) and the website of the National Park Service (nps.gov/places/atchafalaya -national-heritage-area.htm).

Augusta Canal National Heritage Area

State: Georgia

Description: The 1845 Augusta Canal brought the Industrial Revolution to the South, powering textiles mills and other industries; today, the NHA offers a window into this past along with recreational use of the canal and its environs.

Sample Attractions:

- Augusta Canal Discovery Center
- Petersburg Canal Boat Tours
- Savannah Rapids Park
- Trails

Augusta Canal National Heritage Area (Augusta Canal) tells the story of the coming of the Industrial Revolution to the South. This canal was constructed in the city of Augusta in 1845, creating a separate and controlled flow of water from the Savannah River that was used as a source of power, a water supply for the city of Augusta, and a means of safe navigation around the natural rapids of the river. The canal takes advantage of the great "fall line," the 53-foot drop in elevation over four miles between the Piedmont Plateau to the west and the Coastal Plain to the east. The rushing water diverted into the canal provided a steady source of mechanical power that brought textile and other manufacturing to the region. By 1847, the first factories—a saw and grist mill and the Augusta Factory—were built, and many more would follow, eventually lining the banks of the canal. The canal was spearheaded by Augusta native Henry H. Cumming who envisioned the city as "the Lowell of the South" (see John H. Chafee Blackstone River Valley National Heritage Area).

The importance of the canal was magnified by the Civil War. Augusta was one of the few manufacturing sites in the South and was chosen by the Confederates to be their "powder works," manufacturing gun powder for the war; twenty-eight related structures were eventually built along the canal, occupying two miles of canal banks. The Powder Works ultimately produced more than three million tons of gunpowder. After the war, manufacturing grew quickly along the canal; the massive Enterprise, King, and Sibley cotton mills and the Lombard Ironworks were constructed, along with many others. Local farm families, primarily women and children (called "operatives" in the manufacturing mindset), moved to Augusta to work in the mills, enduring eleven and a half hour shifts, work speed-ups and pay reductions. National labor groups organized strikes, but they were ineffective.

As electricity became a more common source of power in the United States, the

A historic photo of the interior of the Enterprise Mill illustrates the scale of the area's textile mills.

canal was used to drive electrical generation facilities. By the early 1890s, the city had electric streetcars and street lighting powered by the canal, and most factories converted from mechanical to electrical power. Periodic improvements to the canal were made over the next several decades, but the textile mills ultimately closed in the 1980s (as they did elsewhere in the United States) and the canal was neglected; consideration was even given to draining the canal and using the bed as the site for a superhighway. But at the same time, interest developed in using the canal for recreation and tourism. Ultimately, the canal and its environs was designated as a National Heritage Area in 1996. The vast Enterprise Mill was redeveloped into an office and residential complex which also houses the Augusta National Heritage Area Discovery Center, an attractive and engaging visitor center and museum. The undeveloped land between the Savannah River and the canal is now a wetland that is habitat for varied plants and animals. The canal still serves as a major source of drinking water for the city and continues to generate electricity from the former textile mills for city residents. Navigation along the canal is now recreational only.

Augusta Canal is managed by the Augusta Canal Authority, a special purpose government agency that has worked with its partner organizations to preserve and develop the canal as a natural, historic, and economic resource. The area is a centerpiece of the city and has become a popular education and recreation destination for visitors and residents. There are many opportunities to learn about the history and significance of the Augusta Canal and to participate in outdoor recreation opportunities including tours of the canal on replica cargo boats and hiking, biking, and paddling on the area's trail system and canal. The canal and surrounding area was designated a National Historic Landmark in 1978.

Attractions

A variety of attractions are found in the NHA, most of them engaging explanations about the history and operation of the Augusta Canal. However, there are opportunities for several types of outdoor recreation as well.

Augusta Canal Discovery Center

This is the grand visitor center of the NHA, cleverly embedded in the repurposed Enterprise Mill. It tells the story of the Augusta Canal, includes an award-winning orientation film (in the Rotary Club of Augusta Centennial Theater, a good example of the many partner organizations that help make this NHA successful), a hydropower demonstration turbine, exhibits on living and working in the textile mills, and lots of other educational materials. And here's where you board the canal boat tours, (see below). All comers should start their visit here.

Savannah Rapids Park

The canal headgates, the mechanisms that control the flow of water from the Savannah River into the canal, are located at the

Replica canal boats offer visitors a tour of the Augusta Canal; this is a highlight for many visitors.

upstream end of the canal. Here you'll find a park operated by Columbia County (another NHA partner) that offers interesting displays on the operation of the canal and access to outdoor recreation opportunities. Facilities and services include picnic shelters, restrooms, water fountains, a playground, and the Savannah Rapids Pavilion Conference Center. A Georgia Regional Visitor Information Center is located in the restored Lockkeepers Cottage.

Petersburg Canal Boat Tours

These canal boat tours are a highlight for most visitors; the boats are replicas of the original vessels that transported cargo through the canal, and tours are conducted with a guide who recounts the period of the 19th-century textile mills, the Confederate Powder Works, and two of Georgia's remaining 18th-century houses, all as you float by them in your open-air boat. Watch for wildlife, including herons, otters, and the occasional alligator. The two 65-foot boats are named in honor of Henry Cumming, the founder of the canal, and William Phillips, the canal's first engineer.

Trails

A network of trails in the NHA support walking/hiking/running, biking, and canoeing/kayaking. The canal's eight-mile towpath is a wide, level trail that was used by mules to pull canal boats through the waterway and is now used by pedestrians and bikers. Other shorter trails explore the wooded and urban areas of the NHA and Augusta. Canoes and kayaks are welcome on the canal, but it may be dangerous to boat on the steep section of the Savannah River. Two bridges span the canal, offering great views and a convenience for trail users. Bicycles and kayaks can be rented in the local area.

Events

An active schedule of events is hosted by the NHA and its community partners. Examples include a local farmers' market, fun runs/walks, and moonlight and music boat cruises—check the Augusta Canal website (see below).

> For more information about Augusta Canal and to help plan your visit, see the area's official website (augustacanal.com) and the website of the National Park Service (nps.gov/places/augusta-canal-national-heritage-area.htm).

Baltimore National Heritage Area

State: Maryland
Description: This NHA celebrates Baltimore's long and diverse history that includes its maritime heritage, contributions of the African American community to its distinctive culture, and the heroic story of Fort McHenry and the Star Spangled Banner.
Sample Attractions:
• Fort McHenry National Monument and Historic Shrine
• Peale Museum
• Inner Harbor
• Scenic Byways

Baltimore is a historic city with a past that's almost as eclectic and rich as the nation. Its location at the junction of America's North and South has marked the city with elements of both, and its major seaport has brought a global influence to its economy and culture. Its status as a National Heritage Area dates to 1997 when the State of Maryland designated the city as a recognized "heritage area" based on its concentration of historic, cultural, and natural resources. After several years of planning and programing, the state enhanced the city's status in 2002 by designating it as "Baltimore City Heritage Area." A feasibility study for status as a National Heritage Area was conducted over the following years, and in 2009 the area was designated by Congress as Baltimore National Heritage Area (Baltimore); this designation applies to much of the city. The NHA is managed by Baltimore Heritage Area Association, Inc. in concert with the National Park Service and many other partners.

Baltimore's history extends back to 1729 when it was founded on the banks of the Patapsco River. Agriculture was the dominant land use and economy, with wheat and tobacco the principal crops. The latter is highly labor intensive and enslaved Africans were brought to the area for this reason. The

slave trade flourished at Baltimore's port; the census of 1790 found that the city's population included twice as many slaves as free blacks. Slaves were used extensively in other sectors of the city's economy, including the marine trades (joiners, caulkers, painters, sailmakers, etc.) and track builders for the Baltimore and Ohio (B&O) Railroad. It's ironic that African Americans were treated so poorly given the importance they—and other minority groups—eventually played in the development of the city's distinctive culture.

Even before the end of the Civil War, most African Americans in Baltimore were free, working alongside white laborers and immigrants from throughout Europe. Communities of free black residents built more than 20 churches, founded more than 30 benevolent societies, and established schools. Some historians think the city was also active in the Underground Railroad. But even after the Civil War, blacks were subject to the indignities of segregation and Jim Crow laws. Nevertheless, the African American population continued to grow and assert itself. Religious leaders were active in the Niagara Movement, an organization

founded to promote racial equality, and members of the community helped form the National Association for the Advancement of Colored People (NAACP) in 1912. African Americans developed a strong cultural component of the city that expressed itself in music, education, literature, art, and law. For example, well-known jazz musicians include Eubie Blake, Cab Calloway, and Billie Holiday. Baltimoreans were active in the modern Civil Rights Movement, working to dismantle segregation. Thurgood Marshall, born and educated in the city, was active in this movement and went on to become the nation's first black Supreme Court Justice. Baltimore's active port encouraged immigrants from across Europe and these people have made important contributions to the multi-racial and ethnic culture of Baltimore.

Many people know Baltimore for its historic role in the War of 1812 when the fate of the young nation hung in the balance as British forces attacked the city by land and sea. The powerful British Navy rained bombs and rockets on the harbor's Fort McHenry for 25 hours, but when the smoke and fog cleared, the American flag was still flying, the American troops remained at their stations,

Fort McHenry, a unit of the National Park System, bravely repulsed a British invasion in the War of 1812 and inspired our national anthem.

and the British forces retreated. Francis Scott Key witnessed the battle and was so inspired that he wrote a poem to commemorate the event, his words later put to music to become the country's national anthem. (It should be noted that Key was a slaveholder and that portions of the anthem (e.g., "the land of the free") are considered by some to be racist.)

Attractions

The richness of Baltimore is found primarily in its diversity; the city exhibits a distinctive synergy that makes it more than the sum of its parts, and its attractions are spread across its neighborhoods and communities—in fact, these neighborhoods and communities are where you can find most of the city's attractions. Here are some examples.

Fort McHenry National Monument and Historic Shrine

This unit of the National Park System celebrates the role this fort played in bravely repulsing a British Invasion and inspiring the national anthem. The facility includes a Visitor and Education Center, an orientation film, a self-guided tour of the fort, interpretive programs, and the Fort McHenry Guard performing drill, musket, and artillery demonstrations.

Star-Spangled Banner Flag House

Mary Pickersgill purchased this home in the early 1800s and established a flag sewing business out of her home. She, her daughter, nieces, and Grace Wisher, an African American indentured servant, sewed the flag that was raised over Fort McHenry during the Battle of Baltimore.

Peale Museum

Opened in 1814, this is the oldest museum building in the country, and is a home for authentic Baltimore stories. The museum works with local historians, artists, educators, and others to craft its exhibits; the museum describes itself as "a new kind of civic museum: both laboratory and a teaching museum—not just a treasure house."

The historic home of Mary Pickersgill doubled as a flag sewing business; now known as the Star-Spangled Banner Flag House, it was here that the flag flown over Fort McHenry during the Battle of Baltimore was made.

The mobile lighthouse, Chesapeake, was launched in 1930 and is now a part of the Historic Ships of Baltimore.

Inner Harbor

Baltimore's Inner Harbor is one the nation's first urban redevelopment projects and is a powerful draw for both residents and visitors. It includes the National Aquarium, Historic Ships of Baltimore, Maryland Science Center, Port Discovery Children's Museum, the Baltimore Visitor Center, and great restaurants; cruises around the harbor are also available.

Scenic Byways

Four Scenic Byways cross Baltimore (NHA). The Charles Street National Scenic Byway is 12 miles long and follows grand Charles Street, connecting the wooded landscapes of Baltimore County with the city's Inner Harbor. Falls River Scenic Byway is 39 miles long and follows the Jones Falls Valley to downtown Baltimore. Maryland's Historic National Road runs 170 miles (in Maryland) and is part of the first federally-funded interstate highway. Star Spangled Banner Byway is 106 miles long and features the events of

1814 when Baltimore fought off the British invasion of the city during the War of 1812.

Walking Tours

Baltimore has developed a series of walking trails that explore the city's most historic and interesting neighborhoods; find descriptions and directions for these trails on the Baltimore website (see below).

Lightship *Chesapeake*

Lightships were once used as mobile lighthouses in the Chesapeake Bay, and this one was launched in 1930, serving mariners for decades. The ship carried two 5,000 pound anchors to help ensure it stayed "on station." The *Chesapeake* is now moored in Baltimore's Inner Harbor and is part of the Historic Ships of Baltimore collection.

B&O Railroad Museum

This important museum is generally considered the birthplace of American railroading. It includes the Mount Clare Station, the oldest passenger and freight station in the United States, and the first railroad complex in the nation. In 1850, the B&O erected an ironworks where the first iron railroad bridge was designed. The museum's large circular roundhouse was completed in 1884.

Steam Tug *Baltimore*
Part of the Baltimore Museum of Industry, the *Baltimore* was built in 1906 and is the oldest steam-powered tugboat in the United States. The tug operated for decades in Baltimore Harbor, ultimately serving as the city's official welcoming vessel.

Parks and Open Spaces
Baltimore is fortunate to have an especially rich system of parks and residential neighborhoods that were influenced by America's great landscape architect, Frederick Law Olmsted and his sons who were also landscape architects. Their philosophy was that parks and landscapes were an essential part of democratic society, and this is evident in Baltimore. Druid Hill Park, home of the Maryland Zoo, is the most well-known park in the city.

USS *Constellation*
This large warship, a 22-gun sloop powered by sail, was commissioned in 1855. It played a central role in ending the foreign slave trade and was an active participant in the Civil War, proving essential to the Union war effort. The ship was decommissioned in 1955 after 100 years of service and is now a National Historic Landmark. (The ship shouldn't be confused with the ship of the same name that was launched in 1797.) The *Constellation* is moored in Baltimore's Inner Harbor and is open to the public.

For more information about Baltimore and to help plan your visit, see the area's official website (explore-baltimore.org) and the website of the National Park Service (nps.gov/places/baltimore-national-heritage-area.htm).

Druid Hill Park reflects the democratic character of Baltimore.

Blue Ridge National Heritage Area
State: North Carolina
Description: Located in the foothills and mountains of North Carolina, this NHA celebrates its rich natural environment, the presence of Cherokee Indians, its distinctive agricultural, crafts, and musical culture, and its outstanding opportunities for outdoor recreation.
Sample Attractions:
- Great Smoky Mountains National Park
- Blue Ridge Parkway
- Blue Ridge Music Trails
- Outdoor Recreation

Cades Cove Baptist Church and Cemetery are part of the reconstructed early American settlement of Cades Cove.

The foothills and mountains of western North Carolina have a longstanding reputation for their distinctive sense of place, defined by their natural and cultural heritage. The Blue Ridge Mountains are among the oldest on Earth, once as high as the Rockies and the Alps, but eroded over deep time to their lower elevations and rounded ridges. And the region is equally defined by its rich human history, featuring the presence of Native Americans, historic sites, agricultural productivity, generous array of historic and modern crafts, and lavish musical tradition. Blue Ridge National Heritage Area (Blue Ridge) was established in 2003 to celebrate, preserve and share all this and more; this is a large geographic area that includes the 25 counties in western North Carolina. It's managed by Blue Ridge National Heritage Area Partnership, a non-profit organization that works with the National Park Service and other partner organizations.

The mountains at Blue Ridge may not be as high as they used to be, but they're impressive in other ways. They include the highest mountain in the eastern United States (Mount Mitchell at 6,684 feet), the deepest gorge in the east (Linville Gorge is sometimes called "the Grand Canyon of the East"), the highest waterfall in the east (Whitewater Falls), and the oldest river in North America (paradoxically called the New River). The area is biologically diverse due to its range of elevations and abundant precipitation. Moreover, this area is far enough south that it was spared the effects of the glaciers of the last several ice ages and has therefore had a million years without major geological change and this has given plants and animals an especially long period to evolve and diversify. Wildflowers can be prolific and include showy mountain laurel and rhododendron. Wildlife includes black bears and elk. The NHA's lovely landscape is on display everywhere, but especially in Great Smoky Mountains National Park and the Blue Ridge Parkway, both among the most heavily visited units of the National Park System.

This region was home to the Cherokee Indians who had an advanced civilization. But they were pushed aside by early European-American settlers and eventually rounded up and marched to present-day Oklahoma; this was the infamous Trail of Tears. Some Cherokee hid in the area's forests and their descendants are called the Eastern Band of Cherokee Indians, and many still live in the area. They purchased land in the 1870s that's called "Qualla Boundary" or "The Qualla" (the meaning of the word "Qualla" is uncertain). This is not a conventional Indian reservation that was set aside by the federal government; it's nearly 83 square miles of land owned by the tribe and is inhabited by more than 8,000 residents. Cherokee culture has had an influence on the region's music and crafts heritage. The early history of the region also includes 16th-century explorers from Spain who were searching for gold.

Beginning in the 18th century, European and African settlers began to occupy the area. The isolation of the region gave rise to local traditions that include distinctive agriculture, music, and crafts. These practices have been highly developed and passed down through generations and draw visitors from around the world. Early settlers adopted some of the Cherokee's farming practices, growing corn, beans, and squash, among other more traditional crops; many of today's farmers have added Christmas trees, ornamental plants, mushrooms, herbs, and wine grapes to their farms.

Distinctive and original forms of music emerged from the region that were derived from the settlers' European and African roots. The resulting "bluegrass" is played throughout the NHA and is influenced by ballad singing, gospel, blues, Anglo-Irish fiddle, old-time, and sacred music. Performances are held regularly throughout the region; check the NHA's website (see below) for a schedule.

Crafts are another important and defining component of Blue Ridge culture. As with music, this art form draws on the area's multi-cultural heritage, including the Cherokee. There are more than 4,000 craft makers in the region who have taken crafts to an art form that focuses on both traditional and contemporary expressions. Genres include blacksmithing, weaving, basket-making from native materials, doll-making, quilting, and woodworking. Once again, check the NHA's website for festivals, galleries, etc.

Attractions

Blue Ridge is widely known for its rich natural and cultural resources, and the area's visitor attractions are high in both number and quality. Examples include national parks and forests, Cherokee history, mountain music and crafts, local foods, museums, colorful towns, and much more. Here are some outstanding examples.

Great Smoky Mountains National Park

This important national park straddles the spine of the Appalachian Mountains with roughly half the park in the NHA. The park is known for its biodiversity, dramatic mountain vistas, rocky streams, impressive waterfalls, old growth forests, iconic wildlife, remarkable array of wildflowers, and remnants of early American settlements. It includes more than 800 miles of trails, including 71 miles of the Appalachian Trail.

Blue Ridge Parkway

Known as "America's favorite journey," this 469-mile-long unit of the National Park System offers a slow, relaxing drive through the Appalachian Mountains of Virginia and western North Carolina. Enjoy stunning long-range vistas and close-up views of rugged mountains and pastoral landscapes. There are frequent turnouts and lots of trails. Special attractions along the parkway include the Folk Art Center (milepost 382), the Moses H. Cone Memorial commemorating the summer estate of the textile magnate (milepost 294), and Linn Cove Viaduct, a seven-mile segment of the Parkway that hugs the face of Grandfather Mountain and is considered an engineering marvel (milepost 304).

Qualla Boundary/Cherokee

As noted above, the Eastern Band of the Cherokee purchased land in the 19th century that is now their home. The area is known as the Qualla Boundary, and visitors are welcome in the town of Cherokee to see traditional crafts, hear ancient stories, and visit the Museum of the Cherokee Indian, the Qualla Arts and Crafts Co-op, and the Oconaluftee Indian Village.

Asheville, Biltmore Estate, Thomas Wolfe Memorial

The small city of Asheville was founded in 1797 and has grown into a trendy town locally known as the "Paris of the South" (with only a slight snicker). Here you'll find 45 sites on the National Register of Historic Places and world-class resorts and mountain retreats. George Vanderbilt built his famous estate, Biltmore, on the outskirts of town and it's the largest private residence in America. Thomas Wolfe, considered a giant of 20th-century American literature, was raised in

The Blue Ridge Parkway, a unit of the National Park System, offers a slow, relaxing, and highly scenic drive through the mountains of North Carolina.

George Vanderbilt built his famous estate, Biltmore, on the outskirts of what is now bustling Asheville.

a Victorian home in Asheville that he celebrated in his autobiographical novel, *Look
Homeward, Angel.*

Carl Sandburg Home National Historic Site

Known as the "poet of the people," Sandburg
offered a popular voice that continues to
speak to readers through his words, activism,
music, and the beauty and serenity of Carl
Sandburg National Historic Site, a unit of
the National Park System.

Blue Ridge Craft Trails

Travel along the Blue Ridge Craft Trails to
visit with artists in their studios and galleries.
The NHA's website (see below) includes 11
itineraries arranged by geographic location.

Blue Ridge Heritage Trail

Use the NHA's website (see below) to design
a journey through the area that connects 70
heritage sites. Use the interactive map and
search by heritage theme, activities/interests,
and towns.

Blue Ridge Music Trails

A bit of a misnomer, this is not a fixed trail
but a collection of sites throughout the NHA
that celebrate the rich musical heritage of
the region. See the website of the NHA (see
below) for a list of sites within the region
that focus on the history and performance of
bluegrass, old-time, gospel, and other traditional music, and then formulate your own
route through the NHA to connect them.

Appalachian Trail

This is the iconic 2,180-plus-mile footpath
along the Appalachian Mountains from

Visitors will find 71 miles of the famous Appalachian Trail
in Great Smoky Mountains National Park; consider walking
a few miles along this iconic trail.

Georgia to Maine. You can find 71 miles of
the trail in Great Smoky Mountains National
Park; consider walking at least a few miles of
this historic trail.

Outdoor Recreation

Visitors will find nearly unlimited opportunities for a range of outdoor recreation activities at Great Smoky Mountains National
Park, Blue Ridge Parkway, Pisgah, Nan-
tahala, and Cherokee National Forests, and
the area's many state parks.

For more information about Blue Ridge
and to help plan your visit, see the
area's official website (blueridge
heritage.com) and the website of the
National Park Service (nps.gov/places
/blue-ridge-national-heritage-area.htm).

Cache la Poudre River National Heritage Area

State: Colorado

Description: This NHA celebrates the lovely Cache la Poudre River as it flows out of the Rocky Mountains, its agricultural heritage, and its colorful western towns.

Sample Attractions:

- Poudre Learning Center
- Poudre Trail
- Picnic Rock Natural Area
- Fort Collins Whitewater Park

The name Cache la Poudre (cash la POO-der) is derived from a group of French trappers who were attacked by Native Americans in the 1820s while traveling the river (another version of the story has it that the men were trapped by a snowstorm); one of the men yelled to the others, "cache la poudre," meaning "hide the gunpowder." At least, that's the most common version of the story. Regardless, the name stuck for this beautiful river that flows out of the Rocky Mountains,

Local residents like to say that "the Cache la Poudre River flows through Colorado history."

dropping 7,000 feet, then spilling onto the Great Plains and then flowing through the towns of Bellvue, Laporte, Timnath, Fort Collins, Windsor, and Greeley before merging with the South Platte River. That's a lot of action for a river that's only 125 miles long! But the river is a vital part of the history and present-day culture of this region, irrigating agricultural lands, writing precedent-setting water law for the western states (where water is scarce and especially valuable), helping to meet the water needs of the half million people who now live along the Front Range of the northern Rockies, and offering beauty and recreation to residents and visitors alike.

The river has received well-deserved attention over the past few decades. The upper portion of the river was designated by Congress as a Wild and Scenic River in 1986, and this designation protects this section of the river from development of dams and related water development projects. It also protects the lower reaches of the river from the potential impacts of such water development projects including water withdrawals and low flows. Shortly after, the nonprofit organization Poudre Heritage Alliance (PHA) was founded and initiated several studies of the lower portion of the river in conjunction with the National Park Service and other groups. Educational projects about the river were also designed and implemented. In 2009, Congress passed legislation establishing Cache la Poudre National Heritage Area (Cache la Poudre) and PHA was designated as the management or coordinating entity.

PHA works with many other partner organizations, including NPS, local towns, regional universities, as well as historic and other attractions in the region. Cache la Poudre covers 45 miles of the lower portion of the river, often referred to as the "working Cache," referencing its historic role in irrigating surrounding lands and serving the water needs of the growing population of the region. It begins in Larimer County at the eastern edge of the Roosevelt National Forest and ends just east of the town of Greeley at the confluence with the South Platte River. NHA designation extends to the lands that make up the 100-year floodplain of the river. The mission of PHA is to provide current and future generations the opportunity to understand and celebrate the area by careful planning and facilitation of educational programs and related amenities in collaboration with residents, the private sector, and government entities.

Attractions

Those involved in Cache la Poudre like to say that "the Cache la Poudre River flows through Colorado history," and this story is told through the work of PHA and its many partner organizations. Drive, bike, boat, and hike this region and you'll see headgates, flumes, water measurement devices, and an intricate network of ditches that signify the importance of the river to agricultural development. And you'll find charming towns that now celebrate the river for its history, beauty, and the recreation opportunities it provides.

Poudre Learning Center
This 65-acre site on the Poudre River offers interdisciplinary learning opportunities that address the history, science, economics, stewardship, and beauty of the river. The center is housed in a historic brick schoolhouse.

Poudre Trail
This multi-use trail allows visitors to experience the historic Poudre River firsthand. The trail connects several of the region's towns that grew up on the river.

Watson Lake State Wildlife Area
Watson Lake was formed during construction of a nearby reservoir and sits at the base of a cliff that is a nesting site for golden eagles and other birds. The lake and surrounding land is a small state wildlife area that is known for attracting hooded mergansers and other migratory waterfowl in spring and fall.

Picnic Rock Natural Area
This developed recreation area on the river offers picnicking, fishing, rafting/kayaking, and hiking. This stretch of river features challenging whitewater, especially during the spring runoff; PHA's "Play it Safe on the Poudre" program cautions boaters to be careful in this area.

Fort Collins Water Works
This historic facility (constructed in 1882-83) provided the growing town of Fort Collins with a reliable supply of drinking water and water to fight fires. The facility sits on a 26-acre site that includes a portion of the historic Cherokee Trail and Overland Stage route. The plant and surrounding area are being restored into an interpretive center.

Fort Collins Museum of Discovery
This innovative museum paints a broad picture of the world, how it works, and the place of visitors within it by using a mix of science

Fort Collins is one of several charming towns along the river with historic "old towns."

and history to discover the interconnectedness of the world.

Great Western Sugar Beet Flume and Bridge

The sugar beet factory that was once located here was one of more than 20 that served Colorado farmers in the early-to-mid 1900s; the flume that carried waste from this plant is all that's left. An innovative and unusual 1926 suspension bridge is also located here. This site is on the National Register of Historic Places.

Fort Collins Whitewater Park

Just north of Fort Collins's appealing and lively Old Town, the city has created a park that brings the river back to a more natural state and offers easy access to the river. The park is well used by kayakers, tubers, and others. As with all such areas, visitors must be cognizant of the inherent dangers of swiftly flowing rivers.

River Bluffs Open Space

This park-like area in the town of Windsor offers access to the Poudre Trail with parking, restrooms, and picnic tables.

Windsor History Museum

Located in the town of Windsor, this museum features historic buildings that illustrate the history of the town. There are exhibits and hands-on activities for all ages in the Train Depot.

Centennial Village Museum

This museum was established in 1976 in the town of Greeley and tells the history of this region—westward expansion, immigrants, and early town life. It includes many historic buildings, some of which are original and some replicas.

> For more information about Cache la Poudre and to help plan your visit, see the area's official website (poudre heritage.org) and the website of the National Park Service (nps.gov /places/cache-la-poudre-river-national -heritage-area.htm).

Cane River National Heritage Area

State: Louisiana

Description: This historic NHA honors its original Native American inhabitants, 18th-century French and Spanish explorers, large cotton plantations, and rich Creole culture as expressed in the area's language, architecture, cuisine, and music.

Sample Attractions:
- Cane River Creole National Historical Park
- City of Natchitoches
- Melrose Plantation
- Cane River National Heritage Trail

The Cane River region of rural western Louisiana is a land of fascinating contrasts: conquest and colonialism, war and peace, wealth and poverty, slavery and freedom, a single culture from many. Even the very geography and place name of the region is a bit of a quandary; the Cane River isn't really a river, but the remnants of one, a large oxbow lake formed by the nearby Red River. (An oxbow lake is created by a river that meanders [bends] sharply; if the river cuts off a meander, it forms an isolated crescent-shaped lake no longer connected to the river.) Nevertheless, this body of water is still called Cane River and it helps define its namesake National Heritage Area. Cane River (NHA) includes 116,000 acres of land that runs along Cane River for about 35 miles, with the historic town of Natchitoches in the north and Monette's Ferry in the south. The history of this place is more complex and interesting than most, though it isn't well known in mainstream American culture.

History began here early by American standards with Caddo Indians who occupied the region, farming corn, beans, squash, and pumpkins, hunting local wildlife (bears, deer, and birds), and fishing. At the beginning of the 18th century, explorers from both France and Spain traveled through this New World region, trading with the Native Americans. A barracks and storage house to support trade were constructed by the French in the winter of 1713-14, and this was the beginning of the present-day historic town of Natchitoches. Both France and Spain claimed large areas of land in the region as colonies for their respective nations and there was tension between these expansionist countries. After the Louisiana Purchase in 1803, when the United States bought vast western lands claimed by France, the western border of this new American land (particularly the border between the eventual states of Louisiana and Texas) was in dispute with Spain and both countries agreed to create a large "No Man's Land" in western Louisiana as a buffer to help keep this tension under control. This further isolated this rural land and the increasingly diverse people who lived there.

The French began to import slaves from Africa and the West Indies to work the area's farms in the early 18th century leading to profound changes to the region for the next two centuries. Initially, growers used enslaved workers to raise tobacco and indigo, but with Eli Whitney's invention of the cotton gin in 1793, growers began to raise cotton; many got rich, establishing large plantations such as Magnolia, Oakland, and Melrose that are now in the NHA (see attractions below). The Civil War brought more change, freeing the enslaved people in particular. However, many former enslaved laborers continued to work on the plantations as sharecroppers or tenant farmers, which often meant that they continued to be indentured to the plantation owners through debt.

The historic mix of diverse cultures in this region—Native American, French, Spanish, African—has given rise to a rich new culture that is often called *Creole*. Creole draws on the 300-year multi-cultural history of all of the peoples who have lived here, adopting and adapting practices that are in keeping with sustainable use of the land and waters that are foundational elements of life in this region. Important dimensions of Creole culture include a distinctive language, architecture, cuisine, music, and other traditions that are the proud heritage of contemporary residents and vital attractions for visitors.

Attractions

The lands, waters, and people of this region in western Louisiana have combined to form a distinctive cultural landscape. Visitors will recognize this throughout Cane River, in the historic plantations, buildings, and communities, and in the land itself, with its lovely parks, forests and waterways.

Cane River Creole National Historical Park

This unit of the National Park System was established in 1994 to preserve the cultural landscape of the Cane River region. The park includes two Creole cotton plantations, Oakland and Magnolia. Both plantations are nearly complete in their historical settings, including landscapes, outbuildings, furnishings, and artifacts. The property on which Oakland was constructed was originally obtained by a land grant from Spain in 1789. In 1859, the plantation included 145 enslaved individuals who lived in 30 dwellings; these people worked in the fields but also were midwives, nurses, cooks, weavers, shoemakers, brick masons, painters, and ginners. The main house was probably constructed by enslaved workers in 1821 and is an example of a raised Creole plantation house constructed of bousillage, an infill material of mud, Spanish moss, and deer hair. Although the land for Magnolia Plantation was acquired in 1753, the main house wasn't built until about 1840, and the plantation has 21 historic buildings and structures. In both plantations, the enslaved population created their own communities where they married, had families, made clothing, furniture, tools and toys, and tended their own gardens where they grew sweet potatoes, watermelons, turnips, and other vegetables. Both Oakland and Magnolia plantations, including many of their outbuildings and grounds, are open to visitors.

City of Natchitoches

Natchitoches is the oldest permanent settlement in the Louisiana Purchase. As noted above, it began as a barracks and storage house constructed by the French in the winter of 1713-14. It's now a charming city with lovely architecture and is the thriving tourist center for the region. The 33-block downtown section of the city is a National Historic Landmark.

The River Walk in the historic town of Natchitoches

Melrose Plantation

A National Historic Landmark, this lovely, historic plantation marks two hundred years of local history. The plantation was started by Louis Metoyer, son of a former

Melrose Plantation, a National Historic Landmark, was started by Louis Metoyer, son of former enslaved woman Marie Therese Coin Coin.

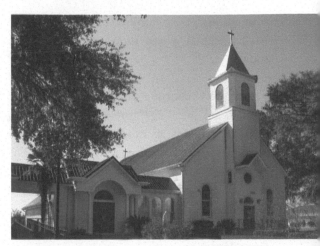

For nearly two centuries, St. Augustine Catholic Church and Cemetery has served members of this multiracial, multicultural community.

enslaved woman, Marie Therese Coin Coin, and French Planter, Claude Thomas Pierre Metoyer. Many descendants of the family live along Cane River today. The site includes nine historic buildings. The plantation also tells the story of Clementine Hunter, one-time Melrose cook, who emerged to become Louisiana's most celebrated primitive artist.

Cane River National Heritage Trail

This driving route that winds through rich farmland, charming villages, forests of live oaks, and southern magnolias and crepe myrtles of Cane River features many of the historic sites of the NHA. Examples include colonial forts, plantation homes, distinctive Creole architecture, and historic landmarks. The trail connects Natchitoches in the north to Cloutierville in the south.

Grand Ecore Visitor Center

The US Army Corps of Engineers, which manages some of the water resources in the region, operates a visitor center at Grand

Ecore, a small community about four miles north of Natchitoches. The visitor center features exhibits on the water and other resources of the region as well as the area's natural and cultural history. The site sits on an 80-foot bluff over the Red River and offers a panoramic view.

St. Augustine Catholic Church and Cemetery

For nearly two centuries, St. Augustine has been the locus of gathering and worshiping and honoring the final resting place for members of this distinctive multiracial, multicultural community.

Los Adaes State Historic Site

In 1716, the Spanish built a presidio, Los Adaes, a few miles west of the French-controlled town of Natchitoches to protect the interests of Spain on the frontier. Los Adaes was 800 miles from the nearest Spanish supply post and was forced to trade with the French at Natchitoches. Many Spanish soldiers and their families ultimately moved to Louisiana, where their descendants live today.

Kisatchie National Forest

This large national forest of more than 600,000 acres is an outdoor playground for residents of the region and visitors alike. Activities include fishing, hunting, hiking, kayaking, camping, mountain biking, and horseback riding.

Fort Jesup

In the early 19th century, there was a dispute between the United States and Spain about the western border between Louisiana and Texas (part of Mexico). Tensions between the two countries led the United States to establish Fort Jesup in 1822 near the "No Man's Land" (see above) between the countries to protect the nation's interests. Portions of the fort have been reconstructed and a visitor center offers information and other services. The fort is a National Historic Landmark.

> For more information about Cane River and to help plan your visit, see the area's official website (canerivernha .org) and the website of the National Park Service (nps.gov/places/cane -river-national-heritage-area.htm).

Champlain Valley National Heritage Partnership

States: Vermont and New York
Description: This grand cultural landscape celebrates its diverse natural and cultural heritage; Lake Champlain and associated waterways served as "corridors of commerce,"

its role in the American Revolution and the Civil War contributed to the "making of nations," and its strong role in environmental protection helps define its theme of "conservation and community."
Sample Attractions:
• Adirondack Park
• Fort Ticonderoga
• Saratoga National Historical Park
• ECHO, Leahy Center for Lake Champlain

Like all NHAs, Champlain Valley National Heritage Partnership (Champlain Valley) is distinctive by virtue of the many characteristics, events, and resources that have shaped this region's history, culture, environment, and economy. But it also includes the area's long devotion to taking a partnership approach to defining and honoring its highly refined sense of place. In fact, the NHA wears the word "partnership" right on its shirtsleeve; Champlain Valley is the only NHA that puts "partnership" right in its name, the word that binds everything together in a metaphoric manner.

Champlain Valley was established by Congress in 2006 to help nurture this region. This is a large area of geography that's bound together by the historic waters of Lake Champlain and associated waterways, including Lake George, the Champlain Canal, and portions of the upper Hudson River. The Champlain Valley lies nestled between Vermont's Green Mountains on the east and New York's Adirondack Mountains on the west. This is a large watershed that covers portions of Vermont, New York, and Quebec. Of course, Quebec isn't part of the United States and therefore can't be an "official" part of Champlain Valley, so the NHA simply invited them to participate, ultimately receiving a letter from the prime minister endorsing the management plan and participating when and where it can. The Champlain Valley region is the ancestral homeland of Algonquin and Iroquois peoples, it played an important role in the establishment of the United States and Canada, its waterways served as routes of travel for early European-American explorers, and it was the site of important battles in the American Revolutionary War and the Civil War.

NHAs are required to have a management entity to guide planning and management and Champlain Valley was fortunate to have one readily available: the Lake Champlain Basin Program (LCBP). This was such an easy choice that Congress wrote it into the enabling legislation of the NHA. LCBP is itself a partnership-based program with its focus a little more narrowly defined on Lake Champlain and its drainage basin. Both LCBP and Champlain Valley prepare and update management plans that guide their activities, but they share this responsibility. Champlain Valley prepares its stand-alone management plan, but this plan is also a chapter within the LCBP management plan.

The management plan for Champlain Valley was completed and approved in 2011. It begins with a thoughtful vision statement, sufficiently broad to address the large collection of natural and cultural resources that contribute to the region's distinctiveness and that invites all of its diverse potential partners to participate:

> The people of the region continue to value and celebrate the significance of their rich heritage. Historic cities, traditional small towns, and picturesque hamlets prosper. Healthy farms and forests are still an important part of community life. Heritage sites thrive. The water and air are clean. We teach and respect the history and traditions of those who have come to live here and are stewards of the place they have settled. We continue to overcome political borders and nurture a robust economy and strong regional identity through thriving collaboration among individuals, organizations, and businesses.

Through its enabling legislation and the deliberations of the partnership members, this vision was then translated into three interpretive themes that guide much of the work of the Champlain Valley. The first is "Corridor of Commerce" which highlights the historic water-based trading routes between the Atlantic Ocean and the St. Lawrence River and the ultimate construction of the Champlain Canal between Lake Champlain and the Hudson River, opening trade to New York City. Later, railroads were built as a more economic form of transportation and steamboats plied Lake Champlain, carrying cargo and tourists from "downcountry." Most recently, a system of interstate highways and country roads (some of them designated as national and/or state scenic byways) carry visitors and residents alike through the NHA and beyond.

The second interpretive theme is "Making of Nations," referencing the role of the Champlain Basin in military campaigns,

The six-million acre Adirondack Park was an early manifestation of the American Conservation Movement.

including the American Revolutionary War, the War of 1812, and the Civil War. Evolution of government and society, from Native American tribes to the birth of American democracy and the Canadian Confederation, along with government that emphasizes local control as a vital component of democracy (e.g., Vermont's distinctive town meetings) are all recognized under this interpretive theme. Native Americans, particularly the Algonquin and Iroquois Tribes, had a strong cultural presence in the Champlain Valley region and even participated in the conflicts that were fought within the region.

"Conservation and Community" is the third interpretative theme. Native Americans farmed in the Champlain Valley, but early European settlers intensified this practice, clearing much of the region's native forests and causing unanticipated environmental damage. Based on this experience, the American Conservation Movement was born and supported in the observations and writings of Vermonter George Perkins Marsh in the mid-19th century and the preservation of the six-million-acre Adirondack Park in upstate New York shortly after. The region is now in the forefront of many modern agricultural initiatives, including organic farming, local food movements, and farmers' markets. More broadly, conservation is supported by thriving parks, forests, and wildlife reserves throughout the Champlain Valley region.

Attractions

The interesting and important cultural landscapes of the Champlain Valley region serve as an attractive home for residents of the area's rural communities, small towns, and growing cities. And the area includes many attractions for visitors in the form of appealing cultural landscapes, historic sites, museums, dramatic mountains, farms, lakes and streams, and parks and recreation areas. The LCBP has developed an inventory of more than 400 cultural heritage, historic, natural, and/or recreation resources in the Champlain Valley (this inventory can be found at: champlainvalleynhp.orgresources.htm). While it's challenging to recommend only a few of these attractions, here are some that would be on just about everyone's "must do" list.

Adirondack Park

Located in upstate New York, the massive Adirondack Park (more than 6 million acres) was set aside for preservation by the state in 1885 as an early manifestation of the American conservation movement. In the park you'll find extensive opportunities for outdoor recreation, including wilderness areas and more than 2,500 lakes.

Fort Ticonderoga

Built in the mid-1700s, this large star-shaped fort guarded the strategic portage route between Lake Champlain and Lake George.

Fort Ticonderoga guards the strategic portage route between Lake Champlain and Lake George.

The British controlled the fort during the early days of the American Revolutionary War until it was captured in a surprise attack by Vermont's Green Mountain Boys and other state militia under the command of Ethan Allen and Benedict Arnold. (However, the British regained control two years later.)

Lake Champlain Maritime Museum

A research and educational institution located on the shores of Lake Champlain, the Lake Champlain Maritime Museum invites visitors to tour its collections, including life-size reproductions of the historic Lake Champlain vessels, *Lois McClure* and *Philadelphia II*. Visitors can also "tour" a Lake Champlain shipwreck using realtime images of a Remotely Operated Vehicle.

Green Mountain National Forest

The nearly 400,000-acre Green Mountain National Forest is found in western Vermont. Managed by the US Forest Service, it offers extensive opportunities for hiking and

Historic Lake Champlain sits at the junction of Vermont, New York, and the Province of Quebec.

other outdoor recreation opportunities, helps maintain the state's clean water, biodiversity and wildlife habitat, and provides timber and other forest products to the state's economy.

Saratoga National Historical Park

Saratoga National Historical Park is a unit of the National Park System and includes the battlefield where American forces won their first significant victory over the British in the Revolutionary War. Visitors can see the battlefield by driving or biking the Battlefield Tour Road, taking a guided tour of the park, visiting the historic Schuler House, walking through Victory Woods, and climbing the stairs to the top of the Saratoga Monument.

ECHO, Leahy Center for Lake Champlain.

ECHO is a visitor and research center on the shore of Lake Champlain at Burlington, Vermont. The facility includes more than 100 interactive exhibits, and its aquarium houses 70 species of fish, reptiles, and amphibians.

Shelburne Farms

Shelburne Farms is a non-profit organization that owns and operates a 1,400-acre working farm, forest, and National Historic Landmark on the shores of Lake Champlain in Shelburne, Vermont. Visitors can walk the farm's extensive grounds and participate in educational programs.

Shelburne Museum

Shelburne Museum offers visitors the experience of human history, art, and design that are a reflection of New England life and culture. Visitors are invited to walk the campus in Shelburne, Vermont, that includes 39 historic structures on 45 acres, each building filled with beautiful, fascinating, and whimsical objects. Highlights for many visitors include the steamboat *Ticonderoga*, a period schoolhouse, a lighthouse, and a round barn.

Burlington Community Boathouse and Greenway (Bike Path)

Burlington, Vermont's Community Boathouse sits at the bottom of College Street on the shore of Lake Champlain and reflects the design of commercial boats that once sailed up and down the Lake. The Boathouse offers great views of the lake and includes a restaurant and marina. The sightseeing vessel the *Spirit of Ethan Allen* ties up here. The adjacent Burlington Greenway (formerly known as the Burlington Bike Path) follows the shore of the lake for eight miles and is an important recreation resource for Vermont residents and visitors alike.

Vermont State Parks

Vermont has 55 state parks offering high-quality opportunities for outdoor recreation that is compatible with the conservation of Vermont's natural resources and aesthetics. The parks provide outdoor recreation opportunities (e.g., hiking, camping, fishing, water sports), environmental education and information, and help support the economies and values of local communities. Many of these parks are found within Champlain Valley.

New York State Parks
New York offers 180 state parks that include campgrounds, hiking trails, beaches, and boat launches. Many of these parks are located in the Champlain Valley and invite visitors to explore the area's natural and cultural history.

Champlain Bikeway
This 363-mile bike route encircles Lake Champlain and the Richelieu River in Quebec. There are also many connecting theme loops. Two bridges and three ferry routes cross the lake and can be used to make a variety of shorter biking adventures.

Champlain Bridge Area
The area around the present-day Champlain Bridge includes a rich cluster of important historic sites, including Crown Point State Historic Site, Chimney Point State Historic Site, and the Champlain Monument. The Lake Champlain Visitor Center located here is a good place to start your visit.

Lake Champlain Ferries
Three historic ferry routes have been operating on Lake Champlain for decades and offer efficient ways to travel through the Champlain Valley. The crossings connect visitor attractions in Vermont and New York, and are visitor attractions in and of themselves.

For more information about Champlain Valley and to help plan your visit, see the area's official website (champlain valleynhp.org) and the website of the National Park Service (nps.gov/places /champlain-valley-national-heritage -partnership.htm).

Crossroads of the American Revolution National Heritage Area

State: New Jersey

Description: New Jersey sat squarely between the British stronghold of New York and the new nation's capital in Philadelphia, making it strategically important to both the British and the Americans, and this played out in the many important battlefields of the state; Crossroads of the American Revolution is the only NHA to focus exclusively on the American Revolution.

Sample Attractions:
- Morristown National Historical Park
- The Old Barracks Museum
- Washington Crossing State Park
- Fort Lee Historic Park

New Jersey stood at the crossroads of colonial America, at the juncture of New England and the southern states, and between the British stronghold of New York and the new nation's capital in Philadelphia. Due to the state's vital importance to both the British and Continental Armies, it was inevitable that New Jersey was central to so much military action throughout the Revolutionary War. Indeed, the record of the war proves the state's importance. The National Park Service's American Battlefield Protection Program lists 296 significant military engagements in the state and hundreds more skirmishes from 1775 through 1783, and General George Washington and his Continental Army spent more time in New Jersey—more than 800 days—than in any other state during the seven years of the war. This includes the Continental Amy's famously storm-plagued encampment in Morristown in the winter of 1779-80. Meanwhile, the Revolution was a civil war in New Jersey, with a third of residents remaining loyal to the British Crown, another third in favor of the revolution, and the other third neutral. New Jersey paid a steep price during the war, including major disruptions to its prosperous farming economy and the violence and damage done to its people and property. The official website of the NHA (see below) includes the well-developed "Meet Your Revolutionary Neighbors" feature, a series of short biographies about how people from all walks of life and regions of New Jersey dealt with the struggles brought on by the war.

Crossroads of the American Revolution National Heritage Area (Crossroads) was established in 2006 as the only NHA to focus exclusively on the American Revolution. Managed by the non-profit Crossroads of the American Revolution Association, Crossroads includes 14 New Jersey counties totaling 2,155 square miles. Given the complexity of the seven-year war for independence, Crossroads interprets the Revolutionary War in New Jersey through a series of 14 storylines:

Road to Morristown: After the Battle of Princeton, the Continental Army faced a long and arduous march to Morristown where the exhausted army camped during early 1777.

Maritime Wars: The battle of the seas is an often untold story of the Revolutionary War. Facing the famously powerful British Navy, the Continental Congress commissioned private merchant vessels to harass and capture British supply ships, seizing valuable cargo.

Defense of the Hudson: The Continental Army defended its control of the Hudson River and ultimately drove the British out of the New York City area.

Retreat Across the Jerseys: General Washington was forced to retreat from Fort Lee on the Hudson and march his troops across New Jersey to the safety of Philadelphia. New Jersey towns along the route provided refuge.

Greater Morristown-Patriot Enclave: The Continental Army spent the winters of 1777-78 and 1779-80 encamped in the vicinity of Morristown, and the latter winter was arguably the most severe on record. The natural features of the Great Swamp and Watchung Mountains offered safety from British forces.

Washington-Rochambeau Revolutionary Route: A series of roads passing through New Jersey carried American and French troops to Yorktown, Virginia, where the British Army surrendered.

Philadelphia Campaign: In the summer of 1777, the British Army planned to invade Philadelphia from the south. General Washington rushed troops to defend the capital and sites in New Jersey played an important role.

Middlebrook and the Defense of New Jersey: New Jersey's Watchung Mountains served as a defensive position and strategic location for the Continental Army to monitor British activities in New York City and on the Hudson River.

Divided Loyalties: Opinion on the war divided New Jersey residents—some opposed the war, some supported it, and some were neutral—resulting in divided families, neighbors, and communities.

Road to Monmouth: British and Continental troops faced the worst of a New Jersey summer as they trekked toward an inevitable collision in June of 1778. When they crossed paths at Monmouth, the newly trained Continental Army fought the British to a standstill, proving they could stand up against the world's premier army.

Delaware River Towns: New Jersey's towns along the Delaware River felt the war's impact when the Continental Army reached Trenton and crossed the river into Philadelphia.

Battles of Connecticut Farms and Springfield: The British Army attempted to reach the Continental Army's Morristown encampment by trying to break through the Watchung Mountains defenses. The resulting Battles of Connecticut Farms and Springfield repelled the attack with help from the New Jersey militia.

Forage Wars: In the winter of 1777, the British established a base at New Brunswick, New Jersey, and troops rode into the surrounding countryside to find forage for their horses. The Continental Army encamped at Morristown harassed these British troops.

Ten Crucial Days: On Christmas Day, 1776, General Washington's army unexpectedly crossed the Delaware River to successfully engage the British Army in Trenton. This was quickly followed by another surprise attack on the British in Princeton. The success of these battles strengthened the morale and resolve of the Continental Army.

Attractions

Crossroads includes many battlefields, historic sites, and museums scattered across much of the State of New Jersey. The following seven locations are "Gateway Sites"—places that offer an introduction to New Jersey's Revolutionary War heritage and are good starting places to begin your visit. While the areas have been preserved because of their historic value, some offer opportunities for hiking and other outdoor recreation activities. The Crossroads website (see below) includes suggested driving and walking tours.

Morristown National Historical Park

Nicknamed "Where America Survived," this unit of the National Park System is where General Washington and his Continental Army encamped during the bitterly cold winter of 1779-80, enduring repeated snowstorms that cut off supply routes for the 10,000 soldiers there. This large park includes

The Washington Museum in Morristown National Historical Park commemorates "the hard winter" encampment of General George Washington's Continental Army in 1779-80.

an attractive landscape of hills and valleys and the streams where the army collected water. It includes a museum and library and offers opportunities for hiking and biking.

Fort Lee Historic Park

This 33-acre park sits atop the Palisades on the Hudson River with overlooks of the river, Manhattan, and the George Washington Bridge. The site includes a reconstructed Revolutionary War encampment, gun batteries, and a visitor center and museum.

Liberty Hall Museum

Built by New Jersey's first elected governor, William Livingston, this Revolutionary-era mansion reflects 250 years of American history through the eyes of one of the nation's oldest families. As a home, it hosted many distinguished visitors, including George and Martha Washington. Enjoy a stroll around the home's impressive gardens.

East Jersey Old Town Village

This village includes sixteen reconstructed and replica 18th- and 19th-century structures that represent farm and merchant architectures typical of communities once found in New Jersey's Raritan Valley region. The site includes exhibits and living history programs and is located along the Washington-Rochambeau National Historic Trail.

Monmouth Battlefield State Park

This New Jersey State Park preserves the story of the Revolution's longest battle. The park includes a restored 18th-century farmhouse and visitor center. The park's landscape includes hilly farmland, fields, and forests and offers opportunities for hiking and horseback riding.

Washington Crossing State Park

On Christmas night, 1776, Washington's army crossed the Delaware River and began their march to Trenton and a surprise attack

Fort Lee Historic Park sits atop the Palisades of the Hudson River and includes a reconstructed Revolutionary War encampment, gun batteries, a visitor center, and museum.

Monmouth Battlefield State Park tells the story of the American Revolution's longest battle.

The Old Barracks Museum was used by both the British and Americans during the Revolutionary War.

Delaware and Lehigh National Heritage Corridor

State: Pennsylvania

Description: This historic transportation corridor through the mountains of northern Pennsylvania and along the banks of the Delaware and Lehigh Rivers includes canals and railroads that carried the region's vast anthracite coal deposits, helping to fuel the American Industrial Revolution.

Sample Attractions:

- National Canal Museum
- D&L Trail
- Hugh Moore Park
- The historic town of Easton

on British troops. The Continental Army moved on quickly to engage the British at the Battle of Princeton on January 3rd. The park on the Delaware River is also a popular place for hiking and wildlife viewing.

The Old Barracks Museum

Constructed in 1758 during the French and Indian War, the building was used by both the British and Americans during the Revolutionary War. It served as a hospital for the Continental Army and housed British prisoners of war. Preserved through the efforts of the Daughters of the American Revolution, the building has been a museum for over a century.

For more information about Crossroads and to help plan your visit, see the area's official website (revolutionarynj .org) and the website of the National Park Service (nps.gov/places/ crossroads-national-heritage-area.htm).

This historic transportation corridor in northeastern Pennsylvania preserves the network of canals and railroads that carried anthracite coal and iron from Wilkes-Barre, Pennsylvania, to Philadelphia in the 19th century and helped trigger America's Industrial Revolution. The corridor runs through the mountains of northern Pennsylvania and along the banks of the Delaware and Lehigh Rivers. Today, a central feature of the region is the 165-mile multi-use D&L Trail that connects the region's canals, railroads, towns, museums, and remnants of the area's industrial heritage. The Delaware and Lehigh National Heritage Corridor (Delaware and Lehigh) was established in 1988 to help preserve the natural and cultural resources of the region, to tell the history of this important place, and to nurture economic development through a program of heritage-based tourism. The NHA includes five counties and more than 100 municipalities and is managed by the non-profit Delaware and Lehigh National Heritage Corridor Commission.

Like most regions of the United States, the story begins with the Native American presence that can be traced back thousands of years. Here, the Susquehannock, Iroquois, Lenape Nation, and other groups of Native Americans lived in villages and subsisted through agricultural practices, hunting, and fishing. However, they were largely displaced by the influx of European settlers in the 18th century who practiced more intense forms of agriculture. The state's namesake, William Penn, promoted religious tolerance and land settlement, attracting thousands of immigrants who left their homelands in search of a better life.

But life in northeastern Pennsylvania changed in 1791 when Philip Grinder found anthracite coal in what is now Carbon County. Anthracite or "stone coal" as it is called locally is formed over millions of years as organic plant debris is compressed under the extreme pressure of many layers of sediment. Anthracite coal is especially hard due to its high carbon content, and its hot, long-lasting fire proved useful in industrial practices. And this rich resource of coal fueled development of one of the nation's earliest and largest iron and steel-making industries, along with associated development such as logging, sawmills, steel mills, cement-making, textiles, slate-mining, and tanneries, and the transportation networks that were needed to ship both the raw materials and the finished products. Canals and then railroads shipped goods to Philadelphia, New York, and beyond. Bethlehem Steel Corporation (sometimes referred to as "The Steel" and "America's Arsenal") grew from a modest iron producer to one of the most lucrative businesses in the United States, providing

steel for icons such as the George Washington and Golden Gate Bridges, naval ships, and Madison Square Garden. During World War II, its shipyards built 1,121 naval and merchant vessels and repaired 38,000 ships; it employed 220,000 workers.

Ultimately, most of these industries declined and the region began to address and rectify some of the environmental impacts of its industrial history; many public parks were established during this period. The underlying natural beauty of the area attracted suburban development, farms were rejuvenated, and technology, culture, and innovation replaced the industrial past. The historic districts of many towns have been revitalized.

In an appropriate nod to the transportation theme of Delaware and Lehigh, the NHA focuses on four "connections" that highlight the region. First, it connects residents and visitors to the pioneering industrial heritage of the area. Second, it connects residents and visitors to the region's outstanding natural environment. Third, it connects residents and visitors to the health and wellness benefits of outdoor recreation. Fourth, it connects the area's towns and cities with economic development opportunities that flow from the region's rich heritage-based tourism and outdoor recreation.

Attractions

This is a large and diverse region that celebrates both its history and its evolution into an attractive, lived-in landscape. The NHA includes nine National Historic Landmarks, six National Recreation Trails, two National Natural Landmarks, and hundreds of sites on the National Register of Historic Places. Its 100,000 acres of public lands and parks are a manifestation of the area's emphasis on outdoor recreation and the quality of life. Here are some places to start your visit.

D&L Trail

The D&L Trail is a long-distance, multi-use trail that runs through the NHA; 140 miles of the trail are now open with plans to extend it to over 165 miles. The trail follows the route that anthracite coal was shipped "from mine to market"; it winds through the northern mountains of the NHA, along the banks of the Lehigh and Delaware Rivers, and through the Lehigh Valley and Bucks County. It passes through towns, industrial centers, and along remnants of the Lehigh and Delaware canals. The NHA has established a Trail Friendly Business program that highlights local businesses that support and cater to the needs of hikers, bikers, and runners.

National Canal Museum

This museum and its associated attractions are a signature feature of Delaware and Lehigh. The museum focuses on America's golden age of canals, a colorful period of American history. It interprets the history

This is an early 20th-century painting of the Delaware Canal.

and culture of these waterways and the science and technology behind their construction and operation. Of course, visitors should tour the museum with its hands-on displays, but one of its most popular "exhibits" is a two-mile canal boat ride that starts on the adjacent Lehigh Canal. Ride the 50-foot, 110-passenger *Josiah White II* canal boat as it's pulled by two sturdy mules that walk the canal's towpath. Visitors should also see the museum's locktender's house and the Abbot Street Lock (Lock 47).

Hugh Moore Park

This 520-acre park (the site of the National Canal Museum described above) is a throwback to America's canal heritage, featuring a restored section of the Lehigh Canal, the Lehigh River, and a section of the D&L Trail. Visitors can walk, picnic, and bird in the park, as well as rent bikes, canoes, kayaks, and paddleboats to explore the canal.

Easton

The historic town of Easton is adjacent to Hugh Moore Park and the National Canal Museum (see above). The town was founded in the mid-1700s and features a large central square; the town sits on the banks of the site where the Lehigh and Delaware Rivers merge. Attractions include the historic town square, the Easton Farmers' Market (thought to be the oldest continually running open-air farmers' market in the nation), Sigal Museum, Nurture Nature Center, the Crayola Experience, walking tours, theater productions, and lots of galleries, restaurants, and boutiques.

The historic town of Easton includes a central square with a large Civil War Memorial; the town is adjacent to Hugh Moore Park, the National Canal Museum, and rides on the *Josiah White II* canal boat.

Jim Thorpe

This town in the scenic mountains of Carbon County was known as Mauch Chunk until 1954 when it was renamed for the famous Native American athlete, Jim Thorpe. Attractions include the Asa Packer Mansion, Mauch Chunk Opera House, and the visitor center inside the town's train station. North of town, the D&L Trail winds through 26 miles of Lehigh Gorge State Park with views of the Lehigh River and canal ruins. Heading south from downtown, the D&L Trail crosses the Mansion House Bridge opened in 2019 to connect the trail to Weissport and south to the Lehigh Valley.

Washington Crossing Historic Park

This Pennsylvania state park lies along the D&L Trail and Delaware Canal and memorializes the world-shaping events of late-December 1776 when George Washington's army crossed the icy Delaware River for a surprise attack on the Hessians, shifting the momentum of the Revolutionary War. The park includes many historic buildings. Each December, visitors can witness a reenactment of Washington's Delaware River crossing.

> For more information about Delaware and Lehigh and to help plan your visit, see the area's official website (delaware andlehigh.org) and the website of the National Park Service (nps.gov/places /delaware-and-lehigh.htm).

Erie Canalway National Heritage Corridor

State: New York

Description: This 500-mile network of canals begun in 1817—an engineering marvel of the times—eventually connected the Hudson River with the Great Lakes; this NHA features the canal, historic vessels, more than 200 canal communities (many with lively Main Streets), and several units of the National Park System.

Sample Attractions:

- Four Units of the National Park System
- New York State Canalway Water Trail
- Canal Towns
- Erie Canalway Trail

The Erie Canalway National Heritage Corridor (Erie Canalway) website trumpets "Start your adventure here!," and that's good advice. You'll find engineering marvels, historic vessels and canal sites, lively Main Streets in more than 200 cities, towns, and villages, great outdoor recreation opportunities, abundant wildlife, and hundreds of festivals and special events. These attractions are strung along more than 500 miles of navigable waterways across the full expanse of upstate New York; there are adventures to be had on land and water. All this began in 1817 when the New York legislature voted to build the Erie and Champlain Canals. Eight years later, the Erie Canal opened from Albany to Buffalo, a daring and profound engineering project that transformed the continent. The canal has been expanded three times to accommodate larger boats and more traffic. Today, the New York State Canal System is a 524-mile network of navigable inland waterways connecting the Hudson River with Lake Champlain, Lake Ontario, Cayuga Lake, Seneca Lake, and Lake Erie, allowing boats to travel from the Atlantic Ocean to the Great Lakes and on to connecting waterways in Canada and the American Midwest.

Originally four feet deep and 40 feet wide, the Erie Canal was cut through fields, forests, rocky cliffs, and swamps. It crossed rivers on aqueducts and lifted and lowered boats with 83 locks. The initial project took eight years of grueling work, most of it powered by laborers (some were Irish immigrants, but most were American born) and animals. Builders adapted and applied design and construction techniques from Europe, but this was a wilderness environment and took on an unprecedented scale. At that time, the only engineering school in North America was at West Point, but the building boom triggered by the canal stimulated universities like Rensselaer Polytechnic Institute and Union College to add engineering to their curricula. The glossary of the canal's technical infrastructure is indicative of its complexity: locks, lift bridges, moveable dams, guard gates, powerhouses, gate cabinets, tow paths, aqueducts. Managing the canal system required water control, toll collection, maintenance and emergency repairs, and administration of property, employees, contractors, and boaters. The Erie Canal opened in 1825 with a ceremonial "wedding of the waters" (officials poured water from Lake Erie into the Atlantic Ocean) performed by the governor and long-term canal supporter, DeWitt Clinton. (Skeptics had dubbed the canal "Clinton's Ditch").

Canal boats carried cargo and passengers. Mules towed freight boats from Buffalo to Albany and steam tugs towed large rafts of canal boats down the tidal Hudson River to New York Harbor. Upstaters and Midwesterners found new markets for agricultural goods, timber, building stone, and dozens of other products in East Coast cities and overseas. Freight rates fell 90 percent compared to ox-drawn wagons. Passengers traveled in relative comfort between Albany and Buffalo in five days—not the two weeks previously needed in crowded, uncomfortable stagecoaches.

History suggests the canal carried more than cargo and passengers—it was a conduit of ideas and progress (perhaps roughly analogous to today's Internet). New York became the "Empire State," generating wealth and prestige, and New York City became America's busiest port, most populous city, and a center of international commerce and finance. As the canal opened America's interior to settlement, it brought new ideas such as abolitionism, women's suffrage, Utopian communities, and religious movements. Stronger connections between the Northeastern and Midwestern states influenced attitudes toward slavery. The canal was one route of the Underground Railroad, used by slaves escaping the South on their way to Canada. It transported soldiers and supplies that helped win the Civil War. The women's rights movement can be traced to Seneca Falls, New York, where the nation's first Women's Rights convention was held in 1848. Evangelical sects, millennialists, and new religious groups such as Latter Day Saints (Mormons) and Seventh Day Adventists were started in canal towns and spread westward. And the canal advanced the idea of America's entrepreneurial "can-do" spirit, an important component of America's then growing reputation and character.

Unfortunately, settlement prompted by the canal accelerated dispossession and removal of Native Americans following the American Revolution. This was a period when "Indian removal" was US policy. Native Americans were seen to interfere with economic progress and settlement of the West. The Erie Canal spanned the traditional territories of five tribes of the Haudenosaunee (Iroquois) Confederacy: the Mohawk, Oneida, Onondaga, Cayuga, and Seneca nations. Members of all five tribes still live in New York, but reservations are far from traditional homelands along the state's waterways and many were forced to move to Canada and the Midwest.

Erie Canalway is managed by the Erie Canalway National Heritage Commission, with members appointed by the Secretary of the Interior, and a non-profit partner, the Erie Canalway Heritage Fund. They work with the National Park Service and other government agencies, non-profit organizations, and businesses. Management objectives include preserving and sharing the canalway heritage, promoting the NHA as a national and international tourism destination, and supporting the vibrant communities connected to the site. The Commission administers a grants program with partner organizations to support creative place-based projects.

Attractions

Erie Canalway is a world-class tourism destination and visitors come from all around the world to experience its natural and cultural heritage. It features the canal itself, many museums and historic sites, boating, hiking, biking and cross-country ski trails, more than 200 canal communities, and several units of the National Park System.

Four Units of the National Park System

The National Heritage Area includes four units of the National Park System. Fort Stanwix National Monument is a reconstruction of the fort that guarded an important portage connecting the ocean with the Great Lakes. It stands near the spot where construction of the Erie Canal began on July 4, 1817. Saratoga National Historical Park preserves and interprets the battlefield where American forces won their first significant victory over the British in the Revolutionary War. It occupies high bluffs overlooking the Hudson River and Champlain Canal. Women's Rights National Historical Park

Saratoga National Historical Park commemorates the battlefield where American forces won their first significant victory over the British in the Revolutionary War.

tells the story of the first Women's Rights Convention held in Seneca Falls, New York, in 1848. It lines both banks of the Cayuga-Seneca Canal. Theodore Roosevelt Inaugural National Historic Site in Buffalo occupies the house where Roosevelt was sworn in as 26th president after the assignation of William McKinley in 1901. Before his rise to national office, Roosevelt served as governor of New York where he was an outspoken champion of enlarging and rebuilding the Erie Canal as the waterway we use today. In addition to these park units, the NPS administers North Country National Scenic Trail that utilizes portions of the old Erie Canal towpath between Syracuse and Rome as part of its 4,600-mile route from Vermont to North Dakota.

The long-distance, multi-use Erie Canalway Trail connects many of the canal's historic towns.

National Historic Landmarks and National Register of Historic Places

Erie Canalway includes 34 National Historic Landmarks (the New York State canal system itself is a National Historic Landmark) and over 800 listings on the National Register of Historic Places.

Festivals, Events, and Programs

Hundreds of thousands of residents and visitors celebrate canal heritage, food, beverages, and traditions at canal-related festivals, events, and programs each year. Check the NHA's official website (see below) for dates.

New York State Canalway Water Trail

This network is comprised of 450 miles of canals and interconnected lakes and rivers that support canoeing, kayaking, and paddle boarding and includes 140 access sites and several sites that alllow camping. This canalway "flows through time and history"

and is a great way to experience the canals and the landscapes and communities through which they flow. The NYS Canalway Water Trail Guidebook and Map Set is a useful resource.

Construction of the 500-mile network of canals connecting the Hudson River and the Great Lakes was begun 1817.

Canal Towns

Many communities were born and grew up along the canal and most feature waterfronts on the canal, historic Main Streets, historic sites, and a variety of visitor services.

Erie Canalway Trail

More than three-quarters of this 365-mile, off-road trail has been developed between Albany and Buffalo. This is a multi-use trail that supports biking, hiking, and cross-country skiing. The trail parallels much of the canal and accesses many canal towns.

> For more information about Erie Canalway and to help plan your visit, see the area's official website (erie canalway.org) and the website of the National Park Service (nps.gov/erie /index.htm).

Essex National Heritage Area

State: Massachusetts

Description: This is the formative story of much of the last 400 years of American history, starting with the experience of the Puritans who landed on the coast of New England in the early 1600s; the region eventually grew into prosperous seaports and its skilled mariners played an important role in the American Revolution.

Sample Attractions:

- National Park Service Regional Visitor Center
- Salem Maritime National Historic Site
- Essex Coastal Byway
- Saugus Iron Works National Historic Site

This story begins in the very earliest period of American history when Puritans landed on the coast of "New England" in the early 1600s and formed small colonies. These immigrants struggled mightily to survive and were helped in their endeavor by the thriving Native Americans who occupied the area in settlements scattered throughout the region; these people taught the new Americans how to farm and hunt. By the early 18th century, the descendants of the European immigrants were beginning to prosper as a result of their focus on the sea for sustenance and trade. The early coastal colonies grew into prosperous seaports specializing in shipbuilding, coastal fishing, and exporting fish overseas. These skilled mariners became leaders of the American Revolution, rebelling against British restrictions and taxes and volunteering their ships to support the nascent American Navy. In fact, some historians consider Essex County to be "the birth place of the American Navy"; the first armed vessel to sail for the Continental Army, the schooner *Hannah* (commissioned in 1775), was built here and sailed by local men. After the war the British banned trade with America, and the New England merchants sent ships to the Far East, importing valuable commodities such as coffee, tea, pepper, and spices. Profits from this trade were used to fund a manufacturing component of the economy with a focus on leather, shoes, and textiles.

Essex National Heritage Area (Essex) was established in 1996 to help tell this formative story of the nation and to preserve the heritage of this important region, including its natural and cultural history. Essex includes the 500-square-mile region north of Boston that is Essex County, Massachusetts, and includes 34 cities and towns, some of which were instrumental in the birth of the American Industrial Revolution. The NHA includes a treasure of natural and cultural resources, including nearly 10,000 historic structures on the National Register of Historic Places, 400 historic farms, 86 museums, 35 National Historic Landmarks, 22 state parks, two units of the National Park System, and a national wildlife refuge. The NHA is managed by Essex Heritage (known in more formal terms as Essex National Heritage Commission), a non-profit organization that takes a community-driven approach to heritage conservation and economic development. Essex Heritage works with the National Park Service and many other partner organizations; its management philosophy is that by engaging people in the nation's past, they help them forge deeper relationships with the communities, institutions, and environments of Essex County, and this improves the quality of life for today and the future for both residents and visitors.

The diversity of this NHA is reflected in the seven cultural districts in Essex County that have been recognized by the State of Massachusetts:

Essex River: This is where the town meets the river and where you can find ancient burial grounds, active shipyards and marinas, the Essex River with its salt marsh borders, the Essex Historical Society and Shipbuilding Museum, and a charming tourist infrastructure.

Harbortown: This is the hub of Gloucester's downtown and the center of the oldest seaport in New England; it's a place for vibrant arts and entertainment that appeals to both visitors and residents. Here you'll find the Cape Ann Museum and the HarborWalk (see below).

Rocky Neck: This district is one of America's oldest artists' colonies. Here you'll find studios and galleries, many featuring the local landscape; artists say it's something about the light. The Gloucester Theatre Company is here as well.

Riverfront: The town of Haverhill is marked by a creative streak that features art, music, and theater. Part of the town's heritage is its history of shoemaking and you'll find giant reproductions of 19th-century shoes and a shoeworkers' memorial.

Central Exchange: The lively core of the city of Lynn is known for its artists, multicultural cuisine, historic buildings, museums, galleries, and street performances.

Newburyport: Located on the Merrimack River, downtown Newburyport is charming and features historic buildings, arts, entertainment, dining, and shopping. This is widely known as the birthplace of the US Coast Guard and is rich in maritime history.

Rockport: This is another great venue for the arts and performances; shop in more than 40 art galleries and studios. The town features the world-class Shalin Liu Performance Center with its stage overlooking the Atlantic.

Salem is an important town in Essex and is known for the infamous witch hunts, since sensationalized. However, public records document the fact that more than 100 residents, mostly women, were accused of being witches in the late 17th century and 20 were put to death (five others died in jail) before the governor of Massachusetts arranged to bring this unfortunate period of history to an end in 1692. The visitor center in Salem (see below) shows a film, *Salem Witch Hunt: Examine the Evidence,* and conducts a walking tour, Myths and Misconceptions.

Attractions

This is a big NHA with an equally big story to tell: the engaging 400-year history of this important region, from the founding of the Massachusetts Bay Colony to the present. The NHA's website describes dozens and dozens of towns, museums, historic sites, tours and programs, and much more. Here are some places to start.

National Park Service Regional Visitor Center

This NPS Visitor Center is also the official visitor center for Essex (NHA). Located in Salem, this may be the most beautiful and interesting visitor center in New England; it features a 27-minute introductory film, exhibits, maps, a gift shop, and knowledgeable staff. Consider starting your visit to Essex here.

Salem Maritime National Historic Site

This is America's first National Historic Site and is a unit of the National Park System. The site preserves and interprets over 600 years of New England's maritime history and includes 12 historic structures along the Salem waterfront. The site features the replica tall ship *Friendship of Salem* designed to present the appearance of an original 1797 Salem-built vessel. When open, visitors can go aboard and speak with volunteers and crew.

The replica tall ship *Friendship of Salem* helps interpret over 600 years of New England's maritime history.

Saugus Iron Works National Historic Site commemorates the European iron workers who brought their special skills to America.

Saugus Iron Works National Historic Site

This unit of the National Park System is known as the "birthplace of the American iron and steel industry." Located on the banks of the Saugus River, European immigrant iron makers brought their special skills to America. The site includes working waterwheels, forges, mills, a historic 17th-century home, and a lush river basin. The site produced wrought iron and cast iron from 1646 to approximately 1670. The National Register of Historic Places calls the site "the first chapter in America's book."

Essex Coastal Byway

This 90-mile roadway links 14 coastal communities from Lynn to Salisbury and makes for a lovely and educational outing. Features include scenic views, period architecture, historic sites, and opportunities for outdoor recreation.

Bakers Island Light Station

This historic lighthouse was built in 1798 on 60-acre Bakers Island in Salem Sound. The lighthouse is now owned by Essex Heritage and has been restored. Day trips to the island are offered on the landing craft *Naumkeag*; overnights can be arranged by camping on the island or staying at the assistant lighthouse keeper's house.

Baker Island Light Station, built in 1798, is a popular visitor attraction.

Theme Guides

Essex Heritage, in cooperation with its partners, has produced a series of Theme Guides to help visitors find their way to and through so many of the NHA's heritage-related attractions. Collectively, these eight guides help define the region: titles include *Guide to First Period Architecture, Maritime Guide, Industrial Trail, Guide to the Great Outdoors, Guide to Farms and Agriculture, Art Escapes Trail, McIntire Historic District Walking Trail,* and *A Visitor's Guide to 1692.* You can find these guides on the official website of Essex Heritage (see below).

> For more information about Essex and to help plan your visit, see the area's official website (essexheritage.org) and the website of the National Park Service (nps.gov/places/essex-national -heritage-area.htm).

Freedom's Frontier National Heritage Area

States: Kansas and Missouri

Description: This vast NHA of more than 31,000 square miles explores the foundational meanings of the American concept of freedom, including the opportunity to make a better life, the historic struggle for freedom among African Americans that led to the Civil War, and the continuing fight for freedom by African Americans during Reconstruction, the Jim Crow era, and to the present day.

Sample Attractions:

- *Brown v. Board of Education* National Historic Site
- Nicodemus National Historic Site

- Negro Leagues Baseball Museum
- National Frontier Trails Museum

What could be more foundational to our nation than freedom? And here, at its namesake Freedom's Frontier National Heritage Area (Freedom's Frontier), you can explore and learn a great deal about the evolution and status of the rich American concept of freedom. In fact, this large NHA, spanning 41 counties in eastern Kansas and western Missouri and totaling more than 31,000 square miles, leads visitors along three dimensions of freedom that have played out in this region and that changed the Unitd States in important ways.

First, the American land itself is a vital dimension of freedom, the opportunity to make a new life without constraints of wealth, class, politics, or religion. This is why a half million pioneers made their way west across the Missouri/Kansas border from civilization to the opportunities of the frontier. This could be a perilous journey because this was the point where river travel ended and great overland treks began along one of several historic routes, including the Santa Fe, California, Mormon, and Oregon Trails. Settlers purchased provisions at border towns and began their historic journeys. However, Kansas was seen by many as permanent Indian Territory because it was occupied by Plains Indians and other tribes forcibly relocated to this area following decades of land disputes. In fact, Native Americans were seen as a threat to the freedom that pioneers were seeking and to the notion of America's Manifest Destiny.

Second, the historic struggle for freedom among African Americans that led to the Civil War had its genesis here in the Missouri/Kansas Border War (often called "Bleeding Kansas") in 1854. The Missouri Compromise was an 1820 act of Congress that allowed the new State of Missouri to be a "slave state," balancing the number of states that allowed slavery with those that didn't ("free states"). But the act also specified that new states located north of the southern boundary of Missouri (which applied to Kansas) would determine for themselves whether or not to allow enslavement. The Kansas-Nebraska Act of 1854 officially opened the Territory of Kansas to settlement and eventual statehood and this caused supporters and opponents of slavery to move to Kansas to participate in determining the outcome of this issue, leading, in turn, to violent and continued conflict over the issue and serving as an important precursor of the Civil War.

And third, the struggle for freedom by African Americans and others didn't end with the Civil War; and this quest continues to test American society. For example, slavery-related fighting in the area defined by Freedom's Frontier continued after the Civil War had officially concluded. Also, after the Civil War, tens of thousands of African Americans relocated to Kansas from southern states to escape the continuing and often violent discrimination they experienced by the Ku Klux Klan and others. This was the "Exoduster Movement," the 1870s exodus of African American people from southern, former slave states to free states. African Americans in Kansas, Missouri, and elsewhere continued to struggle against inequality and segregation during the Jim Crow and Civil Rights eras. One of the NHA's most well-known examples of the fight for freedom is the landmark 1954 Supreme Court ruling, *Brown v. Board of Education* of Topeka, Kansas, ending racial segregation in public schools. This ruling struck down the "separate but equal" doctrine and ushered in the contemporary American Civil Rights Movement. Much of the seemingly eternal search for freedom and equality of all peoples continued to play out in the region defined by this NHA and is an example for the nation.

Freedom's Frontier had its genesis in a grassroots movement to tell the diverse, interwoven, and nationally significant story about how the foundational concept of freedom has evolved and emerged in the region of western Missouri and eastern Kansas. The NHA was established in 2006 and is managed by the nonprofit organization, Freedom's Frontier Board of Trustees. Freedom's Frontier conserves and interprets the history of this region in an effort to inform the citizenry about this issue and to help guide future deliberation and action. Sharing historic and contemporary ideas about freedom and equality with residents and visitors to the area is the primary objective of Freedom's Frontier.

Attractions

Visitor centers, museums, historic sites, natural areas, and other attractions help residents and visitors better understand the foundational concept of freedom and the central role this region has played in exploring and fostering this American ideal.

Brown v. Board of Education National Historic Site

This unit of the National Park System celebrates and interprets what some call one of

Monroe Elementary School is an important location celebrated at *Brown v. Board of Education* National Historic Site; this unit of the National Park System commemorates the Supreme Court decision that led to integration of the nation's public schools.

the most pivotal opinions ever rendered by the American judicial system. Strictly speaking, the ruling ended legal segregation in public schools, but in a more human context, the NHA celebrates the bravery of a group of African American families who insisted on being treated equally.

Nicodemus National Historic Site

Former slaves left Kentucky in organized colonies at the end of the post-Civil War Reconstruction period to experience opportunity in the "promised land" of Kansas. Nicodemus is a manifestation of African American participation in the westward expansion of the nation and settlement of America's great frontier. Nicodemus is the oldest and only remaining Black settlement west of the Mississippi River. This unit of the National Park System includes the five historic buildings that represent the spirit of Nicodemus: church, self-government, education, home,

A young visitor is sworn in as a Junior Ranger at Nicodemus National Historic Site.

The Negro Leagues Baseball Museum helps preserve the history of African American baseball "when only the ball was white."

and business. These buildings illustrate the individual and collective strength of character and desire for freedom of these early pioneers who established Nicodemus. This is a unit of the National Park System.

Negro Leagues Baseball Museum

Founded in 1990, this Kansas City museum celebrates and preserves the rich history of African American baseball which was segregated until the late 1940s. In the words of the museum, visitors can return to the time "when only the ball was white."

Black Archives of Mid-America

The mission of this working museum is to collect, preserve, and make available materials that document the social, economic, political, and cultural histories of African Americans in the central United States.

Constitution Hall State Historic Site— Lecompton

Pro-slavery delegates of the Kansas territorial legislature wrote the Lecompton constitution here. Built in 1856, Constitution Hall

is the oldest wood frame building in Kansas that still stands in its original location. The first land office in the Kansas Territory was located here and the Kansas Supreme Court and the territorial legislature met in this building.

National Frontier Trails Museum

This museum in Independence, Missouri, tells the story of the exploration, acquisition, and settlement of the American West through the perspective of the Santa Fe, Oregon, and California Trails. An award-winning film and extensive use of pioneer diaries are highlights of the museum.

Oregon National Historic Trail

The Oregon Trail was one of several routes that pioneers used to help settle the West. The route travels through portions of Missouri and Kansas on its more than 2,000-mile passage to the West Coast. The National Park Service offers a driving guide to this and other sections of the route.

Battle of Island Mound State Historical Site

This site commemorates the first time African American troops were engaged in Civil War combat. The site encompasses Fort Africa where the 1st Kansas Colored Volunteer Infantry was camped in 1862 before a pitched battle with pro-Confederate forces.

Pony Express National Museum

On April 3rd, a lone rider departed St. Joseph, Missouri, for Sacramento, California, carrying a saddlebag of mail and other materials, and this was the beginning of the iconic Pony Express. Learn more about this American institution designed to help span the vastness of the American West.

Mahaffie Stagecoach Stop and Farm

This historic site is the only remaining stagecoach stop on the Santa Fe Trail preserved for the public. Visitors enjoy 1860s living history activities, including stagecoach rides.

Flint Hills Discovery Center

This site explores the natural and cultural history of the Flint Hills of Kansas, one of the last remnants of the nation's vast tallgrass prairies. Once covering 170 million acres of North America, most of it was plowed under for farmland, and today, less than 4 percent of this ecosystem remains.

For more information about Freedom's Frontier and to help plan your visit, see the area's official website (freedom sfrontier.org) and the website of the National Park Service (nps.gov/places /freedom-s-frontier-national-heritage -area.htm).

Freedom's Way National Heritage Area

States: Massachusetts and New Hampshire
Description: Fueled by the values of freedom, self-determination, and independence, this is where the American Revolution began as marked by the first armed conflict between the American militia and British troops and the famous "shot heard round the world"; in contrast, the landscape is now a peaceful and rich blend of forests, farms, hills, and valleys.
Sample Attractions:
• Minute Man National Historical Park
• Walden Pond State Reservation
• Museums and Galleries
• Outdoor Recreation

This important NHA is marked by "the shot heard round the world," the place where the American Revolution began and a nation was born. The famous Battle of Lexington and Concord on April 19, 1775, the first armed encounter between British troops and the American colonial militia, raged here along a 16-mile stretch of the Battle Road from Boston to Concord, Massachusetts. The spirit of the Americans was stiffened by the passion and eloquence of the compatriots who expounded on the values of freedom, self-determination, and independence. The site of this bloody battle, the first of many over the following seven long years, ultimately led to American independence. And there may be no better way to celebrate American independence than to spend some time in this place that may be the epitome of a grand and glorious cultural landscape.

Freedom's Way National Heritage Area (Freedom's Way) is appropriately large, encompassing 45 communities and nearly

1,000 square miles in northern Massachusetts and southern New Hampshire. As such, it's a model of large landscape-scale conservation, telling important national stories and placing them in their larger context. Freedom's Way is managed by the non-profit organization Freedom's Way Heritage Association; the website offers this eloquent vision statement of this distinctive place:

"The story of Freedom's Way National Heritage Area is intimately tied to the character of the land, as well as those who shaped and were shaped by it. Their stories can be found on village commons, along scenic roadways lined with stone walls, in diaries and artifacts, in a cabin by a pond, along a battle road, or hidden deep within a secret glen by the bank of a meandering river. Known or yet to be revealed, these stories provide a narrative that links the past to the future, reinforcing the region's sense of place. Freedom's Way connects the people, places, and communities of the Heritage Area through preservation, conservation and educational initiatives that protect and promote the natural, historic and cultural resources of the region."

The landscape of Freedom's Way is a rich blend of forests and farms, hills and mountains, and rivers and valleys, dotted with historic towns. This landscape was shaped by glaciers 10,000 years ago and refined by centuries of habitation and cultivation, beginning with Native Americans. Extensive areas of woodlands were cleared in the 18th and 19th centuries by European Americans for farm fields, but most of the region is now reforested. Its history and natural history are intertwined. The thinkers and doers of the American Revolution are complemented by equally revolutionary ideas such as the early conservation impulses of Ralph Waldo Emerson and Henry David Thoreau. It follows that the region has conserved nearly a quarter of its land in permanent protection: three National Wildlife Refuges, one unit of the National Park System, 23 local land trusts, 21 state parks and forests, 17 National Historic Landmarks, 61 national historic districts, and 337 listings on the National Register of Historic Places.

Freedom's Way works to tell the diverse stories of the region through a thematic lens. For example, the NHA recently commemorated the Centennial of the ratification of the 19th Amendment to the US Constitution which provided women the right to vote. It took nearly 80 years of groundwork to make this happen and the women from within the NHA contributed mightily. In celebration, Freedom's Way Heritage Association wrote and published an e-book, *Women Who Made History: Profiles from the Freedom's Way National Heritage Area*, profiling the contributions of 72 women who lived and worked in what is now the NHA. And preparations are already being made to celebrate the 250th anniversary of the American Revolution in 2026.

Attractions

Freedom's Way offers a wide range of attractions that are emblematic of its distinctive sense of place. Of course, its historic and attractive landscape is a prime attraction, admired by both residents and visitors, and a source of many outdoor recreation opportunities. This is complemented by artifacts of

The opening battle of the American Revolution is brought to life through a reenactment at Minute Man National Historical Park.

The famous Old North Bridge is the site of "the shot heard round the world" (Minute Man National Historical Park).

the region's history on display in many of its towns and villages in the form of historical parks, museums, and distinctive architecture.

Minute Man National Historical Park

This important unit of the National Park System preserves the opening battlefield of the American Revolution. The visitor center features the multimedia theater presentation, *The Road to Revolution*, that depicts Paul Revere's ride and the battles at Lexington Green, North Bridge, and along the Battle Road, and the ideals of freedom and independence that led to the Declaration of Independence. Visitors can walk the five-mile Battle Road Trail, visit historic Hartwell Tavern, The Wayside: Home of Authors, and North Bridge where "the shot heard round the world" was fired.

Outdoor Recreation Opportunities

As noted above, nearly a quarter of the NHA is in a conserved status, much of which is open to outdoor recreation—hiking, picnicking,

biking, fishing, canoeing, birding, and more. Prime examples include the Eastern Massachusetts National Wildlife Complex (which includes three National Wildlife Refuges), Middlesex Fells Reservation, Wachusett Mountain State Reservation, Leominster State Forest, Mass Audubon's Wachusett Meadow Wildlife Sanctuary, MassWildlife's Susan B. Minns Sanctuary, and many miles of trails.

Walden Pond State Reservation

This is the famous site where Henry David Thoreau lived in a small cabin for two years in the mid-19th century. His experience here helped inspire his 1854 book, Walden. Many people consider this site the birthplace of the American Conservation Movement.

Concord Literary Tradition

Many writers found inspiration in the region surrounding Concord, Massachusetts. This historic town includes the Orchard House (home of Louisa May Alcott), the Ralph

Visitors can see a replica of Henry David Thoreau's cabin at Walden Pond; his writings helped inspire the American Conservation Movement.

The Shakers' beliefs in gender equality and liberty helped shape the American philosophy of freedom; Fruitlands Museum helps tell this story.

Waldo Emerson House, and the Old Manse (home of Nathaniel Hawthorne).

The Shakers

The Shakers' religious beliefs in gender equality and liberty helped shape the philosophy of the Freedom's Way region. A number of privately owned homes with Shaker heritage can be found at Harvard and the historic Shaker house at Fruitlands Museum.

Farms

Agriculture has played a central role in the development and landscape of the region. Much of the NHA features dairy farms, orchards, market farms, and other specialty forms of agriculture. The region includes farm stands, community supported agriculture, and farm attractions that are patronized by both residents and visitors. The central and western portions of Freedom's Way are especially rich agricultural areas.

Museums and Galleries

Freedom's Way offers several high-quality museums and galleries. Examples include the DeCordova Museum (Lincoln), Tufts University Gallery (Medford), Cyrus E. Dallin Art Museum (Arlington), Fruitlands (Harvard), Concord Museum (Concord), and Fitchburg Art Museum (Fitchburg).

For more information about Freedom's Way and to help plan your visit, see the area's official website (freedomsway .org) and the website of the National Park Service (nps.gov/places/freedoms -way-national-heritage-area.htm).

Great Basin National Heritage Area

States: Nevada and Utah

Description: This large NHA features a portion of the nation's vast Basin and Range topography; it's one of the most sparsely

Great Basin National Park features a 13,000-foot mountain, a small glacier, beautiful alpine lakes, and groves of ancient bristlecone pines.

populated regions of the country and shows off its Native American and ranching heritage.

Sample Attractions:
- Great Basin National Park
- Nevada Northern Railway National Historic Landmark
- Great Basin Museum
- Pahvant Valley Heritage Trail

Deep within the vast Basin and Range geographic province of the American West lies Great Basin National Heritage Area (Great Basin). As the name suggests, this landscape is characterized by high-elevation desert valleys surrounded by generally narrow, north-south oriented mountain ranges reaching more than 13,000 feet. America's great 19th-century geologist Clarence Dutton famously described the area as resembling "an army of giant caterpillars marching toward Mexico."

Curiously, the rivers and streams in the area don't flow into any of the oceans, but disappear underground or pool in shallow lakes and marshes, where the water eventually evaporates. Even though this NHA is big—at 16,000 square miles, it's larger than several states combined—it's still just a microcosm of the Basin and Range region that occupies much of the western United States. And with fewer than 25,000 residents, it's one of the most sparsely populated regions of the country. Another marker of this geography on a grand scale is that the NHA occupies just two counties (White Pine County, Nevada, and Millard County, Utah) plus the Duckwater Shoshone Reservation in Nye County, Nevada. This is a classic American cultural landscape featuring distant horizons, colorful people and associated history, distinctive landforms, and night skies that are truly startling.

Archeological evidence suggests that humans have occupied this region for more than 13,000 years. Many of their descendants now live on four small reservations scattered around the region—the Duckwater Shoshone, Ely Shoshone, Confederated Tribes of the Goshute, and the Kanosh Band of the Utah Paiute. Their long traditions of dance, music, and art contribute to the rich cultural heritage of the NHA. European-American settlement began in the late 19th century. Pony Express riders traversed the region for a short period of time and prospectors followed. Copper was found near Ely, Nevada, in 1900 and mining towns were quickly established in several locations. The Nevada Northern Railroad was built to carry ore to smelters. The vast open spaces of the area were used by farmers, cattle ranchers, and sheepherders; some ranches have remained in the same family for generations. Ghost towns are all that remain of dozens of communities that went bust in this remote and arid area.

In 1998, residents of the region joined together to form the Great Basin Heritage Area Partnership in an effort to preserve its landscape and history. This grassroots organization successfully lobbied for establishment of Great Basin in 2006, and the partnership is the management entity. Great Basin includes nationally significant archeological, historical, cultural, natural, scenic, and recreational resources that are emblematic of the vast Great Basin region. Establishment of Great Basin has helped protect and interpret the heritage and traditions of this large and unique region.

Attractions

This is a big land with lots to see and do. It's a classic western landscape that includes high desert valleys surrounded by biologically rich mountains, multi-generational ranches, historic mines and railroads, and colorful towns. The NHA also includes a national park, three National Historic Landmarks, and several state parks. Enjoy the wide-open spaces of this remote region that offers visitors lots of elbow room. Here are several attractions that shouldn't be missed.

Great Basin National Park

From a natural history and recreation standpoint, this grand national park is the crown jewel of the NHA. Located in central Nevada near the Utah border, this remote park features a 13,000-foot mountain, a small glacier, beautiful alpine lakes, and groves of ancient bristlecone pines. The park also includes Lehman Caves, an impressive system of caverns best known for its elaborate shields, large stone disks that are sometimes connected with stalactites and draperies. The park offers campgrounds and 60 miles of hiking trails. Most visitors reach the park on US Route 50, known as "the loneliest road in America."

Nevada Northern Railway National Historic Landmark

The Nevada Northern Railway was built over a century ago to service what would become one of the largest copper mines in North America. Today, several of the original coal-fired standard-gauge steam locomotives that were ordered and delivered to the railroad over 100 years ago are still in operation and offer train rides. The site consists of the

The Nevada Northern Railway was built over 100 years ago to carry copper ore, but today offers scenic train rides to visitors.

Great Basin NHA includes Topaz National Historic Landmark, a World War II Japanese internment camp.

original railway locomotives, rolling stock, track, passenger station, and buildings that served the historic copper mining region of central Nevada for over a century. This attraction is in Ely, Nevada.

Topaz National Historic Landmark

Every nation has dark periods of history and we're reminded of this at Topaz, a World War II Japanese internment camp. In 1943, 11,000 Japanese-Americans living in California were forced to relocate to this bleak outpost near Delta, Utah, for the remainder of the war. A museum in Delta tells this story. The Unitd States eventually issued a formal apology and monetary compensation to all living survivors of this and other internment camps.

Territorial Statehouse State Park

Representative of Utah's early history, this park celebrates the state's oldest existing government building, and this building now houses exhibits that help tell the story of Utah's territorial history. Park grounds include Old Rock Schoolhouse and historic cabins.

Cove Fort

Cove Fort was built in the mid-19th century to protect and refresh settlers and travelers. The fort was constructed in the southeast corner of Millard County, Utah, and is made of lava rock found near the site of the fort.

Great Basin Museum

Located on Main Street in Delta, Utah, Great Basin Museum tells the story of the surrounding region, including its natural and human history. Exhibits include information on geology, Native Americans, agricultural development, Spanish explorers, Mormon settlers, and pioneer architecture.

Ward Charcoal Ovens State Park

This large forested park is found in the mountains of eastern Nevada and features six distinctive beehive-shaped charcoal ovens that were used from 1876-1879 to help process silver ore. The ovens were later used to shelter travelers and had a reputation for harboring

The handsome Territorial Statehouse of Utah houses exhibits on the history of the state.

stagecoach bandits. The park also offers hiking, camping, picnicking, and fishing.

White Pine Public Museum and McGill Drugstore

This museum complex is located in Ely, Nevada, and interprets the history of the area, including that of Native Americans, mining, and ranching. The museum also includes the historic McGill Drugstore (12 miles north in McGill, Nevada) with its displays of period merchandise.

Pahvant Valley Heritage Trail

Consider an adventure on the roads and trails that traverse land managed by the federal Bureau of Land Management. Here, you'll find a diverse set of natural and cultural sites, including Fort Deseret, Great Stone Face, Sunstone Knoll, Clear Lake, Devils Kitchen Petroglyphs, Pahvant Butte, Lace Curtain, Lava Tubes, and Hole-in-the-Rock

Petroglyphs. The Heritage Trail is bounded by the town of Delta, Utah, and Highways 50 and 6 to the north, the town of Fillmore and Interstate 15 to the east, the town of Kanosh and the Kanosh Road to the south, and Highway 257 to the west. Be advised that a four-wheel-drive vehicle is required and you should check on local conditions before setting out on this adventure.

> For more information about Great Basin and to help plan your visit, see the area's official website (greatbasin heritage.org) and the website of the National Park Service (nps.gov/places /great-basin-national-heritage-area .htm).

Gullah Geechee Cultural Heritage Corridor

States: North Carolina, South Carolina, Georgia, and Florida

Description: The thousands of African people enslaved in the isolated lowcountry and islands of the American Southeast developed a distinctive culture as manifested in language, food, arts and crafts, architecture, music, and spirituality; this NHA celebrates these people and their heritage.

Sample Attractions:
- Cumberland Island National Seashore
- McLeod Plantation Historic Site
- Charles Pickney National Historic Site
- Timucuan Ecological & Historic Preserve

During the decades surrounding the beginning of the 18th century, thousands of African people were captured, brought to the "lowcountry" and barrier and sea islands of the American Southeast, and enslaved, forced to do agricultural work and other tasks. Most of these people were from a number of ethnic groups in central and west Africa and had firsthand knowledge of the moist climate and fertile soils in both their African homelands and south Atlantic coastal area. In fact, these people were valued for their knowledge of growing rice and other crops that were important in the lowland areas of the four states that now comprise Gullah Geechee Cultural Heritage Corridor (Gullah Geechee Corridor)—North Carolina, South Carolina, Georgia, and Florida.

Because the lowcountry and islands were so remote and isolated, the Gullah Geechee people were able to retain much of their indigenous African heritage—language, food, arts and crafts, architecture, music, and spirituality—and combined these customs and traditions with elements of American culture to form a distinctive heritage that endures through the present time. For

This woven basket is an example of the distinctive arts and crafts of the Gullah culture.

example, a new language emerged, Gullah, a form of creole that's spoken nowhere else in the world. The language began as a simplified form of communication among people who spoke many languages, including those of European slave traders, slave owners, and diverse African ethnic groups; Gullah has influenced contemporary vocabulary and speech patterns in the South. Gullah is still spoken by about 5,000 people in the region. Contemporary Gullah Geechee arts and crafts are adaptations of their deep history applied to items necessary in daily life such as cast nets for fishing, basket weaving for agriculture, and textiles for clothing and warmth. Their deeply rooted music was adapted to the conditions of slavery and has influenced contemporary American spiritual and gospel music, ragtime, rhythm and blues, soul, hip hop, and jazz. Traditional Gullah Geechee foods focused on what was locally available, including vegetables, fruits, game, seafood, and livestock. This was supplemented with foods imported from Africa during the slave trade, including okra, rice, yams, peas, hot peppers, peanuts, sesame "benne" seeds, sorghum, and watermelon, and Native American foods such as corn, squash, tomatoes, and berries. The African tradition of "stretching" limited food supplies (by supplementing with local fish and game and leftovers from butchering) continued, as did African cooking methods and seasonings. Since many enslaved women cooked in plantation kitchens, some of these practices were adopted into what is now called "Southern" cooking.

They, with their strong spiritual traditions, adopted like-minded Christian concepts of God, community over individuality, respect for elders, kinship bonds and

Cumberland Island National Seashore is an exemplar of the barrier islands along the southeastern coastline of the United States.

ancestors, respect for nature, and the continuity of life and the afterlife. The plantations where they worked and lived often had a "praise house" for their use.

While these indigenous adaptations have added value and variety to American culture, they can't be celebrated without recognition of and empathy for the tragedy of slavery. Perhaps the atrocity of the enslavement of these people is best expressed in Dr. Anne Bailey's book, *The Weeping Time*, which tells the story of the single largest slave auction in US history. In 1859, 436 Gullah Geechee men, women, and children from plantations in Darien and St. Simons Island, Georgia, were put up for sale. These families and friends were separated, likely never seeing each other again. Heavy rain fell over the three-day auction and the slaves and others reflected afterward that even God "wept" at this abomination.

Gullah Geechee Corridor was established in 2006 to help commemorate and preserve this history and culture and to recognize the ingenuity, pride, and perseverance of the Gullah Geechee people. Many of the descendants of these people still live in the area, perhaps as many as 200,000, along the Southeastern coast. Gullah Geechee Corridor is administered by the federal Gullah Geechee Cultural Heritage Corridor Commission that partners with the National Park Service and other public, private, and non-profit organizations. The corridor is vast, running along the American coast from Pender County, North Carolina, to St. John's County, Florida, encompassing 12,000 square miles, and focusing on sites that are historically and culturally important to the Gullah Geechee people. Years of research by Derek Hankerson and other descendants of the Gullah Geechee people were instrumental in establishment of the NHA. Gullah Geechee Corridor focuses on 79 Atlantic barrier islands and adjoining areas within 30 miles of the coastline.

Attractions

Of course, most of the attractions in this NHA are focused on the history and culture associated with the Gullah Geechee people. However, many attractions also feature broader educational and historic themes and offer opportunities for outdoor recreation.

Charles Pinckney National Historic Site

This unit of the National Park System tells the story of Charles Pinckney, an author and signer of the United States Constitution. Twenty-eight acres of his coastal plantation, Snee Farm, are preserved and his life of public service is documented. The history of slavery on South Carolina plantations is also addressed.

Cumberland Island National Seashore

This large unit of the National Park System is the biggest and southernmost barrier island in Georgia. The largely undeveloped island offers wonderful opportunities for hiking, biking, and beachcombing. The island's history includes the life and work of enslaved African Americans.

Fort Sumter and Fort Moultrie National Historical Park

These two forts were part of the nation's early coastal defense system. They played a pivotal role in the American Revolution; patriot troops defeated the British Navy here. But locals fought on the side of the Confederates in the Civil War.

This plantation was established in 1851 and was built with money earned from sea island cotton grown with slave labor.

Historic Harrington School

Built in the 1920s, this building served as the main educational structure of three African American communities on St. Simons Island. It accommodated grades 1-7 until desegregation in the 1960s.

McLeod Plantation Historic Site

Established in 1851, this plantation was built with money earned from sea island cotton grown with slave labor. While the site tells many stories, it's a powerful tribute to the African American men and women who endured slavery and ultimately persevered in their quest for freedom, equality, and justice.

Moores Creek National Battlefield

This small unit of the National Park System celebrates the February, 27, 1776, victory of American patriots over British forces; this was the first significant victory for the Americans in the Revolutionary War. It also marked the last broadside charge by Scottish Highlanders in the war.

Fort Mose Historic Site

In 1738, the Spanish governor of what would become the state of Florida proclaimed the area a free black settlement, the first that was legally sanctioned in what would become the United States. The site is a National Historic Landmark and is a stop on the Florida Black Heritage Trail. The area also offers outdoor recreation in the form of picnicking, hiking, boating, and birding.

Timucuan Ecological & Historic Preserve

Locally known as "where the waters meet," this diverse unit of the National Park System is one of the last unspoiled wetlands on the Atlantic coast. It includes salt marshes, coastal dunes, and hardwood hammocks. It also includes Fort Caroline and Kingsley Plantation.

Pinpoint Heritage Museum

For nearly 100 years, the community of Pinpoint was isolated on the banks of the Moon River, just south of Savannah, and here you can experience Gullah Geechee culture firsthand. Located in the old A. S. Varn & Son Oyster and Crab Factory, a modern museum complex now features the area's history.

Programs and Events

The Gullah Geechee Cultural Heritage Corridor Commission, in conjunction with its partner organizations, has developed a series of programs and events that are presented throughout the year; videos of many of these programs can also be found on the Commission's website (see below). Examples include *Tracing the African Diaspora: Colonoware, Lives of the Enslaved on Kingsley Plantation*, and *Preserving Traditional Arts: Gullah*

Timucuan Ecological & Historic Preserve is a unit of the National Park System and preserves one of the last unspoiled wetlands along the Atlantic Coast.

Geechee and African Basketmaking. The Commission also sponsors an annual ceremony that celebrates the anniversary of January 1, 1863, when enslaved people of the lowcountry and sea islands and throughout the United States officially emerged from bondage as a result of the signing of the Emancipation Proclamation.

For more information about the Gullah Geechee Corridor and to help plan your visit, see the area's official website (gullahgeecheecorridor.org) and the website of the National Park Service (nps.gov/places/gullah-geechee -cultural-heritage-corridor.htm).

Illinois and Michigan Canal National Heritage Area

State: Illinois

Description: In the mid-19th century, men hand-dug a nearly 100-mile canal that connected the Great Lakes and fledgling city of Chicago to the Illinois and Mississippi Rivers, the final link in a national transportation network; this NHA preserves this canal, features the "canal towns" that sprung up along the waterway, and offers a long-distance trail on the canal towpath.

Sample Attractions:

- I&M Canal Visitor Center and the Canal Boat *Volunteer*
- Canal Towns
- Illinois and Michigan Canal State Trail
- Midewin National Tallgrass Prairie

There can only be one inaugural National Heritage Area and this is it! Established in 1984, President Ronald Reagan, a native of Illinois, traveled to Chicago to proudly sign legislation establishing the Illinois and Michigan National Heritage Corridor (now known as the Illinois and Michigan Canal National Heritage Area (Illinois and Michigan Canal)). In his remarks at the bill signing, President Reagan presciently remarked to those in attendance that they were helping to establish a "new kind of national park."

It all started in 1827 when the federal government gave 300,000 acres of prime farmland to the State of Illinois; sale of the land was to fund construction of a great canal to be used to transport both people and goods in the region of northern Illinois. (Such land grants were commonly used by the federal government to fund public works projects, including railroads and educational institutions.) Shortly after, workmen literally "dug in" to the project, hand-digging a nearly 100-mile canal connecting Lake Michigan and the fledgling city of Chicago to LaSalle, Illinois, where the canal entered the Illinois River.

The canal was completed in 1848 and was the final link in a national transportation system that tied together many regions of the developing nation. New York City and the Atlantic Ocean were linked to Chicago via the Erie Canal (see Erie Canalway National Heritage Area) and the Great Lakes. And the Illinois and Michigan Canal extended this network to the Midwest, the Illinois River, St. Louis, the Mississippi River, New Orleans, and the Gulf of Mexico. In a bit of a pun, the canal opened the floodgates to an influx of travelers and goods through much of the nation.

Travelers could use this "water highway" as a faster, more efficient, and more comfortable way to move through much of the nation rather than traveling the rough and slow overland routes. For example, packet (passenger) boats carried travelers along the 400-mile journey from Chicago to St. Louis in three days, and at a cost of $9.00. Freight could travel from St. Louis to New York City in 12 days. Farmers had a reliable way to get their crops to market which stimulated agricultural production. Mining of minerals such as limestone, coal, sand, and gravel expanded in response to the canal's ability to economically ship large quantities of materials, including grain and lumber.

The opening of the canal made Chicago and the surrounding area a key crossroads of American commerce; in fact, the canal helped transform Chicago from a small frontier town to what may have been the fastest growing city on earth, and ultimately one of North America's great cities. The canal siphoned off trade from St. Louis, self-proclaimed "Queen City" of the West, to the commercial rival of Chicago. The canal also spurred growth of other towns along the canal that industrialized and contributed to the reputation of northern Illinois as the western end of the American Manufacturing Belt. Like many American canals, a railroad was eventually built along its general route, but unlike most of these areas, the Illinois and Michigan Canal continued to thrive for several decades until commercial traffic began to decline in the 1880s. Nevertheless, the canal remained open to commercial use until 1933.

It's interesting to note that the canal enjoyed active support from Illinois resident Abraham Lincoln, who advocated for improvements in the nation's transportation systems in general. He believed that waterways held the key to economic success of the nation and the northern Illinois region in particular. As president, he actively supported construction, use, and expansion of the Illinois and Michigan Canal. Recognizing his support, at least three canal boats carried his name: *Rail Splitter*, *Old Abe*, and *A. Lincoln*.

After the canal was retired from commercial use, it fell into disrepair and was replaced by the more modern Illinois Waterway, still used today for shipping between the Great Lakes and the Mississippi River. The easternmost section of the Illinois and Michigan Canal was used for construction of an expressway and the State of Illinois was preparing to sell extensive real estate holdings along the canal. However, the canal was recognized for its importance to Chicago, northern Illinois, and the nation when it was designated a National Historic Landmark in 1964. In 1975, the State of Illinois created the I&M Canal State Trail along the original towpath, and shortly after that a local coalition, including the nonprofit conservation

group Openlands, formed to consider the future of the area in a more comprehensive way. Illinois and Michigan Canal was established in 1984 and is managed by the nonprofit group, Canal Corridor Association, with help from a number of public, private, and nonprofit entities. Its success helped lead to other NHAs around the country.

Attractions

Illinois and Michigan Canal might best be thought of as an outdoor museum that extends nearly 100 miles; it includes 862 square miles, encompasses five counties and 60 communities, and offers a great range of attractions for residents of the area and visitors from afar. Of course, the primary attraction is the restored canal itself, including locks and other historic structures; there's lots to learn and enjoy. The NHA also includes a number of parks and nature reserves.

I&M Canal Visitor Center and the Canal Boat *The Volunteer*

The canal's visitor center is located at Lock 16 in LaSalle and is a good place to start a visit; the facility includes exhibits, a large map of the NHA, and an 8-by-40-foot mural that tells the story of the canal. And this is the place to start your canal boat experience on the replica *The Volunteer* pulled by a mule along the restored towpath and narrated by guides in period clothing.

Canal Towns

Many towns grew up and prospered along the canal and each has its own character. Examples include Morris (a quintessential rural Midwestern town as well as an important agricultural center with historic

The replica canal boat *The Volunteer* offers visitors rides along the historic canal.

built the canal" and offering interesting history, architecture, and trails), Ottawa (this historic town includes the large Fox River Aqueduct and the canal's last remaining tollhouse), and La Salle (the western end of the canal where it meets the Illinois River).

Illinois and Michigan Canal State Trail

This 79-mile biking and hiking trail connects the historic canal towns of La Salle and Lemont as it follows the reconstructed towpath. This is a popular recreation trail that includes educational markers that tell the story of the canal and associated history.

Pullman National Monument and Chicago Portage National Historic Site

Illinois and Michigan Canal includes two units of the National Park System. Pullman

buildings and visitor facilities right on the water), Lemont (a picturesque and historic town known for its church spires, historic limestone buildings, and a walkable downtown), Lockport (known as "the town that

The Illinois and Michigan Canal offers lots of opportunities for outdoor recreation.

This historic photo shows the Locktenders House at Lock 1 on the Illinois and Michigan Canal.

Riddick Mansion was constructed in 1855 in the historic canal town of Ottawa.

National Monument tells the story of the Pullman train car company and the nation's first model planned community. Chicago Portage National Historic Site marks the western end of the historic portage linking the Great Lakes to the Mississippi River.

Midewin National Tallgrass Prairie

This restored tallgrass prairie ecosystem that once dominated this region of Illinois is part of a 20,000-acre conservation area managed by the US Forest Service. A small herd of bison graze a portion of the area and is part of a study of the ecological relationships between bison and this historic landscape. Medewin is a Potawatomi Native American word for the tribe's healers who it was believed kept the tribal society in balance.

Reddick Mansion

The lovely Reddick Mansion was constructed in 1855 in Ottawa and anchors Washington Square, the site of the first Lincoln-Douglas Debate.

Isle a la Cache Museum

This museum illuminates the canal region's natural and cultural history. It transports visitors back to an 18th-century "Illinois Country" home of French voyageurs and Potawatomi Indians. The museum includes a forest preserve.

Navy Pier

The Navy Pier was constructed in Chicago in 1916 and was designed by famed architect Daniel Burnham to accommodate both shipping and public access to Lake Michigan. The pier projects more than 3,000 feet into the lake, the longest pier in the world. With its visitor attractions and facilities, it's a popular place for residents and visitors.

For more information about Illinois and Michigan Canal and to help plan your visit, see the area's official website (iandmcanal.org) and the website of the National Park Service (nps.gov/places /illinois-and-michigan-canal-national -heritage-area.htm).

John H. Chafee Blackstone River Valley National Heritage Corridor

States: Massachusetts and Rhode Island

Description: Development of a cotton mill on the Blackstone River marked the beginning of America's Industrial Revolution, changing the nation economically and socially; the now peaceful countryside of this NHA includes lovely New England villages, farms and forests, and a distinctive culture that is enriched by the immigrants who came to work in the mills.

Sample Attractions:

- Blackstone River Valley National Historical Park
- Blackstone Valley Heritage Corridor Visitor Center
- Blackstone River and Canal Heritage State Park
- Self-guided Mill Village Tours

In 1789, Pawtucket, Rhode Island, entrepreneur Moses Brown was struggling with the innovative idea of how to use the power of the Blackstone River to help spin cotton. Having only limited success, he hired Samuel Slater, a recent immigrant who had worked for seven years in a textile mill in England. A year later, an experimental mill was operating on the Blackstone River using water power to spin cotton, marking the beginning of America's Industrial Revolution. Soon, cotton mills were built throughout the Blackstone River Valley and then New England more widely. This story of American industrialization—and the cultural changes it precipitated—is told at John H. Chafee Blackstone River Valley National Heritage Corridor (Blackstone River Valley).

To take maximum advantage of water power, mills were built where rivers dropped in elevation and this meant that many were built in rural areas, often on agricultural and forested lands, a symbolic manifestation of the conversion of much of New England from a rural, agrarian landscape to an industrialized one. Developers constructed these mills, along with homes, schools, and churches to serve the needs of their workers. Hopedale and Whitinsville are good examples of these paternalistic company towns. Moreover, the lives of these former farm families who now worked in the mills changed dramatically. Lives that had been determined by the rhythm of nature—the seasons and the sun—were now governed by the mill bell, and productivity was measured by long hours tending the machines that worked around the clock and throughout the year.

New and larger mills were built throughout much of the 19th century, making America a leading economic power on the international stage. But more workers were needed, and mills recruited immigrants who were anxious to take advantage of this economic opportunity. Irish immigrants came first, working in the mills and helping to build the Blackstone Canal (linking Worcester, Massachusetts, with the port of Providence, Rhode Island) and making a series of improvements to the river that would aid the passage of commercial freight. Later, immigrants came from Quebec and throughout eastern and western Europe, and this tradition continues today; many of the newest immigrants are from Central America and Southeast Asia. The contemporary Blackstone River Valley is a rich mix of cultures that contributes to the area's diverse cultural heritage.

Of course, water power was eventually replaced by steam and electricity, and canals were superseded by railroads, bringing an end to this early manifestation of America's Industrial Revolution. But this heady period of American history can still be found in this region of New England: the landscape is studded with historic mills, some "repurposed" to other uses and some refurbished to help tell the story of this vital period of American history. The Blackstone River still flows 48 miles from Worcester, Massachusetts, to the Seekonk River just north of Providence, Rhode Island. Recent attention has been placed on the water quality of the river badly damaged in the industrial period; it's said that the river used to flow red one day and blue the next, depending on the activity of the mills. But water quality has been greatly improved. Charming New England towns have grown up around the original mill communities, and much of the rural landscape has returned to its original farms and forests.

Blackstone River Valley was established in 1986 to tell the important story of America's industrialization. The coordinating entity is the dynamic non-profit group, Blackstone Heritage Corridor, Inc. which partners with the National Park Service, municipalities, businesses, residents, and non-profit groups up and down the 48 miles of the river. The name of the NHA was later modified to honor John H. Chafee, Governor of Rhode Island, Secretary of the Navy, and US Senator from Rhode Island who did so much to support the NHA. Blackstone River Valley is large, encompassing 25 cities and towns in Rhode Island and Massachusetts, including two of New England's largest cities, Providence, Rhode Island, and Worcester, Massachusetts, and the NHA is 465,000 acres. Blackstone River Valley has been so successful that Congress established a new unit of the National Park System, Blackstone River Valley National Historical Park, in 2014 to honor and emphasize the importance of the region; the National Park Service and Blackstone River Valley work together closely to protect the region and tell this vital story of American history.

Attractions

Blackstone River Valley includes lots of attractions that follow the important history of the region and its effects on the American economy and society. The beauty of the river, its historic and charming villages, and the pastoral character of the countryside add to the enjoyment of experiencing this NHA.

Blackstone River Valley National Historical Park

This unit of the National Park System tells the nationally important story of what it calls the "Birthplace of the American Industrial Revolution." The park includes Old Slater Mill, the original mill site on the river where the American Industrial Revolution began. Step inside Old Slater Mill and hear the rumble of the machinery and learn about the mill and the families that worked here. Samuel Slater recognized the changes his and other mills were having on society when he said "I gave out the psalm and they have been singing to the tune ever since."

Slater Mill used the water power of the Blackstone River to weave textiles marking the beginning of America's Industrial Revolution.

The company town of Whitinsville includes the massive Whitin Machine Works.

Self-Guided Mill Village Tours

Several villages along the historic Blackstone River offer self-guided tours. Slatersville was America's first planned mill village, a model for mill towns that followed. The original village was created in 1807, but has been transformed twice, the latest in 2007 when the original mill was repurposed to housing. Whitinsville is also interesting, the original mill village expanding several times to accommodate growth of the massive Whitin Machine Works. The village tells the story of its evolution from agrarian settlement to industrial giant, and the company town that was controlled by the Whitin family for more than 100 years. The village of Hopedale began as a commune, but ultimately became the home of Draper Corporation, the country's largest loom manufacturer. The historic factory housing here is some of the finest in the valley, with streets that reference the town's name and original philosophy: Freedom, Social, Union, Peace, and Hope. Walk through Parklands, the recreation area built by the Draper family for their workers.

Blackstone River and Canal Heritage State Park

This 1,000-acre park on the Blackstone River is part of the Massachusetts state park system and offers insights into the history of Blackstone River Valley, with an emphasis on the role of canals in transporting raw materials and manufactured goods and the valley's transition from farm to factory economy. It also includes trails, picnic areas, canoe access to the Blackstone River, and fishing.

The Blackstone Canal was constructed to carry freight between Worcester, Massachusetts, and Providence, Rhode Island.

Blackstone River State Park

Located between the Blackstone River and Blackstone Canal, this riverfront park includes walking and bike paths, canoe portage, and fishing access. Historic walking tours along the canal are available. The Captain Wilbur Kelly House Transportation Museum features exhibits on transportation, including canals, railroads, and highways.

Blackstone River Valley Heritage Center

This modern and multifunction heritage center in Worcester sits on the banks of the Blackstone River and is a gateway for visitors to Blackstone River Valley. The center functions as a museum and orientation center for visitors to the NHA and surrounding areas and is located at the start of the Blackstone River Greenway/Bikeway.

Blackstone River Greenway/Bikeway

This is an ambitious plan for a 48-mile paved path through much of the Blackstone River Valley, eventually linking with the 3,000-mile East Coast Greenway. The greenway/bikeway is partially completed, so visitors should check the NHA's website for up-to-date information. The Greenway/Bikeway is suitable for walking and biking.

Museum of Work and Culture

This interesting museum focuses on the lives of the thousands of immigrants searching for a better life in America. Visitors explore the lives of immigrants at home, work, and school through nine immersive exhibits.

Blackstone River Paddling

Paddlers are welcome to use their canoes and kayaks on the Blackstone River and the Blackstone Canal. The river includes rapids and portages in places and demands expertise and experience; the canal has no current and is a good opportunity for beginners.

For more information about Blackstone River Valley and to help plan your visit, see the area's official website (black stoneheritagecorridor.org) and the website of the National Park Service (nps.gov/places/blackstone-river -valley-national-heritage-corridor.htm).

Journey Through Hallowed Ground National Heritage Area

States: Maryland, Pennsylvania, Virginia, and West Virginia

Description: This is a 180-mile-long, 75-mile-wide swath of land through four states that runs from Gettysburg National Military Park in the North to Thomas Jefferson's Monticello in the South; the area teaches us about many of our nation's leaders, the historic conflicts we've faced, and how we might best learn from these people and places.

Sample Attractions:
- Journey Through Hallowed Ground National Scenic Byway
- Civil War Battlefields (Gettysburg National Military Park, Fredericksburg and Spotsylvania National Military Park, Antietam National Battlefield, Manassas National Battlefield Park)
- Harpers Ferry National Historical Park
- Monticello

In the early 1990s, there was a proposal to develop a theme park near the Civil War's Manassas Battlefield in Virginia where Confederate forces won a solid victory over the Union at great expense to both armies. Historians and concerned citizens worried that this development would desecrate this important historic site, a part of the National Park System. Grassroots organizations of citizens, including the National Trust for Historic Preservation, the Civil War Trust, the Piedmont Environmental Council, and Scenic America joined forces in an effort to protect the area around Manassas Battlefield and many of the other significant sites that make up the especially rich cultural landscapes of the larger region. Through these efforts, Journey Through Hallowed Ground National Heritage Area (Journey) was established in 2008. The NHA is managed by the nonprofit organization, Journey Through Hallowed Ground Partnership and the number of partner organizations has expanded to more than 300.

Journey's slogan is "Where America Happened," and they've got a good point. Yes, it's a big area—a 180-mile-long, 75-mile-wide swath of land through fifteen counties in four states that runs from Gettysburg National Military Park in Pennsylvania in the North to Thomas Jefferson's Monticello in Virginia in the South—but it's an especially rich region that addresses many of the nation's leaders, the historic conflicts we've faced, and how we might best learn from these people and places. A brief inventory includes:

1. Nine presidential homes
2. Thirteen units of the National Park System
3. Two World Heritage Sites
4. The largest collection of Civil War sites in the nation including Gettysburg, Harpers Ferry, Manassas, Antietam, Wilderness, and Monocacy
5. Sites from the Revolutionary War, French and Indian War, and the War of 1812
6. The largest collection of National Historic Districts in the country
7. Thirty historic Main Street communities
8. Hundreds of African American and Native American heritage sites
9. Sixteen National Historic Landmarks
10. Over a million acres on the National Register of Historic Places

All this is scattered over a diverse, bucolic landscape of rolling hills and mountain views, farms and orchards, woodlands and forests, and rivers and streams. And tying all this together is the Journey Through Hallowed Ground National Scenic Byway (see attractions below), an automobile route that wanders through this remarkable cultural landscape. Even more importantly—and as suggested in the very name of this NHA—Journey ties this area together metaphorically; it gives structure and facilitates understanding of the story of so much of American history. Moreover, this is a history that's taught in the very locations where it happened, which adds a vital component of engagement and capitalizes on the power of place. Journey contributes a valuable component of synergy to the many sites that comprise this large NHA, challenging visitors to confront the meaning of foundational American ideas such as freedom, duty to country, and conservation. What was it about these people and places that spawned the Declaration of Independence, US Constitution, Emancipation Proclamation, Gettysburg Address, Monroe Doctrine, and the Marshall Plan? NHAs tend to do well at these kinds of questions, and it's particularly important and well done at this one.

Journey is especially active in public education and programming. For example, its National History Academy attracts high-performing high school students to its five-week residential program each summer. This ambitious program is at least partially driven by data from the National Assessment of Educational Progress which found that just 23 percent of high school students were proficient in their knowledge of US history. The academy teaches the foundations of American democracy through place-based education.

Attractions

Of course, most of the attractions in Journey are historical and educational—and they're some of the most important in the nation—so take the time to experience the power of this history "in place." But don't overlook the natural beauty of this grand cultural landscape and opportunities it offers to get out of the car and walk. The following attractions are important, but are only a sampling.

Journey Through Hallowed Ground National Scenic Byway

As noted above, this 180-mile automobile route defines the heart of Journey, tying together many of the NHA's most important sites and offering a scenic drive of several days if you take advantage of the many important places along the way. The route you follow was an important transportation corridor during the Revolutionary War, a transition zone for the Underground Railroad, and a key battleground during the Civil War. Literature describing the scenic byway notes that "this early corridor was the literal 'roadbed' for the creation of our country and American ideals."

Civil War Battlefields (Gettysburg National Military Park, Fredericksburg and Spotsylvania National Military Park, Antietam National Battlefield, Manassas National Battlefield Park)

Journey includes many of the most significant battlefields of the Civil War. Certainly all visitors to the NHA should stop at Gettysburg, a turning point of the war and the northernmost point reached by Confederate troops, often called the "high water mark of the rebellion." This was one of the bloodiest battles of the war and the inspiration for Lincoln's "Gettysburg Address." The

Gettysburg National Military Park commemorates a turning point of the Civil War and was the inspiration for Lincoln's Gettysburg Address.

Harpers Ferry National Historical Park sits at the confluence of the Potomac and Shenandoah rivers and was of great military significance during the Revolutionary War.

battlefields at Fredericksburg and Spotsylvania mark the last phases of the war and were traumatic for all concerned—the many soldiers who died or were wounded and the local residents whose lives were disrupted, terrorized, or ruined. The battle at Antietam ended the Confederate Army's invasion of the North, but at a cost of 23,000 soldiers killed, wounded, or missing. The battle led Lincoln to issue the Emancipation Proclamation. Battles took place twice at Manassas and proved that the Civil War would be long and costly. All these battlefields are part of the National Park System.

Harpers Ferry National Historical Park

This unit of the National Park System focuses on the historic and charming town of Harpers Ferry. The town sits at the confluence of the Potomac and Shenandoah Rivers, was of great military significance during the Revolutionary War, and was the northernmost point of Confederate-controlled territory. It's also known as the location of "John Brown's raid," an effort by Brown to initiate a slave revolt in the southern states by taking over the US arsenal.

Chesapeake & Ohio Canal National Historical Park is a unit of the National Park System and a harbinger of America's Industrial Revolution.

Monticello was the plantation home of Thomas Jefferson, author of the Declaration of Independence.

Eisenhower National Historic Site

This unit of the National Park System preserves the farm of General and 34th President Dwight D. Eisenhower that served as a weekend retreat for the president and first lady. The site is adjacent to Gettysburg National Military Park.

Chesapeake & Ohio Canal National Historical Park

The C&O Canal is a harbinger of America's Industrial Revolution. Begun in 1828, the 185-mile canal runs along the Potomac River from Georgetown in Washington, DC, to Cumberland in western Maryland. Avoiding the rapids of the river, the canal transported goods including coal, lumber, and agricultural products between the East Coast and the midwest. The towpath of the canal has been restored into a delightful walking and biking trail and offers historic canal boat tours.

Monticello

This is the plantation home of Thomas Jefferson, author of the Declaration of Independence and third president of the United States. The home is part of his 5,000-acre plantation and was designed by Jefferson; the home is built on a small hill and the name means "little mountain" in French (Jefferson spent several years in France serving as Minister of the United States). Jefferson is largely responsible for the purchase from France of the Louisiana Territory (doubling the size of the United States) and for commissioning the Lewis and Clark Expedition. Though Jefferson was influential in advancing human rights, he kept hundreds of slaves to work on his plantation; Monticello is making a good faith effort to help visitors understand the complexities of Jefferson, human rights, and his stance on slavery by prominently sharing stories of the enslaved community. Monticello is a National Historic Landmark and a World Heritage Site.

> For more information about Journey and to help plan your visit, see the area's official website (hallowedground.org) and the website of the National Park Service (nps.gov/places/journey-through-hallowed-ground.htm).

Kenai Mountains-Turnagain Arm National Heritage Area

State: Alaska

Description: This beautiful and dramatic NHA on Alaska's Kenai Peninsula showcases its rich history, including land and water routes traveled by indigenous people, routes used by prospectors and miners looking for gold and other minerals, dramatic and scenic roads and railroads that now serve the area, and an extensive system of trails that offer

The Harding Ice Field is an impressive 700 square miles, the largest such formation in the United States.

opportunities to appreciate the area on foot, bicycle, and horse.

Sample Attractions:

- Kenai Fjords National Park
- Iditarod National Historic Trail
- Seward All American Scenic Highway
- Alaska Railroad

Kenai Mountains-Turnagain Arm National Heritage Area (Kenai Mountains) is the first and only national heritage area in Alaska, established in 2009. But given the interesting history and the vast and spectacular resources of the state, there will probably be more NHAs in this state that's more than twice the size of Texas. The NHA is in south-central Alaska on the Kenai Peninsula, about 100 miles south of Anchorage. The peninsula extends for 150 miles and is separated from the mainland on the west by Cook Inlet and on the east by Prince William Sound. The colorful name of the area—Kenai Mountains-Turnagain Arm—is derived from its history. Kenai (the original spelling was *Kenaitze*) is the name of the Native American Tribe that inhabits this area and this name was given to the rugged and glacier-covered mountain range that rises up to 7,000 feet and dominates the peninsula. The Kenai called the peninsula *Yaghanen*, meaning "the good land."

Turnagain Arm is the name of the wide river that flows into Cook Inlet from the east. The name was given in frustration by William Bligh, Sailing Master of the HMS Bounty (captained by James Cook) in 1778. Searching for a Northwest Passage, the ship entered Cook Inlet and Bligh was ordered to send a party up what is now Knik Arm, but the party discovered it was only a river

(and not a passage) and turned around to return to the ship. The party then explored the other large water body that extended off Cook Inlet, only to find that it too was a river and had to "turn around again" to return to the ship, thus the name. Turnagain Arm experiences remarkably large tides of up to 40 feet, the largest in the United States. The flood tide often begins with a "tidal bore" (especially on large tides with a strong east wind) which can have a height of 6 feet and travel at a speed of 5–6 miles an hour. At low tide, the arm becomes a broad mud flat, cut by stream channels, and hikers are advised not to attempt to walk on these quicksand-like mudflats. Kenai Mountains is unusual in that it's mostly public land; nearly 90 percent of the NHA is in the vast Chugach National Forest. But this is logical considering that the vast majority of all land in Alaska is publicly owned in the form of national parks, national forests, national fish and wildlife refuges, and lots of state lands.

The NHA is managed by the Kenai Mountains-Turnagain Arm Corridor Communities Association and works with many partner organizations, including the National Park Service and the US Forest Service. The primary theme of the NHA is the history of transportation on the Eastern Kenai Peninsula. This is a rich history that includes the land and water routes traveled by indigenous people, the routes used by prospectors and miners looking for gold and other minerals, the dramatic and scenic roads and railroads that now serve the area, and an extensive system of trails that offer opportunities to appreciate the area on foot, bicycle, and horse. And, of course, this is a beautiful and distinctive landscape of mountains,

Large and impressive Kenai Fjords National Park sits hard on the mighty Gulf of Alaska.

lakes, rivers, glaciers, fjords, and frontier communities.

Attractions

Kenai Mountains includes many visitor attractions that are based on its history, natural features, and stunning land and seascapes. Drive its scenic roads, take the historic train, visit its historic towns, boat its waterways, hike its trails, and much more.

Kenai Fjords National Park

This large and impressive park sits hard on the mighty Gulf of Alaska and features a signature system of large finger-like fjords reminiscent of those in Norway; the fjords are narrow inlets with steep sides or cliffs created by glaciers. But the park is even more than this with the largest ice field in the United States (the Harding Icefield is an impressive

700 square miles!), nearly 40 glaciers (several of which flow directly into the sea), a staggering 545 miles of wild coastline, towering peaks that rise right out of the sea, and a collection of iconic terrestrial and aquatic wildlife that only Alaska can offer. Be sure to take the short hike to Exit Glacier (you can see it up close and personal) and consider hiking the more challenging route to the massive Harding Ice Field.

Iditarod National Historic Trail

The famous Iditarod Trail is the only winter trail in the US National Trails System. It's actually a system of trails comprised of a 1,000-mile main trail between Seward and Nome, and an additional 1,400 miles of side/connecting trails that link communities and historic sites, or provide parallel/alternative routes. Consider walking or biking the first

The main stem of the famous Iditarod National Historic Trail runs 1,000 miles between Seward and Nome; consider walking the first mile of the trail as it departs from the Alaska SeaLife Center in Seward.

The Coastal Classic Route of the historic Alaska Railroad offers a great way to enjoy the scenery of Turnagain Arm and the Kenai Peninsula.

mile of the trail (it's paved) as it departs from the Alaska SeaLife Center in Seward.

Seward All American Scenic Highway

Recognized for its scenic, natural, historical, and recreational values, the 127-mile Seward Highway holds the distinction of being an All-American Road. The road skirts the base of the Chugach Mountains and the shore of Turnagain Arm where you may see beluga whales, Dall sheep, waterfalls, and eagles. The remainder of the drive courses through the mountains, offering dramatic views of wild Alaska.

Alaska Railroad

The historic Alaska Railroad connects many visitor attractions and Alaskan communities over hundreds of miles of track. The Coastal Classic route winds its way south from Anchorage along Turnagain Arm before joining the Kenai Peninsula, eventually reaching Seward. This 114-mile trip takes around four and a half hours as the line winds its way over mountains.

Seward

Seward is a small town (population of about 3,000) on the shore of beautiful Resurrection Bay with glacier-clad mountains behind; it's approximately 120 miles south of Anchorage and was a former Russian colony. It's the southern terminus of the Alaska Railroad (see above) and the historic starting point of the Iditarod National Historic Trail (see below). It's a popular cruise destination and houses the visitor center for Kenai Fjords National Park. If time allows, take a day cruise on Resurrection Bay and into one of the national park's fjords. Seward is also a stop on the Alaska Marine Ferry System.

Trails

The vast public lands of Kenai Mountains boast lots of trails that are in keeping with the historic transportation theme of the area. The Iditarod National Historic Trail is famous enough to warrant its own entry above, but there are lots of other good choices that include day hikes and backpacking trips. Primrose Lake/Lost Lake is a 15-mile route that features lots of alpine lakes and can be done as a long day hike or short backpack.

Russian Lakes Trail is 21 miles, but offers a shorter option of only 2.4 miles to Russian River Falls. Three Forest Service cabins are available by reservation. Gull Rock Trail is 5.7 miles and is nicely representative of the Turnagain Arm area. There are numerous overlooks of the waterway, but don't be tempted to walk on the extensive mudflats that appear at low tide as they can trap hikers. Byron Glacier Trail is just 1.4 miles of varied trail, including ferns, creeks, and snowfields, and the glacier is easily visible at the end of the trail; climbing on the glacier can be dangerous. Palmer Creek is 1.5 miles to lakes and the historic town of Hope with the remnants of gold mining and a few current claims. Some stream crossings may be required. This is just a sampling.

Trail Towns

The NHA has worked hard to showcase the historic towns that dot the landscape and that are connected to the area's many trails (see above). Trail Towns support trail users with services, promote the trails to residents and visitors, and celebrate trails as a resource to be protected. Examples include Seward (see above), Moose Pass, Cooper Landing, Hope, Sunrise, Whittier/Portage (see below), Gridwood, and Indian/Bird Creek.

Prince William Sound/Whittier/Valdez

A large body of water off the Gulf of Alaska, Prince William Sound is on the east side of the Kenai Peninsula. It's a large, historic, and beautiful body of water that offers outstanding fishing and plentiful marine mammals. It's the southern terminus of the Trans-Alaska Pipeline and includes the town of Whittier as well as two small native villages.

Large and lovely Prince William Sound offers spectacular scenery and plentiful marine mammals.

The area experienced a magnitude 9.2 earthquake and associated tsunami (the most powerful ever registered in North America) in 1964, causing many deaths and great damage. (The earthquake is known as the Great Alaskan Earthquake and the Good Friday Earthquake, and it damaged many Alaskan towns and villages.) In 1989, the Exxon *Valdez* ran aground on Bligh Reef resulting in a historically large oil spill. The spill affected 1,300 miles of coastline and despite massive clean-up efforts, less than 10 percent of the oil was recovered. Whittier is accessible by car and train through the Anton Anderson Memorial Tunnel (often called the Whittier Tunnel), constructed in 1941-42; the tunnel is two-and-a-half miles long. Whittier is a popular port for cruise ships, sightseeing boats, and fishing charters; it's served by the Alaska Marine Ferry System.

For more information about Kenai Mountains and to help plan your visit, see the area's official website (kmta corridor.org) and the website of the National Park Service (nps.gov/places /kenai-mountains-turnagain-arm -national-heritage-area.htm).

Lackawanna Valley National Heritage Area

State: Pennsylvania

Description: This historic valley in northeastern Pennsylvania produced much of the nation's anthracite (hard) coal that heated homes and helped to power much of America's Industrial Revolution.

Sample Attractions:

- Steamtown National Historic Site
- Lackawanna River Heritage Trail
- Anthracite Heritage Museum
- Lackawanna Coal Mine Tour

Steamtown National Historic Site is part of the National Park System and features a large collection of steam powered locomotives and related equipment.

Pennsylvania's historic Lackawanna Valley lies in the northeastern part of the state. The valley's rich deposits of anthracite ("hard") coal—a relatively clean and hot-burning mineral—powered much of America's Industrial Revolution, including mining, iron and steel production, steam-powered transportation, food processing, large-scale fabrication, and textile manufacturing of the 19th and 20th centuries. This region produced 80 percent of the world's anthracite coal. Countless railcars of this coal were sent from Scranton, the industrial hub of the valley, to the cities of the Northeast and in barges across the Great Lakes to the Midwest to help heat households around the nation. The rugged Lackawanna Valley was settled in the early 1800s, but by the 1880s, the Scranton area had become one of the nation's leading industrial centers, attracting entrepreneurs and laborers from around the country and the world.

The Lackawanna Valley region was established as Pennsylvania's first State Heritage Park in 1991, and this was complemented with designation by Congress as a national heritage area in 2000. The current-day

Lackawanna Valley National Heritage Area (Lackawanna Valley) includes the Lackawanna River watershed as it flows through the towns of Carbondale and Scranton to its junction with the mighty Susquehanna River at Pittston, and includes portions of Lackawanna, Susquehanna, Wayne, and Luzerne Counties. Lackawanna Valley is managed by the Lackawanna Heritage Valley Authority, a Pennsylvania Municipal Authority of Lackawanna County. (Because this area is both a national and state heritage area, it is sometimes called Lackawanna Heritage Valley National and State Heritage Area.) The focus of this management and coordinating entity is renewal—renewal of the natural environment from its large-scale development in the 19th century; renewal of the area's historic and diverse economic base from industry to heritage-based tourism, and renewal of the sense of place and pride of the area's residents. Partnership agencies, organizations, and individuals represent historic and cultural sites, environmental organizations, educators and students, municipal governments, and residents and visitors. Lackawanna Valley supports and coordinates a diverse array of projects that preserve, enhance, interpret, and promote the region's historic, cultural, natural, and recreational resources. As both a national and state heritage area, Lackawanna Valley receives funding from the National Park Service, Pennsylvania Department of Conservation and Natural Resources, and other sources.

Attractions

Lackawanna Valley offers a glimpse into America's Industrial Revolution, much of it powered by coal mined in northeastern Pennsylvania. However, it also suggests the future of such places as residents take pride in their heritage and share it with visitors. Many of the NHA's attractions are historical and cultural in nature, but the area also celebrates the natural beauty of the landscape and the recreational opportunities of the Lackawanna River watershed.

Steamtown National Historic Site

This unit of the National Park System features a substantial collection of steam-powered railroad locomotives, freight and passenger cars, maintenance-of-way equipment, and related items located on 40 acres at the Scranton railroad yard. Much of this equipment was the private collection of entrepreneur F. Nelson Blount. This historic site encourages visitors to "feel heat from the firebox, smell hot steam and oil, hear the whistle, feel the ground vibrate, and watch as one-ton drive rods turn the steel wheels."

Steamtown offers seasonal passenger excursions to various local destinations.

Lackawanna River Heritage Trail

The 40-mile Lackawanna Valley Heritage Trail joins with the Northeast Pennsylvania Rail Trail to form the 70-mile Lackawanna River Heritage Trail System, linking urban and rural communities and serving as the premier recreational asset for residents and visitors. The trail system travels through four counties and 30 municipalities, including the cities of Carbondale, Scranton, and Pittston. The trail uses abandoned railroad corridors and former coal mining lands, access roads, flood control levees, municipal parks, public sidewalks, and streets to help revitalize the region's natural resources and reclaim forgotten sites for public recreation. The trail is popular with bicycle riders, walkers, and runners. The trail is not yet complete, so check the NHA website (see below) for up-to-date conditions. The trail hosts many races and other events. Confluence Sculpture Park is a popular stop on the trail.

Scranton Iron Furnaces

These four massive stone blast furnaces are remnants of the Lackawanna Iron and Steel Company. This once extensive facility had the highest iron production capacity in the United States by 1865. The South Scranton site is located along Roaring Brook, a short hike from Steamtown National Historic Site, and is accessible via the Lackawanna Trolley (see below).

Anthracite Heritage Museum

This educational facility is located in Lackawanna County's McDade Park and tells the

The 1884 Lackawanna County Courthouse includes a five-story clock tower and is listed on the National Register of Historic Places.

Take the adventurous Lackawanna Coal Mine Tour and observe for yourself the working conditions that men and boys endured.

stories of the coal mining and associated industries in the Lackawanna Valley and the people who came from Europe to work here. These people endured harsh working conditions, but created proud communities filled with tradition. Visitors can tour family's homes, a pub, and the local church.

Lackawanna Coal Mine Tour

Visitors are lowered in an authentic mine car down a 300-foot slope below the surface of the earth in a once-abandoned, but now restored anthracite coal mine. Observe for yourself the working conditions that men and boys endured to help power the Industrial Revolution.

Lackawanna County "Electric City" Trolley Museum

This engaging museum is housed in a restored 19th-century mill building on the grounds

of Steamtown National Historic Site (see above). The museum displays vintage trolleys and has interactive exhibits and displays. Antique trolley rides are offered over Roaring Brook, through a more than mile-long curved tunnel, and along the original "Laurel Line" Electric Railroad.

Lackawanna County Courthouse

This impressive public building was constructed in 1884 and occupies a nearly 5-acre site in downtown Scranton. The building includes a five-story clock tower and is listed on the National Register of Historic Places.

Lackawanna Historical Society at the Catlin House

The historic Catlin House, the former residence of financier George H. Catlin, is one of the architectural treasures of Scranton and houses the local historical society. Built in 1912, the Tudor Revival home has been restored and most of the furniture is original to the home.

The Everhart Museum of Natural History, Science, and Art challenges visitors to ponder the connections between art and science.

Carbondale Historical Society and Museum

This historical society was formed by a group of local citizens to preserve and interpret the history of their town and the surrounding area. It's a membership-based society that maintains a genealogical and local history research center and exhibition galleries in the Carbondale City Hall (listed in the National Register of Historic Places).

Everhart Museum of Natural History, Science and Art

Part of the early 20th-century museum movement, the Everhart Museum was founded in 1908. Exhibits and programs stimulate visitors to think about creative expressions and active engagement between art and science.

For more information about Lackawanna Valley and to help plan your visit, see the area's official website (lhva.org) and the website of the National Park Service (nps.gov/places/lackawanna-heritage-valley.htm).

Maritime Washington National Heritage Area

State: Washington

Description: This large and diverse NHA celebrates the maritime heritage of northwest Washington with its impressive 3,000 miles of coastline, Native American presence, naval bases, units of the National Park System, recreational harbors, and contemporary industrial seaports.

Sample Attractions:
- Olympic National Park
- Ebey's Landing National Historical Reserve
- San Juan Island National Historical Park
- Seattle Waterfront

Maritime Washington National Heritage Area (Maritime Washington) celebrates the nationally important story of the maritime heritage of northwestern Washington. This story begins with Native American canoe cultures and continues to the contemporary times of industrial seaports and explains why and how this coastal heritage shaped western Washington and contributed to development of the nation. Maritime Washington includes approximately 3,000 miles of western Washington's saltwater coastline from Gray's Harbor County to the Canadian border and includes 18 federally recognized Native American tribes, 13 counties, 32 incorporated cities, and 30 port districts, as well as innumerable harbors, inlets, peninsulas, island shores, and parks—all connected by the nation's largest ferry system and an extensive network of highways. Maritime Washington was established in 2019 and the Washington Trust for Historic Preservation is the coordinating entity for the many public, private, and nonprofit groups that participate in the NHA.

Long before there were roads and railroads in the Pacific Northwest, boats were the primary source of transportation. Native Americans established sophisticated cultures based on canoe journeys and salmon cycles. Spanish, English, Russian, and American explorers used boats to search for new lands and shipping routes. The region's natural harbors and commercial ports were used to trade the rich natural resources including timber, marine life, and minerals. More recently, naval bases were built to guard the continent. This history has left a coastline that's rich with historic buildings and vessels, museums and historical archives, outdoor recreation opportunities, and the area's maritime industry is a vital component of the region's economic base. Today, tribal nations continue to promote traditional culture and practices and together with modern shipyards, container ports, cruise ships, tugboats, marinas filled with pleasure craft, national parks, lighthouses and other aids to navigation help tell the story of the past, present, and future of maritime Washington.

This large and diverse NHA is often considered to have four relatively distinct geographic areas: the Olympic Peninsula, Puget Sound, the North Coast, and the Salish Sea Islands. The Olympic Peninsula is the large landmass surrounded by the Pacific Ocean, the Strait of Juan de Fuca, and Puget Sound's Hood Canal. The peninsula includes historic ports, coastal communities, and tribal lands, but its namesake and defining feature are the iconic Olympic Mountains and national park—a real powerhouse (see the "attractions" below).

Puget Sound is a complex collection of land and water that makes up the third largest estuary (places where rivers meet the sea and create large areas of brackish water) in the nation. In prehistoric times, indigenous people used the sound to reach the sea, but the sound is now marked by tribal lands, maritime industry, military bases, small coastal communities, and the cities of Everett and Olympia (the state capital). The Kitsap Peninsula and associated islands lie in the interior of Puget Sound.

The Northern Coast runs along the western edge of Skagit and Whatcom counties and features protected bays that extend to the Canadian border. Traditional aquaculture and fishing remain important components of the area's economy. Northern coastal cities such as Bellingham provide traditional jumping-off points to Alaska by means of the Inside Passage.

The Salish Sea—defined by the Strait of Juan de Fuca, Puget Sound, and Canada's Strait of Georgia—is home to more than 400 islands that are the traditional homelands of native tribes and habitat for diverse marine life. Whidbey Island and the San Juan archipelago are diverse, often remote and rugged, and include bustling harbors and popular vacation destinations.

Attractions

Given the size and diversity of Maritime Washington, it's not surprising that its visitor attractions are large in number and high in appeal. Enjoy the area's parks, historic sites, museums, thriving cities, diverse culture, and a myriad of outdoor recreation opportunities. Here are some places to start.

Olympic National Park includes 60 miles of wild Pacific Ocean beach.

Ebey's Landing National Historical Reserve is a unit of the National Park System and includes rich farmland, a lovely harbor, and outstanding opportunities for outdoor recreation.

Olympic National Park

Square in the middle of America's nearly million-acre Olympic National Park rises Mount Olympus, nearly 8,000 feet high and cloaked in the glaciers that helped shape the mountains and this park. Follow these glaciers and their meltwater downstream toward the Pacific Ocean through subalpine meadows of wildflowers to find this national park's emerald valleys that hold some of the world's most impressive and beautiful old-growth rain forests; some trees are more than 300 feet tall and 70 feet around, and everything is covered in moss and lichens. Just a little farther west, walk along the park's more than 60 miles of wild Pacific Ocean coastline with its sea stacks, tide pools, and driftwood. It's no wonder the park is also a World Heritage Site.

Ebey's Landing National Historical Reserve

This is an unusual unit of the National Park System designed to protect a rural community and its significant natural and cultural resources. This striking landscape at the gateway to Puget Sound includes rich farmland, a lovely harbor, and outstanding opportunities for outdoor recreation. The park is located on Whidbey Island and celebrates the history of both the Native and Euro-America presence.

Klondike Gold Rush National Historical Park (Seattle Unit)

Gold was discovered in Canada's Yukon Territory in the late 1800s, setting off one of the world's great gold rushes. Seattle instantly became the primary point of departure to reach the gold fields by ship, and its port and local merchants prospered. The city became known at the "Gateway to the Gold Fields," supplying prospectors with the (literal) "ton of provisions" they would need to cross into Canada. This small unit of the National Park System offers two floors of exhibits and ranger-led gold-panning demonstrations. A larger unit of Klondike Gold Rush National Historical Park is located in Skagway, Alaska, where most ships docked.

San Juan Island National Historical Park

San Juan Island is well known for splendid vistas, saltwater shorelines, quiet woodlands, orca whales, and one of the last remaining native prairies in the Puget Sound/Northern Straits region. This unit of the National Park

The Seattle historic waterfront district includes Seattle Aquarium, the Great Wheel, historic piers, and Pioneer Square.

System focuses on the sites of the British and US Army camps during what is commonly called the Pig War, a boundary dispute over the ownership of the island in 1859 between the United States and Great Britain (the park's interpretive displays will explain the meaning of the conflict's unusual name).

Fort Worden State Park
One of nearly a hundred Washington State Parks in Maritime Washington, this 432-acre park includes more than two miles of saltwater shoreline and a variety of facilities and services. The park also features the early 20th century Fort Worden, including hidden gun emplacements, expansive parade grounds, and restored Victorian-era officers' homes. The area has been designated a National Historic Landmark District.

Northwest Maritime Center
Located along the waterfront in downtown Port Townsend and within the Port Townsend National Historic Landmark District, NWMC offers boatbuilding classes and educational programs, and hosts the annual Port Townsend Wooden Boat Festival (one of the largest in the world), and the annual Race To Alaska.

Seattle Waterfront
This historic district includes the Seattle Aquarium, Seattle's Great Wheel (a giant ferris wheel that provides great views of the waterfront), historic piers, and Pioneer Square (Seattle's "first neighborhood" that includes Renaissance Revival architecture and a wide variety of tourist-friendly facilities and services).

Tribal Museums
Celebrating its Native American heritage, Maritime Washington includes several tribal museums, including the Makah Museum (part of the Makah Cultural and Research Center), the Squaxin Island Museum Library

& Research Center (a living eco-museum demonstrating the relationship between nature and Squaxin Island tribal culture), the Suquamish Museum, featuring the home of the Suguamish people since time immemorial and the Chief Seattle gravesite.

For more information about Maritime Washington and to help plan your visit, see the area's official website (preservewa.org) and the website of the National Park Service (nps.gov/places /maritime-washington-national-heritage -area.htm).

Maurice D. Hinchey Hudson River Valley National Heritage Area

State: New York

Description: This historic and dramatically beautiful NHA is centered on a 150-mile stretch of the Hudson River that features thriving cities, lovely compact hamlets, rolling farm and forest land, the Hudson Highlands, and the grand residences of some of the most famous names in American history, including Roosevelt, Rockefeller, and Vanderbilt.

Sample Attractions:
- Saratoga National Historical Park
- Home of Franklin D. Roosevelt National Historic Site
- Vanderbilt Mansion National Historic Site
- United States Military Academy (West Point)

New York's Hudson River Valley includes a string of natural and cultural resources that are important to the nation. The region includes thriving cities, lovely compact hamlets, rolling farm and forest land, the Hudson Highlands with some of the most dramatic rural scenery in the East, distinctive parks and gardens, many remarkable historic homes and sites, and fanciful architecture, all set in the context of the long and powerful Hudson River and the gentle Catskill Mountains. The valley played an important part in the American Revolution, gave birth to significant developments in American art and architecture, and was instrumental in reimagining the aesthetic value of the American landscape. This is a big landscape that includes 154 miles of the Hudson River from the New York Capital District in Albany/ Troy downstream to New York City, totaling approximately four million acres and including more than 250 communities in ten counties bordering the river. It includes five units of the National Park System and the grand residences of some of the most famous names in American history, including Roosevelt, Rockefeller, and Vanderbilt.

All this and more is part of the overachieving Maurice D. Hinchey Hudson River Valley National Heritage Area (Hudson River Valley). Originally designated Hudson River Valley National Heritage Area in 1996, it was renamed in 2019 to honor local Congressman Hinchey who did so much to help create and advance the NHA. Hudson River Valley is managed by Hudson River Valley Greenway (the "Greenway"), a state entity formed to facilitate a coordinated regional approach to preserving the natural, historic, cultural, scenic, and recreational resources of the NHA. The Greenway has identified several themes that tie this landscape together

A reenactment of the American victory over the British at Saratoga National Historical Park

and highlight its contributions to American history, culture, and environment: settlement and migration, corridor of commerce, American and Industrial revolutions, freedom and dignity, and nature and culture. The Greenway partners with many public, private, and non-profit entities to conduct and coordinate its work. A network of more than 100 designated Heritage Sites, classified by theme and amenities, has been created to better interpret and celebrate its attraction sites and the "big picture" stories they help tell and illustrate.

The lands and people of Hudson River Valley represent a long and eventful history. It's estimated that there may have been over 17,000 indigenous people living in the Hudson River Valley at the time Europeans began exploring the area; these people called the river Mahicanituck meaning "the river that flows both ways," a reference to the river's

tidal action. European-American exploration began in 1609 when Henry Hudson and crew set off from the Netherlands in the ship *Half Moon* and arrived (mostly by accident) at the mouth of a great river where he decided to sail upstream. Later, the region was settled mostly by the Dutch and English and became a popular destination for immigrants. The Hudson River was a primary strategic target during the Revolutionary War; the British tried but ultimately failed to take control of the waterway, the Americans thwarting their attempt to separate New England from the other colonies. The battles at Saratoga were also a turning point for the patriots. Later, the natural beauty of the Valley helped establish the original American artistic movement that celebrated the wildness or sublimity of the American landscape, in contrast to a more traditional European focus on the pastoral in landscape painting;

appropriately, this became known as the Hudson River School of Art, prominently represented by Hudson River Valley residents Thomas Cole and Frederick Church. In the late 19th and early 20th centuries, the Hudson River Valley became home to wealthy industrialists who built their great mansions and estates with money earned from the Industrial Revolution. However, the industries of large-scale mining, foundries, mills, manufacturing, railroads, and shipping degraded portions of the river and surrounding landscape, and this, along with a proposal for a large hydro-electric generating facility in the early 1960s, contributed to an environmental movement that continues today and is well represented in the NHA.

Attractions

Where to begin? This large and dynamic NHA features more than 100 heritage sites that include early American history, architecturally important homes and gardens of influential American families, innovation in American and modern art, and a string of parks and outdoor recreation areas. The following are only representative examples.

Home of Franklin D. Roosevelt National Historic Site

This unit of the National Park System in Hyde Park was home to America's longest-serving president, and Roosevelt often returned here to where he was born. This site preserves the homes of Franklin and Eleanor Roosevelt, the nation's first presidential library and museum, over a thousand acres of gardens and trails, and Val-Kill, Mrs. Roosevelt's retreat.

Saratoga National Historical Park

This unit of the National Park System includes the battlefield where American forces won their first significant victory over the British in the Revolutionary War. Visitors can see the battlefield by driving or biking the Battlefield Tour Road, taking a guided tour of the park, visiting the historic Schuler House, walking through Victory Woods, and climbing the stairs to the top of the Saratoga Monument.

KyKuit (Rockefeller Family Home)

This majestic hilltop residence and estate with sweeping views of the Hudson River was home to four generations of the Rockefeller family, beginning with industrialist and philanthropist John D. Rockefeller, founder

KyKuit is the historic home for four generations of the Rockefeller family; the home, its art collection, and terraced gardens are open to the public.

Stroll the lovely grounds and gardens of the many historic homes along the Hudson River Valley (Vanderbilt Mansion National Historic Site).

The view from Olana State Historic Site, the home of Hudson River School painter Frederick Church

of Standard Oil. Meticulously maintained for more than 100 years, the home and its art collection and terraced gardens are open to the public.

Vanderbilt Mansion National Historic Site

One of the many stately homes built by the Vanderbilts, the Vanderbilt Mansion at Hyde Park was constructed for the aristocratic lifestyle of this wealthy and legendary family. This home was built for Frederick and Louise Vanderbilt and is an understated masterpiece of American design. This is a unit of the National Park System.

Thomas Cole National Historic Site and Olana State Historic Site

Among the founders of America's distinctive and original Hudson River School of Art, Thomas Cole and Frederick Church lived and painted in the Hudson River Valley. Cedar Grove, the home and studio of Cole near Catskill, is featured at Thomas Cole National Historic Site, a unit of the National Park System. Olana State Historic Site includes the impressive estate of Church, the

distinctive home designed by Calvert Vaux, and lovely grounds that include five miles of carriage roads. The Cole and Olana sites are linked across the Hudson by the Sky Walk Trail; the bridge across the Hudson has bump-outs so artists can stop and sketch/draw/paint.

Storm King Art Center

Storm King Art Center is a 500-acre outdoor museum located in New York's Hudson Valley, where visitors experience large-scale sculpture and site-specific commissions under open sky. The center includes the lovely hills, meadows, and forests that comprise the surrounding landscape.

United States Military Academy (West Point)

Founded in 1802 and the oldest of the five US military academies, the United States Military Academy (often called West Point) sits on strategic high ground on the tall banks of the Hudson River. The area features Revolutionary War fortifications. The central campus is comprised of mostly Norman-style buildings and is a National Historic

The United States Military Academy sits on strategic high ground on the banks of the Hudson River.

Landmark. Visitors are welcome at the visitor center, museum, and walking tours.

Empire State Plaza Art Collection

This site enjoys the reputation of "the greatest collection of modern American art in any single public site that is not a museum." The collection was formed under the direction of Governor Nelson A. Rockefeller during construction of the Empire State Plaza (1966–1978). Ninety-two works of abstract expressionist art are on permanent display throughout the plaza.

Bear Mountain and Harriman State Parks

Hudson River Valley is graced with a number of state parks. Bear Mountain and Harriman are among the largest and most well known. Bear Mountain is situated in the rugged mountains rising from the west bank of the Hudson River near Highlands and Stony Park. It offers opportunities for hiking, fishing, swimming, picnicking, and many other outdoor recreation pursuits. Harriman State Park is large and includes 31 lakes and reservoirs, 200 miles of hiking trails, beaches, and camping.

Hudson River Valley Ramble

This annual event, conducted in September, celebrates the natural, cultural, historic, and recreational resources that are part of Hudson River Valley. Tour historic homes, appreciate the area's history, enjoy the scenic landscape, learn about the American Revolution, walk the region's parks, trails, and grand gardens, and lots more. Celebrate this diverse and important NHA in the company of like-minded visitors.

For more information about Hudson River Valley and to help plan your visit, see the area's official website (hudson rivervalley.com) and the website of the National Park Service (nps.gov/places /hudson-river-valley-national-heritage -area.htm).

Mississippi Delta National Heritage Area

State: Mississippi

Description: The Delta is the defining natural feature of this large NHA, the vast alluvial floodplain of the Mississippi River; other themes include the area's historic period when "cotton was king," Civil War Battle-fields, distinctive blues music that's played in the NHA's many "jukes," and the modern Civil Rights Movement.

Sample Attractions:
- Vicksburg National Military Park
- Mississippi Freedom Trail
- Mississippi Blues Trail
- B. B. King Museum and Delta Interpretive Museum

As the name suggests, Mississippi Delta National Heritage Area (Mississippi Delta) focuses on the vast alluvial floodplain of the Mississippi River, one of America's great natural phenomena, and includes 18 counties that are located fully or partially on this floodplain. The NHA is bound together by several themes that have affected American history and culture. It was once where "cotton was king," founded on the backs of slave labor, and played an important role in the Civil War. It was the birthplace and incubator of distinctive forms of music, including American blues and rock and roll. And the region played a central role in the modern Civil Rights Movement. Many of its African American residents left the state in the early and middle 20th century as part of America's Great Migration. Grassroots efforts to designate the NHA began in 2003 and Congress established the area in 2009. The management entity is the Delta Center for Culture and Learning at Delta State University, and this has given the stories of Mississippi Delta a strong and award-wining scholarly foundation that's translated into its conservation and educational programs.

Of course, the story of Mississippi Delta has to begin with the Delta. This distinctive feature is comprised of the sediment carried south by the Mississippi River—the largest river system in the nation—over millions of years and deposited near the mouth of the river. The Delta is enormous, 200 miles long and 87 miles at its widest point, an area of nearly 7,000 square miles. The Delta was home to Native Americans who left many mounds as evidence of their prehistoric occupation. Choctaws and Chickasaws lived there in historic times, but relatively little is known about them.

Early European-Americans began settling the region in the early 19th century and found much of the Delta covered in forest, but most of the trees were cut to create what would become the most productive cotton-growing area in the nation, thanks to the fertile soils of the Delta. As the local saying goes, "the river bore the alluvial plain that is the Delta, and the Delta bore fruit," But the cotton-growing heritage of the region was based on slave labor and then sharecropping, and because of their mistreatment of African Americans, these agricultural systems were unsustainable. In their stead agricultural crops have become more diverse and managed according to the dictates of contemporary "precision agriculture" and the application of modern spatial and temporal information technologies that guide crop management. Agriculture remains vital to the region's economy.

The Delta has been productive in other ways as well, especially in music. Abuse of African Americans gave rise to the blues, an original form of music. This music originated with African Americans shortly after the end of slavery and incorporates African musical traditions such as spirituals, gospel, work songs, and field hollers. Lyrics are often related to historic mistreatment. Blues are traditionally played in the region's many "jukes," informal music and dance establishments operated primarily by African Americans. Blues is a uniquely American musical form and is played throughout the NHA. The Delta region is also known for its contribution to rock and roll music, an outgrowth of the blues. This creativeness extends to other cultural forms as well, including art, food, painting, architecture, and literature.

The Civil War had an enormous effect on Mississippi, where some of the most important battles were fought. For example, the 1863 Siege of Vicksburg ended in Union victory and meant that the close of the war was near. Ultimately, slaves were freed, but they remained at a substantial disadvantage during the Reconstruction and Jim Crow periods. This contributed to the Great Migration period of American history in which an estimated six million African Americans moved from rural areas of the southern states to urban areas in the North between 1916 and 1970. Continuing racial discrimination led to the modern Civil Rights Movement after World War II, and much of this movement played out in Mississippi Delta. Prominent examples include the brutal murder of Emmett Till, Freedom Summer, and the Poor People's Campaign. Leaders and activists include Amzie Moore, Fannie Lou Hamer, the delegates of the Mississippi Freedom Democratic Party, and the Freedom Riders.

Attractions

This historic and colorful region includes a great variety of attractions that celebrate its history and culture. The following includes some great options, but be sure to leave time to wander some of the backroads and walk through historic towns. Find a juke, eat some BBQ, enjoy southern hospitality. As the locals suggest, "it all runs on Delta time and no one is watching the clock."

Vicksburg National Military Park

The Mississippi River port city of Vicksburg was vital to both the Confederates and the Union because it was a lifeline of supplies for the southern army. Confederate President Jefferson Davis called it "the nailhead that holds the South's two halves together" and Abraham Lincoln called the city "the key." The city was well fortified and defended,

Vicksburg National Militray Park commorates the weeks-long Union siege and capture of the port city of Vicksburg.

but the 47-day siege by General Grant's army resulted in an important victory for the Union and hastened the end of the Civil War. The park's grounds include over 1,300 monuments to those who fought; the site is informally called "the largest outdoor art gallery in the world."

Mississippi Freedom Trail

A large collection of roadside markers that celebrate and interpret the Civil Rights Movement have been placed throughout the state and many are found in Mississippi Delta. Examples include the site where Emmett Till was murdered, the Fannie Lou Hamer gravesite, the Amzie Moore home, the home of Dr. T. R. M. Howard, and a marker honoring activist Unita Blackwell.

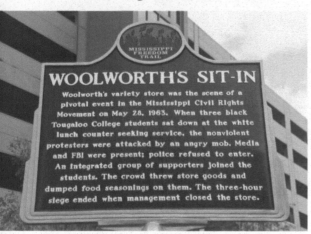

Roadside markers throughout the NHA commemorate the modern Civil Rights Movement.

Mississippi Blues Trail

This collection of roadside markers celebrating American blues is also found throughout the state, with the largest number located in Mississippi Delta. Markers are found in a great diversity of locations, including city streets, cotton fields, cemeteries, churches, and jukes.

Delta National Forest

This national forest north of Vicksburg is one of the few hardwood forests remaining in the Mississippi Delta. Visitors are welcome to hike, camp, picnic, and enjoy the beauty of this area.

2000-Year-old Bald Cypress Tree

These trees with their distinctive "knees" that grow from the trees' roots are found in abundance in the swamps and wetlands of the Delta region. At Sky Lake Preserve, see a remarkable specimen that is at least 2,000 years old. Walk to the tree on a boardwalk and enjoy the beauty of this wetland.

Mississippi River Boat Launch

Access to the Mississippi River is rare, but can be found at a site locally known as "the Asphalt," near the town of Mayersville. Dip your feet in the river and wait for a tow boat to come along.

Scenic Drive from Sardis to Batesville

Drive MS-315 S on this two-lane blacktop as it meanders through lovely rural Mississippi. Take a break at large Sardis Lake State Park which includes a reservoir and surrounding lands: you can hike, bird, camp, and fish. Continue on MS-35 S to Batesville and enjoy the attractive and tourist-friendly town square.

GRAMMY Museum

Celebrate the most important award in music at the GRAMMY Museum in

Cleveland, Mississippi. This 28,000-square-foot museum located on the campus of Delta State University honors all forms of music. Interactive exhibits encourage learning about the creative and technological processes of recording and the history of the GRAMMY Awards.

B. B. King Museum and Delta Interpretive Museum

Riley B. King, professionally known as B.B. King, grew up in a poor town in the Delta but became an internationally recognized blues musician. This facility tells his story, including his career, as well as stories of the Delta, race relations, and his professional success and legends.

B.B. King grew up in a poor town in the Delta, but became an internationally recognized blues musician; the B.B. King Museum tells his story.

Delta Blues Museum

For more than 40 years, this museum in Clarksdale has been preserving the history of blues and exploring the future. Established in 1979 by the Carnegie Library Board of Trustees, this is the oldest music museum in the state.

> For more information about Mississippi Delta and to help plan your visit, see the area's official website (msdelta heritage.com) and the website of the National Park Service (nps.gov/places /mississippi-delta-national-heritage -area.htm).

Mississippi Gulf Coast National Heritage Area

State: Mississippi

Description: This diverse NHA features a long stretch of the Gulf Coast with its inviting white sand beaches and biologically rich wetlands; the history and culture of the area is also diverse, affected by Native Americans, early French and Spanish explorers, and African American slaves, and is manifested in local foods, historic homes and downtowns, and local museums.

Sample Attractions:
- Gulf Coast Blueways
- Biloxi Lighthouse & Visitor Center
- Infinity Science Center
- Gumbo

When is a National Heritage Area like a good bowl of gumbo? Given that we're talking about Mississippi Gulf Coast National Heritage Area (Mississippi Gulf Coast), then I guess the answer's easy. This NHA is diverse, but it really seems to hang together in an enjoyable way, just like the good bowl of gumbo that you'll find here. Mississippi Gulf Coast is comprised of the six Mississippi counties that occupy the Gulf Coast of the state and it celebrates the region's history, nature, innovation, and flavors. Visitors are offered authentic cultural experiences that reflect this diverse region, and residents have become more aware and appreciative of the special character of where they live.

Given the diverse character of the region, Mississippi Gulf Coast has helped develop a unified story of the region, distilling and promoting its unique culture. Management of the NHA is guided by several themes.

Let's begin with history. Archeologists have documented the presence of Native Americans in the region for more than 10,000 years, though not much is known about this prehistoric period; however, they lend their names to many of the area's communities and natural landmarks, such as Biloxi. French and Spanish explorers arrived very early in American history. Famed French explorer Pierre Le Moyne D'Iberville explored and colonized the Mississippi Sound in 1699 and the city of Biloxi briefly served as the capital of French Louisiana. During the past 300 years, flags of six nations flew over the Mississippi Gulf Coast: French, English, Spanish, the Republic of West Florida, the Confederate States of America, and the United States of America. Native American, Spanish, and French cultures established a presence in the region as part of its heritage, along with other cultural elements. Today, the region's long and diverse history is found in its historic homes and downtowns and local museums; take time to stroll.

Of course, much of the heritage of the region is derived from the presence of the Gulf of Mexico and other natural features. In this case, the land is largely defined by the water at its doorstep. There are miles after miles of sandy beaches along with many bays, rivers, creeks, swamps, marshes, and islands. The gulf offers ecological niches and riches that are coveted throughout the nation and beyond, and many residents rely on the bounty of the sea for their livelihoods and family dinners. Wetlands are biologically rich, supporting a great variety of plants and animals; the area is a birder's heaven.

The region is also marked by an interesting streak of innovation. Local people build great ships that help defend our nation. Modern ports ship goods around the world. Rockets that send satellites and astronauts into space are tested here. And arts and crafts—painting, pottery, and sculpture—are defined by a strong element of creativity.

We've already started the conversation about what locals call their "flavorful culture," a mix of cultural derivations using seafood and other local sources. We're fortunate that residents are pleased to share their bounty with visitors in seafood houses, gourmet kitchens, backwoods barbecue joints, and various dives. And there's that gumbo again.

Though they don't advertise this, the people of the region are also resilient, a useful quality when you live in a place subject to hurricanes. Hurricane Katrina devastated much of the area in 2005, but local people and communities have rebounded. And to their credit, Mississippi Gulf Coast has recently worked with the Gulf of Mexico Alliance Coastal Resilience Team and the Nature-Based Tourism Task Force to craft a Nature-Based Tourism Plan for the region.

Attractions

Given this region's eclectic character, it shouldn't be surprising that Mississippi Gulf

Coast includes an equal variety of attractions. Consider the following as good options to jump start your visit.

Infinity Science Center

This contemporary museum offers a blend of space, Earth science, engineering, and technology content. It's also host to the NASA Stennis Visitor Center. The museum is designed for all ages and takes advantage of its location in an area that contributes to space exploration.

Biloxi Lighthouse & Visitor Center

Erected in 1848, this lighthouse was one of the first cast-iron lighthouses in the South and serves as the city's scenic symbol. The lighthouse was operated by civilians until 1939 and is notable for its several female light keepers, including Maria Younghans who tended the light for 53 years. Hurricane Katrina's storm surge reached a third of the way up the 64-foot structure; the lighthouse sustained damage but withstood the event and is back open for tours.

Gulf Coast Blueways

Considering the omnipresent waters of the region, there may be no better way to see the sights than by paddling in a canoe or kayak. And Mississippi Gulf Coast has helped create seven "blueways," water-based trails that explore the area's rivers, creeks, and bayous. Each blueway includes an established route, mileage markers, and points of interest. Maps are available locally.

Beauvoir

This lovely summer home (the name is French for "beautiful view") on the Gulf

Biloxi Lighthouse was one of the first cast-iron lighthouses in the South and serves as the city's scenic symbol.

This lovely summer home on the Gulf Coast is named Beauvoir, meaning "beautiful view."

Coast was built by a plantation owner and completed in 1852. It changed hands several times until ownership passed to Jefferson Davis, the president of the Confederacy.

Davis occupied the home while he wrote his two-volume memoir, *The Rise and Fall of the Confederate Government*. The home and outbuildings were badly damaged in recent storms, but have been reconstructed and are now open to the public.

Charnley-Norwood House

This distinctive home was built on the Gulf Coast in 1890 by architect Louis Sullivan of Chicago for a vacation house for the Charnley and later the Norwood famlies. Sullivan employed one of his young draftsman, Frank Lloyd Wright, to assist in the design. The home has a distinctive long, low orientation that blends into the natural surroundings of the Coastal Plain and exhibits what are now considered to be classic elements of modern architecture. The home has been subject to fire and storm surges but has been painstakingly restored to its original specifications and is open to the public upon request.

Bay St. Louis L&N Train Depot

Designated a Mississippi Landmark, this building was constructed in the late 1920s and houses both the Bay St. Louis Mardi Gras Museum and the Alice Moseley Folk Art & Antique Museum. The building is surrounded by park-like grounds.

Walter Anderson Museum of Art

Walter Anderson was a master artist who loved to capture images of plants, animals, and life along the Gulf Coast of Mississippi. The museum features permanent and changing exhibits and showcases other artists as well.

Crosby Arboretum

This large arboretum is designed to protect and display plants native to the Gulf Coast. Three basic habitats of the local area are featured—savanna, woodland, and aquatic.

La Pointe Krebs House & Museum

First constructed in 1757, this house built of tabby and bousillage construction techniques is determined as the oldest standing building in Mississippi. The house and museum interpret the history of Jackson County, Mississippi.

Gumbo is a metaphoric culinary mashup of the region's engaging natural and cultural history.

Gumbo

You know the story by now: gumbo is a metaphoric culinary mashup of the region's engaging natural and cultural history. But it's really a flavorful, signature dish that's on the menu nearly everywhere you go.

For more information about Mississippi Gulf Coast and to help plan your visit, see the area's official website (msgulf coastheritage.ms.gov) and the website of the National Park Service (nps.gov /places/mississippi-gulf-coast-national -heritage-area.htm).

Mississippi Hills National Heritage Area

State: Mississippi

Description: This large expanse of hills dotted with towns in the northeastern quadrant of Mississippi features its Native American heritage, monumental battles of the Civil War, the contemporary Civil Rights Movement, the world's greatest blues artists, and outstanding opportunities for outdoor recreation.

Sample Attractions:

- Brices Cross Roads National Battlefield Site and Shiloh National Military Park
- Natchez Trace Parkway
- Elvis Presley Birthplace and Museum
- University of Mississippi Lyceum and Civil Rights Monument

The Mississippi Hills occupy the northeastern quadrant of the Magnolia State and offer a distinctive cultural landscape that is marked by a large expanse of hills dotted with small towns and a noteworthy blend of cultures. Much of this large region is forested and the area's largest towns are Tupelo and Columbus. Mississippi Hills National Heritage Area (Mississippi Hills) was established in 2009 and is a sizable area of geography that includes 19 counties and portions of 11 more. This designation commemorates the region's impact on American history and culture. The area is managed by Mississippi Hills Heritage Area Alliance, a non-profit group that works with the National Park Service and a host of other partner organizations.

Mississippi Hills celebrates the diverse components of its nationally distinctive heritage. The area sits at the intersection of the nation's Appalachian and Mississippi Delta regions and its culture has been shaped by these regions in distinguishing and interesting ways. The history of the region starts with the area's Native Americans who left a rich heritage of sacred burial mounds found throughout the area. The region was also shaped by monumental battles of the Civil War and includes Brices Cross Roads National Battlefield Site and Shiloh National Military Park, both units of the National Park System. As a complement to its role in the Civil War, the area also played an important role in the modern-day Civil Rights Movement as exemplified by James Meredith and Ida B. Wells-Barnett. In addition, a number of cultural icons representing powerful southern literature and vibrant music have emerged from this culture that include Nobel Prize-winning novelist William Faulkner, popular novelist John Grisham, and famed playwright Tennessee Williams, as well as Elvis Presley, Jerry Lee Lewis, Tammy Wynette, and some of the world's greatest blues artists (be sure to explore the Mississippi Blues Trail markers within the NHA). This is a culture that has touched and inspired millions.

And the land is inspiring too, a heavily forested and mostly rural area that offers both beauty and adventure. Outdoor recreation opportunities abound in the region's parks, forests, and rivers. Examples include the National Park Service's Natchez Trace Parkway, the huge Tennessee Tombigbee Waterway, and the long-distance Tanglefoot Trail.

Attractions

Mississippi Hills' attractions are both numerous and diverse: a beautiful landscape,

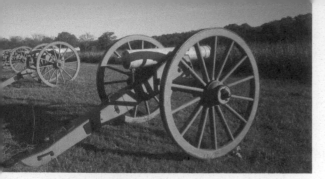

More than 23,000 casualties were sustained at the famous Civil War battlefield commemorated at Shiloh National Military Park.

Mississippi Hills National Heritage Area includes a portion of the Natchez Trace National Scenic Trail, a unit of the National Park System.

Nobel Prize–winning author William Faulkner lived and worked for more than 40 years at his home, Rowan Tree.

Elvis Presley was born in 1935 in this modest home in Mississippi Hills NHA.

colorful history, welcoming communities, museums of natural and cultural history, historic homes and architecture, Civil War sites, lovely drives, and lots of opportunities to get out of the car and into nature at the area's parks, forests, and rivers. There's a wide range of places to go, things to see, and culture to experience. As Mississippi Hills writes, "We invite you to get lost in these hills—you never know what you might find!" But in case you don't want to get lost, the NHA has developed four driving itineraries through the region and posted them on their website (see below); the tours address Native American History, Civil War, Civil Rights, and Cultural Icons. The website also notes more than a dozen annual festivals and events.

Brices Cross Roads National Battlefield Site

This Civil War battlefield is a unit of the National Park System and is an example of the brutality of the war; 12,000 soldiers joined the battle and there were 3,000 casualties. Though the Confederates won the battle, it was costly. The nearby National Park Service Visitor Center for the Natchez Trace Parkway interprets the battle.

Shiloh National Military Park

This 4,200-acre unit of the National Park System tells the story of the famous 1862 Civil War battle where there were more than 23,000 casualties. A separate unit of this park includes the Corinth Civil War Interpretive Center.

Natchez Trace Parkway
A unit of the National Park System, the Natchez Trace Parkway is a 444-mile road and scenic drive through three states and includes a portion in Mississippi Hills. The route roughly follows the "Old Natchez Trace," a historic travel corridor used by Native Americans, European settlers, slave traders, and armies. The Parkway Visitor Center is located in Tupelo.

Natchez Trace National Scenic Trail
Also a unit of the National Park System, the trail runs parallel to the Natchez Trace Parkway in five sections that total more than 60 miles. The trail offers opportunities to explore wetlands, swamps, hardwood forest, rock outcroppings, overlooks, and the history of the area.

William Faulkner's Rowan Oak
This modified Greek Revival home sits on 29 heavily wooded acres just south of the historic Oxford Square. This was Faulkner's home for more than 40 years and served as inspiration for much of his writing. He won the Nobel Prize for Literature in 1949 and the Pulitzer Prize and a National Book Award in 1954.

Elvis Presley Birthplace and Museum
Elvis Presley's father borrowed $180 to build a small family home in 1934 in East Tupelo, and this is where the King of Rock 'n Roll was born on January 8, 1935. Elvis lived in Tupelo for 13 years and attended the Assembly of God Church; it was here and

The University of Mississippi Lyceum includes a civil rights monument commemorating James Meredith, who bravely integrated the university in 1962.

in the nearby Shake Rag community that he was exposed to gospel music that played an important role in his musical career.

University of Mississippi Lyceum and Civil Rights Monument
James Meredith bravely integrated the University of Mississippi in 1962, an iconic moment in the Civil Rights Movement, and a monument commemorating Meredith is located near the university's Lyceum. This is a stop on the State of Mississippi's Freedom Trail.

Historic Oxford Square and Lafayette County Courthouse
Oxford was chosen as the name of this county seat in 1837 in hopes that it would become the center of higher learning; this aspiration materialized when the University of Mississippi was founded here in 1848. Oxford Square remains the cultural and economic hub of the city and is very visitor friendly.

Tennessee Williams Home and Welcome Center
The early home of playwright Tennessee Williams is located in the town of Columbus; the house was the rectory of St. Paul's

Popularly known as the Tenn-Tom, the Tennessee-Tombigbee Waterway is a large water development project that offers opportunities for water-based outdoor recreation.

Episcopal Church where Williams's grandfather served. The Victorian home has been moved to a new site on the town's Main Street Historic District where it honors Williams and serves as the town welcome center.

Tennessee-Tombigbee Waterway

Popularly known as the Tenn-Tom, this 234-mile-long waterway was completed in 1984 at a cost of $2 billion and connects the Tennessee River with the Gulf of Mexico. The waterway was constructed for navigation and includes ten locks and dams. The lands surrounding the waterway are managed for wildlife habitat and extensive opportunities for outdoor recreation.

Tanglefoot Trail

Constructed on the bed of a historic railroad, this 43.6-mile trail meanders through the Mississippi Hills, passing fields, forests, meadows, and wetlands. The trail accommodates hikers and bikers and is served by a number of interesting towns along the way.

For more information about Mississippi Hills and to help plan your visit, see the area's official website (mississippihills .org) and the website of the National Park Service (nps.gov/places/mississ ippi-hills-national-heritage-area.htm).

Mormon Pioneer National Heritage Area

State: Utah

Description: This is a large NHA that interprets the westward migration of Mormon pioneers in the late 1800s; the area includes some of the finest scenery in the West and truly outstanding opportunities for outdoor recreation.

Sample Attractions:

- Five units of the National Park System
- Utah State Route 12 All American Highway
- Hole-in-the-Rock Expedition
- Anasazi State Park Museum

Mormon Pioneer National Heritage Area (Mormon Pioneer) celebrates the Mormon pioneers who migrated westward, settling much of Utah and the American West. In the latter part of the 1800s, tens of thousands of Mormons from New England, England, Scandinavia, and elsewhere traveled 1,400 miles from Illinois to the Great Salt Lake and eventually settled and colonized Utah, Nevada, the southwest corner of Wyoming, the southeast corner of Idaho, southeast Oregon, and a large portion of southern and eastern California. This large NHA spans a 400-mile area along US Highway 89, Utah State Route 24, and Utah State Route 12 and stretches from central Utah to the state's southern border. It's the only NHA focused on and named for a specific people—the Mormon pioneers—offering a window into their colonization and settlement experience in the western United States.

Mormon Pioneer was established in 2006 and is managed by the Utah Heritage Highway Alliance. According to its management

Bryce Canyon National Park includes a remarkable "forest of stone," a large collection of geologic hoodoos.

objectives, the NHA "preserves, interprets, promotes, and enhances Utah's pioneer heritage ... working to increase tourism, encourage economic development, revitalize communities, provide heritage educational opportunities, and improve the quality of life." The Alliance works with the National Park Service, local travel councils, and others to achieve its objectives.

Travel the NHA roads that wander through the region and enjoy some of the finest scenery in the West. You may recognize some of the area as the backdrop for the many Hollywood westerns filmed in this iconic portion of the American "Wild West," including *Butch Cassidy and the Sundance Kid* and *Jeremiah Johnson*. Stop in the towns the settlers built along the way to get picturesque insights into Mormon life and their role in settling and developing the region. Much of the local architecture was influenced by the large number of Scandinavian and British immigrants who relocated to Utah in the 1800s, including stonemasons who quarried the local limestone as a building material. Peruse the region's museums to learn more about the pioneer and Mormon life; you might even find a lost relative or two while looking through the family histories, life stories, photographs, and family genealogies found in several of these museums. Find truly outstanding opportunities for outdoor recreation; the NHA features an impressive five units of the National Park System—Bryce Canyon National Park, Zion National Park, Canyonlands National Park, Capitol Reef National Park, and Cedar Breaks National Monument—along with national forests and several state parks. Learn about the original inhabitants of the region—Paiute, Ute, and San Pitch Native American tribes. Camp or stay at a historic B&B. You'll find artisans, innkeepers, park and forest rangers, outfitters, local residents, descendants of pioneers, and others who will be happy to welcome you to Mormon Pioneer.

Attractions

This large NHA is stocked with lots of attractions, and one of the best is the scenic roads that link these sites; they're among the most dramatic in the nation. Take the time to enjoy them. There are lots of stops to be made along the way, including the following parks and other sites.

Utah State Route 12 is an All American Highway that offers a spectacular drive through a portion of Mormon Pioneer NHA.

The Virgin River Narrows is one of the most popular visitor attractions at Zion National Park.

Utah State Route 12
All American Highway

One of the main attractions is the spectacular drive along Utah State Route 12, an All American Highway. This designation means that the road includes features that don't exist elsewhere in the United States and are important enough to be tourist attractions unto themselves; there are only 31 All American Highways in the US. Route 12 connects with Highway 24 to form the attractive Boulder Loop.

Bryce Canyon National Park

Erosive forces over millions of years have carved a series of canyons, horseshoe-shaped bowls, and amphitheaters filled with colorful rock spires called hoodoos, some as much as 200 feet high. This is a crown jewel national park and not to be missed.

Zion National Park

This is another crown jewel national park of great and colorful slickrock canyons, towering cliffs, and magical spires and arches. Be sure to visit Zion Canyon and walk at least a few steps into striking Virgin River Narrows (but be prepared to get wet!).

Canyonlands National Park

As the name suggests, this grand national park is a seemingly boundless network of canyons carved into the vast Colorado Plateau. It's divided into several "districts" and the Maze District and detached Horseshoe Canyon area are most accessible to NHA visitors (though they require a long drive over dirt roads and have few facilities).

The Horseshoe Canyon portion of Canyonlands National Park features "The Great Gallery" and its world-famous rock art sites.

The lovely Mormon settlement of Fruita is the heart of Capitol Reef National Park.

This important temple was constructed by the Church of Jesus Christ of Latter-day Saints in Manti and was completed in 1888.

Capitol Reef National Park

This is the fourth national park in Mormon Pioneer and is not as well known as the others, but it's filled with colorful canyons, massive rock domes, twisting slot canyons, buttes, monoliths, arches, and a rich collection of the region's historic and prehistoric artifacts. Spend time in the historic Mormon village of Fruita.

Cedar Breaks National Monument

This national monument is a unit of the National Park System and offers a dramatic half-mile-deep amphitheater with a stunning collection of hoodoos. Other features in the 10,000-foot-high park include bristlecone pines, subalpine forests, meadows of wildflowers, and fabulous night skies.

Fairview Museum of History and Art

Appropriately located in Fairview, Utah, this museum was founded in 1859 and offers two main buildings. The more than 100-year-old schoolhouse features historical collections and the works of sculptor Dr. Avard T. Fairbanks, and the more contemporary building houses regional art, the Colombian Mammoth (named Spirit), historical displays, and the Clark Bronson bronze collection.

Manti Temple

This is the fifth temple constructed by the Church of Jesus Christ of Latter-day Saints (Mormons) and is located in Manti, Utah. This impressive temple was completed in 1888.

Casino Star Theatre

This historic building in the Gunnison Valley opened in 1913 as the Casino Theatre.

The large performance site hosted movies and occasional live productions. The building included chandeliers, terra cotta rosettes, and an ornate Beaux-Arts facade with columns and statuary from Philadelphia.

Moroni Opera House
This building was constructed in 1891 and is one of only two surviving 19th-century Utah opera houses. It included a large stage, orchestra pit, and seating for as many as 1,000 people. Located in the town of Moroni, it's listed on the National Register of Historic Places.

Hole-in-the-Rock Expedition
An effort to create a new settlement along the San Juan River in the southeast corner of Utah turned into a challenging, six-month struggle to reach the area by wagon train. A narrow path was carved into the rock for the expedition's 83 wagons, and a ferry was constructed to ford the Colorado River. Learn more about this at the Interagency Visitor Center in the town of Escalante.

Freemont Indian State Park
Construction of Interstate 70 unearthed a large Fremont Indian village and a treasure of rock art, pottery, baskets, and arrowheads that are now on display at this Utah state park. The park also offers hiking and camping.

Butch Cassidy Cabin
Just south of the tiny town of Circleville you'll find a small cabin that was the childhood home of the infamous outlaw Butch Cassidy. Born Robert Leroy Parker, Cassidy changed his name and robbed his first bank in Telluride, Colorado, in 1885.

Kanab/Little Hollywood
The iconic southwestern landscape in and around the town of Kanab, Utah, and surrounding Kane County served as the backdrop for more than 100 Hollywood movies. Consequently, the area has been dubbed "Little Hollywood" (though the Mormon culture of the area sometimes clashed with the Hollywood lifestyle).

Anasazi State Park Museum
This site includes an Ancestral Puebloan (Anasazi) village that was likely occupied from AD 1050 to 1200, and one of the largest communities west of the Colorado River. Tour a life-sized, six-room replica of an ancient dwelling and view a portion of the original site. Inside, see artifacts excavated from this site, offering insights to how these ancient people lived.

Grand Staircase-Escalante National Monument
This large and remote area is administered by the federal Bureau of Land Management and includes slot canyons, natural bridges and arches, as well as rock art panels, occupation sites, campsites, and granaries left by ancient Native Americans. Due to its remote location and rugged landscape, the monument was one of the last places in the continental United States to be mapped. This area is best explored on foot.

Escalante Petrified Forest State Park
This Utah state park features fascinating deposits of petrified wood (do not remove

any petrified wood from the park) as well as Wide Hollow Reservoir and a campground.

> For more information about Mormon Pioneer and to help plan your visit, see the area's official website (mormonpioneerheritage.org) and the website of the National Park Service (nps.gov/places/mormon-pioneer-national-heritage-area.htm).

MotorCities National Heritage Area

State: Michigan

Description: The auto industry is a vital component of American history, culture, and economy and this NHA tells this story, including emergence of the big three auto companies and the many ways in which the industry has helped shape American society.

Sample Attractions:
- Detroit Historical Museum
- Henry Ford Museum of American Innovation
- Gilmore Car Museum
- Tours and Programs

The American automobile industry is a triumph of inventiveness, engineering, technology, business management, and marketing. Just as importantly, it changed the course of American history, settlement patterns, and culture. This foundational story is told in engaging ways in appropriately named MotorCities National Heritage Area (MotorCities), a 10,000-square-mile area in southeast and central Michigan. The NHA was established in 1998 and is managed by the non-profit group, MotorCities National

Heritage Area Partnership, Inc., which works with the National Park Service and a host of other organizations.

Though Americans may not have invented the automobile, we enthusiastically embraced it, adding innovation to both the machines and how they're manufactured and marketed. Out of the very early chaos of many small car companies in the first part of the 20th century, the "big three" car companies—Ford, General Motors, and Chrysler—emerged to dominate the market by the end of the 1920s. Ford was founded in 1903, General Motors in 1908, and Chrysler in 1925. The innovation of the assembly line dramatically contributed to the success of these companies, allowing for increased production at a lower price per unit. These powerhouse companies thrived for decades until environmental and safety concerns arose in the 1960s, followed by the 1973 and 1979 oil crises and sharply rising gas prices. American auto companies were slow to adapt and foreign car sales soared based on perceived quality issues and low gas mileage of American cars. The great recession of 2008 also dealt a blow to the American auto industry. While the auto industry is still a vital part of the American economy, it is no longer as dominant as it once was.

The ways in which the automobile have helped shape the American landscape and culture are equally important. Given the comparatively low population density of the United States and its rural character over much of the landscape, cars were important to Americans as a basic means of transportation, helping to stimulate the demand for "automobility." A massive American program of road building, epitomized by construction of the Interstate Highway System, also helped increase demand for cars. Improvements in both cars and roads fueled development of the suburbs, large residential and service centers outside the crowded living conditions of large urban areas, and helped build America's middle class through the affordability of cars. Automobiles changed American society in other ways as well, introducing the purchase of expensive consumer goods on credit and planned obsolescence of consumer goods based on rapid changes in styling.

The auto industry played a critical role in both World Wars by shifting production to military vehicles and other wartime-related products. The industry manufactured several million military vehicles in World War II. President Franklin Roosevelt called the auto manufacturers the "Arsenal of Democracy." More recently, the auto industry aided production of face masks, ventilators, and medical equipment in the Covid pandemic; some called the industry the "Arsenal of Health." The industry has declined in the postwar period due to perceived quality deficiencies (compared with some foreign manufacturers), its slow embrace of fuel efficiency, massive carbon emissions, and strong international competition. However, some observers note that the traditional auto industry is evolving into a "mobility" industry that includes autonomous and electric vehicles.

MotorCities is deliberate in addressing the many dimensions of the American automobile industry, including the inherent tension between the auto companies and their workers. The United Automobile Workers or UAW (more formally known as the International Union, United Automobile, Aerospace and Agricultural Implement Workers of America) was founded in 1935 and is one of the oldest and largest labor unions in the nation with more than 400,000 active members and nearly 600,000 retired members. The UAW and the industry have negotiated many successful contracts, but this has occasionally involved high-profile strikes and other labor actions. The union has also been a leader in social movements designed to secure economic and social justice for all people.

The auto industry is an important component of American history, culture, and economy. It helped lead to a consumer goods society and economy, and by the 1980s it was responsible for one out of six jobs in the nation (including the demand for all the component car parts and related businesses), it helped drive the national and international oil industry and the nation's steel industry, it helped facilitate a growing tourism industry, it mediated rural isolation, it contributed to better health care and schools, and it altered the architecture of the American home. These and related stories are told at MotorCities.

Attractions

To quote the old adages, the American auto industry "put the world on wheels" and was founded by "tinkerers who became titans." This long and multifaceted story is told at MotorCities, in the very places where this history was made. The NHA includes auto factories, labor organizations, museums, archives, automobile collections, homes and gardens, tours, and programs and events. Here's a sampling.

Detroit Historical Museum

This important museum was founded in 1928 and has become one of the leading cultural institutions in the Midwest. Its collections and exhibits feature a sweeping history of Detroit and the surrounding region, including "America's Motor City" and "Detroit: The Arsenal of Democracy."

Henry Ford Museum of American Innovation

Located in Dearborn, this museum explores the many ways that innovative ideas have changed our world. Examples are wide-ranging and include the automobile, the Wright brothers' airplanes, Buckminster Fuller's circular Dymaxion House, and Rosa Parks's decision to sit rather than stand.

Old Mill Museum

Henry Ford converted the historic Dundee grist mill into his tenth village industry plant in the 1930s. Today, it offers three floors of museum collections and exhibits that help bring the history of the Dundee area to life. Materials range from the 1807 Macon Native American Reservation to everyday life in a Victorian-era village, and to the community's love affair with the automobile.

R. E. Olds Transportation Museum

Located on the Grand River in Lansing and housed in the original factory of the Bates and Edmonds Motor Company, the museum interprets the history of the auto industry through the eyes of Ransom Eli Olds, one of the industry's great pioneers.

The Henry Ford Museum of American Innovation celebrates the many ways that innovative ideas have changed the world; here we see what may be the world's oldest school bus.

The Gilmore Car Museum features 200 historic automobiles, including this 1954 Cadillac.

Gilmore Car Museum

This 90-acre historic campus is located in bucolic Hickory Corners and interprets automotive history and Americana. The museum features nearly 200 historic autos and two dozen beautifully restored buildings, including a 1930s service station and a functioning 1941 diner.

Alfred P. Sloan Museum

This museum tells the history of the Flint area, including early fur trading, pioneer life,

The Ford Piquette Avenue Plant is the country's oldest purpose-built automobile factory.

The 60-room lakeside mansion of Edsel and Eleanor Ford offers an inside look at the Ford family.

lumbering, carriage making, and the automobile boom of General Motors.

Ford Piquette Avenue Plant
Located in Detroit, this is the first building built and owned by Ford Motor Company and is the birthplace of the famous Model T. It's a National Historic Landmark and is open for tours of 10 or more visitors by appointment.

Ypsilanti Automotive Heritage Museum
This museum focuses on several elements of automotive history that have Ypsilanti connections, including Tucker, Hudson, Kaiser-Frazer, General Motors Hydra-matic, and the Chevrolet Corvair. A featured car is the 1952 Hudson Hornet race car owned by NASCAR champion Herb Thomas.

Edsel and Eleanor Ford House
This 60-room lakeside mansion in Grosse Pointe Shores, with lovely views and grounds, offers an inside look at the Ford family. Edsel Ford was the only son of Henry and Clara Ford and became president of Ford Motor Company in 1919 at age 25. The home is a

National Historic Landmark and is open to the public.

Automotive Hall of Fame
Located in Dearborn, this facility celebrates the men and women whose automotive innovations changed the world and revolutionized our way of life. Permanent and changing exhibits explore the early days of the automobile, the rise of the auto industry, and the beauty of automobile styling.

Tours
MotorCities partners with Detroit-area tour operators to offer public tours related to the automotive and labor union heritage of the region. Tours might include riding in a vintage Ford Model A, riding a bicycle, and kayaking on the Detroit River, all the while learning the story of how the region put the world on wheels. The MotorCities Moguls, Mansions, & Automobiles Tour paints a picture of Detroit's "Golden Age of the Automobile" where auto-related power brokers amassed fortunes and auto workers enjoyed substantive raises in wages and benefits.

Programs

MotorCities has worked with partners to create a rich slate of programs and other opportunities for residents and visitors to learn more about the diverse heritage of the region. Examples include the annual Michigan Auto Heritage Day; Awards of Excellence presented to community members who have rendered outstanding service; establishment of Fort Street Bridge Interpretive Park that tells the story of the Ford Hunger March in 1932 that led to the formation of the United Auto Workers; and the website, Making Tracks, that describes the struggles of African Americans who moved to Michigan from the South to work in the auto industry.

> For more information about MotorCities and to help plan your visit, see the area's official website (motorcities.org) and the website of the National Park Service (nps.gov/places/motorcities -national-heritage-area.htm).

Mountains to Sound Greenway National Heritage Area

State: Washington

Description: Threatened by booming regional development, this NHA has helped preserve and restore the area's lush forests, rugged mountains, wild rivers, alpine wilderness, flower-strewn meadows, and habitat for endangered salmon and other wildlife; it's cultural heritage includes numerous Native American tribes, diverse people, vibrant cities, small towns, and working farms.

Sample Attractions:
- Interstate 90 National Scenic Byway
- Snoqualmie Falls
- Pioneer Square-Skid Road and Pike Place Market Historic Districts
- Roslyn Historic District

In 1990, a group of local citizens hiked from Snoqualmie Pass in Washington's Cascade Mountains to the shores of Puget Sound to highlight their vision of preserving this scenic corridor in the face of booming development. Soon after, the Mountains to Sound Greenway Trust, a non-profit organization, was formed to help make this dream come true. Over the next three decades, the Greenway Trust led a coalition of non-profit, business, and government leaders who worked together to conserve public lands, restore native habitat, and connect an expansive network of trails across what is now known as the Mountains to Sound Greenway. The Greenway is an iconic 1.5-million-acre cultural landscape that spans three watersheds and extends nearly 100 miles from Seattle and Puget Sound on the west, across the Cascade Mountains, and on to Ellensburg and central Washington in the east. With hard work and broad support from local people and the area's congressional delegation, Mountains to Sound Greenway National Heritage Area (Mountains to Sound Greenway) was established by Congress in 2019. The Greenway Trust serves as the managing (or "coordinating") entity to promote collaborative care for the region's distinctive historical, cultural, and natural resources.

Native Americans have lived here for thousands of years, traveling and trading along rivers and footpaths through the area, some of which are now used as roads and trails. But it's Interstate 90 that most people will recognize as the primary travel route through the area today. In fact, this busy road is the first interstate highway that's been designated a National Scenic Byway, a testament to the region's natural beauty. Following signing of treaties with Native American tribes in the 1850s, the federal government "checkerboarded" the landscape into a mosaic of public and private land-ownership by granting every other section of land to railroad companies as an incentive for them to extend service in the region. When the Northern Pacific Railroad connected the Pacific to the rest of the United States, new residents plundered the region's astonishing old-growth forests and extracted minerals such as coal. Conservation efforts over the last half century have reassembled public ownership of critical lands to preserve and restore the region's natural resources and scenic beauty. Today, Mountains to Sound Greenway symbolizes the commitment of local people to protecting the region's history and outstanding natural environment. The NHA includes a treasure of vast and lush forests, rugged mountains, wild rivers, alpine wilderness, flower-strewn meadows, and habitat for endangered salmon and other wildlife. Its cultural heritage includes numerous Native American tribes, diverse people, vibrant cities, small towns, working farms, and an extensive network of outdoor recreation facilities that support hiking, boating, skiing, and biking. The result is pride of place among its two million residents, an enduring stewardship ethic, and a heritage-based tourism economy that's good for both residents and visitors.

Attractions

Mountains to Sound Greenway offers an unusually diverse set of attractions that feature everything from the complex and interesting history of the area to the region's inherent natural beauty and diverse outdoor recreation opportunities. The following attractions are representative examples.

Klondike Gold Rush National Historical Park (Seattle Unit)

Gold was discovered in Canada's Yukon Territory in the late 1800s, setting off one of the world's great gold rushes. Seattle instantly became the primary point of departure to reach the gold fields by ship, and its port and local merchants prospered. The city became known at the "Gateway to the Gold Fields," supplying prospectors with the "ton of provisions" they would need to cross into Canada. This small unit of the National Park System offers two floors of exhibits and ranger-led gold-panning demonstrations. A larger unit of Klondike Gold Rush National Historical Park is located in Skagway, Alaska, where most ships docked.

Interstate 90 National Scenic Byway

Interstate 90 forms the backbone of Mountains to Sound Greenway, running from the Seattle area through the Cascade Mountains. It was the first interstate highway to be named a National Scenic Byway. Follow this route to appreciate this National Heritage Area, to reach many of its attractions, and to find outstanding opportunities for outdoor activities such as hiking, biking, and skiing/snowboarding.

Pike Place Market Historic District includes over 600 vendors of fresh produce and seafood.

Pioneer Square-Skid Road and Pike Place Market Historic Districts

Pioneer Square and Skid Road were early centers of activity in the city of Seattle. A disastrous fire in 1889 burned much of the city's original wooden business district, but it was rebuilt of fireproof bricks, iron, and stone. Architect Elmer Fisher designed many of the buildings in the Richardsonian Romanesque style that led to the aesthetically pleasing appearance of the area today. The vast timber resources in the region were processed and shipped from Seattle and were skidded down the town's steep hills known as the Skid Road area of the city. Pike Place started as a public market in Seattle in 1907 to offer residents fresh and fairly priced food directly from farmers and fishermen. It's expanded over the years to become a visitor attraction with over 600 vendors as well as a culturally diverse meeting area.

Roslyn Historic District

Nestled in the eastern foothills of the Cascade Mountains, Roslyn is known among the outdoor recreation community as the gateway to the Alpine Lakes Wilderness Area.

It's also celebrated for its historic importance as a coal-mining company town; many of its architecturally significant buildings remain, along with artifacts of its mining heritage. It was designated a National Historic District in 1978. Viewers of the popular television series *Northern Exposure* will recognize the town where the show was filmed.

South Cle Elum Rail Yard National Historic District

Railroad access to the Pacific Northwest expanded rapidly in the early 1900s when the Milwaukee Road train line built 1,300 miles of tracks in a mere four years. The Cle Elum Depot was the local hub of operations, and the Beanery (now the Depot Cafe) fed the train crews and locals. Walk the Interpretive Rail Yard Trail to see the locomotive roundhouse.

Kittitas County Historical Museum

Founded in the 1960s by descendants of early pioneers of Kittitas County, the Kittitas County Historical Museum now offers an extensive and wide-ranging collection of

Kittitas County Historical Museum's 15,000 artifacts help tell the story of this rural area.

The Snoqualmie Tribe considers Snoqualmoie Falls sacred but welcomes visitors to this iconic place.

15,000 objects that help tell the story of this rural area. Museum themes include geology, Native Americans, historic photographs, and household items.

Washington State Ski and Snowboard Museum

The WSSSM celebrates the history and prominent legacy of skiing and snowboarding in the Pacific Northwest. The museum is appropriately located at Snoqualmie Pass in the Cascade Mountains and features exhibits and artifacts of snow sports in the State of Washington.

Snoqualmie Falls

From time immemorial, the Snoqualmie Tribe has considered this place sacred—it's the birthplace of creation. Mists from the thundering 268-foot waterfall carry prayers to ancestors, and the falls provide the gifts of food, water, life, and healing. Today, the tribe warmly welcomes all visitors to this sacred place to experience its power. The falls are a short walk from the parking lot and are wheelchair accessible.

Hiram M. Chittenden Locks

The Lake Washington Ship Canal and associated Hiram H. Chittenden Locks were constructed by the US Army Corps of Engineers in the early 20th century to connect Lake Washington, Lake Union, and Salmon Bay to the tidal waters of Puget Sound, enhancing navigation for both commercial and recreational boaters. Chittenden was the Seattle District Engineer for the Corps of Engineers, but the site is known locally as Ballard Locks after the neighborhood to the north. The site includes a visitor center and a fish ladder where visitors can see migrating salmon.

The Lake Washington Ship Canal and associated Hiram H. Chittenden Locks connected Lake Washington, Lake Union, and Salmon Bay to the tidal waters of Puget Sound, enhancing navigation; stop by the Visitor Center and fish ladder to see migrating salmon.

Snoqualmie Point Park

This eight-acre park off Exit 27 of Interstate 90 offers what may be the grandest view of the Snoqualmie Valley, Mount Si, and the Cascade Mountain Range. Immediately adjacent to the park is the trailhead for Rattlesnake Mountain.

Thorp Grist Mill

This mill was constructed in the late 1800s and has been restored and maintained as a symbol of the history of settlement in Washington State. The mill produced flour and livestock feed, powered a nearby lumber mill, and housed a turbine that made the nearby city of Thorp the first community in central Washington with electricity. An interpretive center provides information about the mill, pioneering families, and local history.

For more information about Mountains to Sound Greenway and to help plan your visit, see the area's official website (mtsgreenway.org) and the website of the National Park Service (nps.gov /places/mountains-to-sound-greenway -national-heritage-area.htm).

Muscle Shoals National Heritage Area

State: Alabama

Description: This region of Alabama is known for its Native American inhabitants, its rich musical heritage and modern-day recording industry, and the Tennessee River that flows through it; the area offers outstanding opportunities for outdoor recreation.

Sample Attractions:

- Roots of American Music Trail
- Natchez Trace Parkway
- Trail of Tears National Historic Trail
- Wilson and Wheeler Dams

Local lore suggests that the Tennessee River has been called "the singing river," a reference to the pleasing sounds—the music, really—that the river and its tributaries make as they flow freely over rocks and rapids. And this legend might be seen as a precursor to the region's musical heritage. Muscle Shoals is one of the largest towns along the river and its name seems to have been derived from a shallow zone of the Tennessee River where mussels were traditionally gathered (though the spelling has obviously changed). Regardless, Muscle Shoals National Heritage Area (Muscle Shoals) was established in 2009 to celebrate this six-county area in northwest Alabama (Colbert, Franklin, Laughterdale, Lawrence, Limestone, and Morgan counties—all historically connected to the Muscle Shoals stretch of the river). Primary themes of this NHA are Native American heritage, music, and the Tennessee River. As with all NHAs, the management objectives are to protect the region's important natural and cultural resources and to build a sustainable tourism industry around these resources.

The area is administered by the University of Northern Alabama in cooperation with the National Park Service and other partners.

Paleo-Indian people migrated across a land bridge between Asia and North America some 20,000 years ago and found their way to the Tennessee River by following herds of large mammals; a Native American presence in the Muscle Shoals area has been traced back some 10,000 years. These people were hunters-gatherers, but later adopted a more sedentary, agricultural lifestyle, growing corn, beans and squash, while continuing to hunt and fish. When European explorers and settlers encountered these Indians, primarily the modern-day tribes known as the Creek, Cherokee, and Chickasaw, conflicts were frequent and often dangerous. The US Indian Removal Act of 1830 spelled doom for most of the regional tribes, 125,000 of whom (known as the "Five Civilized Tribes"—the Chickasaw, Choctaw, Seminole, Cherokee, and Creek) were forced to move to reservations in Oklahoma. The horrific journey of the Cherokee is known as the "Trail of Tears" in which many suffered and died.

Native American legends of the "singing" Tennessee River might be considered the beginning of what has now become the music tradition of Muscle Shoals. Many of the white settlers who migrated into northwest Alabama were of Scotch-Irish descent and brought their Celtic musical traditions and fiddles with them. African slaves brought to the area to help work the fields came with their musical traditions as well, including chants, field hollers, and spirituals. Later, the region contributed to development of the blues. These and other styles of music were mixed and blended (becoming a "musical melting pot") into a unique genre that became the heart of the contemporary music industry of the region. More than a dozen recording studies were established, including the Muscle Shoals Sound Studio and FAME Studio. Diverse stars such as Aretha Franklin, Rolling Stones, Cher, and Willie Nelson recorded their music here. More recent performers include Martina McBride, George Strait, Alicia Keys, and Kenny Chesney. Muscle Shoals was transformed into the "Hit Recording Capital of the World."

The Tennessee River is one of the primary forces that binds this region of Alabama. This is a long river—652 miles, running through four states, and one of the most significant river systems in the United States—and 80 miles are included in the NHA. The watershed is filled with limestone sinkholes, caves, and underground streams, and is exceptionally biodiverse. The river attracted Native Americans, earlier settlers, and contemporary people. A canal was constructed along the river in the 19th century for purposes of navigation (the Muscle Shoals stretch of the river was impassible most of the year), but more recent development has focused on a series of dams and reservoirs to provide electrical power to the region. The dams were built by the Army Corps of Engineers and the federal Tennessee Valley Authority in response to the chronic underdevelopment of the region, and the reservoirs have become magnets for outdoor recreation.

Attractions

Muscle Shoals is exceptionally diverse, featuring important historic and cultural resources and associated attractions. Here,

The Alabama Music Hall of Fame honors the musical accomplishments of Alabamians.

The Natchez Trace Parkway, a unit of the National Park System, is a recreational road and scenic drive through three states.

you'll find wonderful music, beautiful rivers and lakes, and great outdoor recreation opportunities.

Roots of American Music Trail

The Roots of American Music Trail takes visitors to where musical history was made. The trail travels through Muscle Shoals and includes museums, recording studios, live music venues, and festivals. Plan your trip along the trail using the following website: http://musictrail.una.edu

Alabama Music Hall of Fame

This 12,500-square-foot exhibition hall opened in 1990 and is designed to honor the musical accomplishments of Alabamians. The facility includes the spectrum of musical genres. Musicians inducted into the Hall of Fame are featured with a bronze star on the building's walk of fame.

Natchez Trace Parkway

The Natchez Trace Parkway, a unit of the National Park System, is a 444-mile recreational road and scenic drive through three states, a portion of which runs through Muscle Shoals. It roughly follows the "Old Natchez Trace," a historic travel corridor used by American Indians, European settlers, soldiers, and others. Today, it can be enjoyed as a scenic drive, but also offers opportunities for hiking, biking, horseback riding, and camping.

Trail of Tears National Historic Trail

As noted above, the Trail of Tears is the infamous forced relocation of Cherokees to "Indian Territory" (reservations in Oklahoma); it's now a unit of the National Park System. Waterloo Landing and Tuscumbia Landing are sites on the route where some Native Americans boarded steamboats that carried them along sections of the Tennessee River, and some were transferred to railroad cars. Little remains of these sites except some interpretive panels and an opportunity to remember this and other historic mistreatment of Native Americans.

Contemporary Cherokee people retrace the route of the infamous Trail of Tears.

Florence Indian Mound is an impressive 43-foot prehistoric Native American feature.

Florence Indian Mound and Museum

Visitors to this site will find an impressive 43-foot-high prehistoric Indian mound. A museum displays artifacts—spear points, fish hooks, necklaces carved from river-bottom shells, animal effigy pipes, pottery, and textiles—that have been collected from this region of Alabama.

Oakville Indian Mounds Museum and Education Center

Sited adjacent to the William B. Bankhead National Forest, this museum and education center focuses on human occupation of this region over thousands of years. The adjacent national forest is one of the premier sites for petroglyphs, prehistoric drawings, and rock carvings. The museum and education center have a park-like campus that encourages picnicking, hiking, and fishing.

Pond Spring

Pond Spring is the home of Joe Wheeler who was a Confederate lieutenant general, a US congressman, and a general in the Spanish-American War. The 50-acre site includes 12 historic buildings, gardens, and archeologic features.

Ivy Green

This is the birthplace of Helen Keller. Though blind and deaf, Keller learned to read, write, and speak in this home, taught by her companion, Anne Sullivan (Macy), and went on to be an international advocate for those with disabilities. The home is on the National Register of Historic Places and is also a National Historic Landmark.

Red Bay Museum

This museum includes artifacts of the town's history and an extensive collection of items donated by Tammy Wynette, the "First Lady of Country Music." Wynette called the Red Bay area her home.

Wilson and Wheeler Dams

These are two of the largest hydroelectric dams on the Tennessee River. Wilson Dam was completed in 1924 and Wheeler Dam in 1936. Both are on the National Register of Historic Places. The reservoirs behind these dams are popular recreation areas.

For more information about Muscle Shoals and to help plan your visit, see the area's official website (msnha.una.edu) and the website of the National Park Service (nps.gov/mush/index.htm).

National Aviation Heritage Area

State: Ohio

Description: Orville and Wilbur Wright's first flight in 1903 changed the world, and this NHA celebrates this story in the brothers' hometown of Dayton, Ohio, and surrounding area; here, visitors will find a center of American aircraft development and aeronautics that spans the "bicycle shop to the surface of the moon."

Sample Attractions:

- Dayton Aviation Heritage National Historical Park
- National Museum of the United States Air Force
- National Aviation Hall of Fame
- Wright "B" Flyer

"From bicycle shop to the surface of the moon" is the phrase that's often used to describe the National Aviation Heritage Area (National Aviation) centered in Dayton, Ohio, and extending into the southwestern part of the state. And this place lives up to its ambitious legacy and objectives! Most people probably remember from their American history class that the airplane was invented and flown—the first sustained and controlled heavier-than-air powered flight—in 1903 by Orville and Wilbur Wright. But many may not recall that the Wright brothers ran a bicycle shop in Dayton at the time. And many historians suggest that their invention has changed the world to a degree that few others have. Dayton was—and still is—a center of American aircraft development and aeronautics, its rich history spread across the Dayton and western Ohio landscape and in the culture.

The US Army took an early interest in the possibilities of aircraft and the Wright brothers won their 1907 bid for construction of airplanes; the Army awarded the $25,000 contact to the Wright brothers in 1908. The federal government purchased land in Dayton in 1917 and developed North Field (now known as McCook Field) for experimental engineering work. This work transformed the airplane from a fragile wood-and-fabric machine powered by a four-cylinder radial engine into a low-wing, streamlined, all-metal aircraft with a supercharged engine. After World War I, Wright Field was developed in Dayton, and shortly after the Army established Patterson Field. In 1948, these two facilities were combined into today's powerhouse Wright-Patterson Air Force Base. The local paper declared Dayton "Air City." Over the ensuing years, several aeronautical research and development companies, along with many military scientists, have called Dayton and the adjacent Miami Valley home. Consequently, the Dayton region is known in the aircraft and aeronautical community as the global center of aviation heritage.

National Aviation was established in 2004 to celebrate the area's remarkable aviation and aerospace technology and heritage. Its objectives are to preserve and promote the rich aviation heritage of the area and to educate and inspire the public about this through a program of aviation-based heritage tourism. The NHA encompasses an eight-county area in southwest Ohio and includes Dayton Aviation Heritage National Historical Park (a unit of the National Park System), along with hundreds of sites listed on the National

Register of Historic Places and several sites that are National Historic Landmarks. The NHA is managed by the National Aviation Heritage Alliance, a non-profit corporation designated by Congress. The vision of the alliance is to make the Dayton region the widely recognized global center of aviation heritage and premier destination for aviation heritage tourism, thereby sustaining the legacy of the Wright brothers.

Attractions

National Aviation features a stunning array of aviation-related attractions. But be prepared to choose carefully because it would take weeks to see and experience them all. The official National Aviation website (see below) includes several sample itineraries and an innovative "create your own" itinerary feature. All visitors will learn how the Wright brothers unlocked the millennia-old secret of human flight and appreciate how our nation's aviation heritage extended into space flight over the subsequent decades.

Dayton Aviation Heritage National Historical Park

This unit of the National Park System in Dayton is an integral part of National Aviation and features several attractions, including the Wright Cycle Company Complex (with Wright Cycle Company Building), Huffman Prairie Flying Field (where the Wright brothers perfected their airplanes in 1904 and 1905), the Wright Brothers National Museum at Carillon Historical Park, Hawthorne Hill (the 1914-1948 residence of Orville Wright), the Wright Brothers Museum, the 1905 Wright Flyer III, a large Aviation Trail Parachute Museum,

and Paul Laurence Dunbar State Memorial (Dunbar was a noted African American writer and poet who was a contemporary and neighbor of the Wright brothers).

Carillon Historical Park

A beautiful 65-acre campus, this area tells the story of the Dayton region's innovation and industrialization, including the Wright Brothers National Museum, the 1905 Wright Flyer III, Hawthorne Hill, and a large carillon.

Huffman Prairie Flying Field and Interpretive Center

This is the place where the Wright brothers developed and tested the world's first practical airplane, and includes a memorial built to honor the brothers. It's located on the grounds of Wright-Patterson Air Force Base and is open to the public.

Air Camp

Air Camp offers immersive experiences in aviation and aeronautics for students and teachers; these camps range from a day to a week.

Vectren Dayton Air Show Summer Event

This is an annual air show at Dayton International Airport and is one of America's premier air shows.

National Aviation Hall of Fame

This facility honors the iconic men and women of aviation and space travel; an enshrinement ceremony is held each year. There are also changing exhibits and interactive displays such as hands-on experience in landing an aircraft on a Navy aircraft carrier,

A replica Wright Flyer decorates the Dayton-Wright Brothers Airport.

The massive National Museum of the United States Air Force is the oldest and largest aviation museum in the country.

controlling the movement of a helicopter, docking in space with the Hubble Space Telescope, and taking the controls of a historic aircraft on one of four flight simulators.

Champaign Aviation Museum
The museum offers close-up inspection of a range of historic aircraft, many of which have been or are being restored to fly again.

Armstrong Air and Space Museum
In Wapakoneta, Ohio, this museum celebrates the accomplishments of native son, Neil Armstrong, the first person to walk on the moon, as well as other astronauts who called Ohio home.

Historic WACO Field
This site celebrates the Golden Age of Aviation with numerous historic aircraft and a 2,400-foot grass airstrip. Visitors can experience an open cockpit flight in one of two aircraft.

National Museum of the United States Air Force
This vast site is the largest and oldest military aviation museum, illustrating the Air Force and military aviation progress. The collection

includes hundreds of aircraft and aerospace vehicles and thousands of historic aviation artifacts. There is also a six-story 3D digital theater, flight simulators, and visitors can "walk in space" thanks to the ongoing support of the Air Force Museum Foundation.

Wright Cycle Company
Several of the original Wright Brothers Bicycle Shops were lost to urban development, but this is the fourth location of their bicycle shop. Fittingly, Dayton has one of the largest network of paved bicycle trails in the nation—340 miles—so consider honoring

Wright Cycle Company is one of several locations of the Wright Brothers bicycle heritage.

the Wrights by biking to a number of the National Aviation sites.

Hawthorne Hill

This is Orville Wright's home from 1914 to 1948 and is open to the public for guided tours by visiting Carillon Historical Park. The mansion welcomed dignitaries such as Charles Lindberg, Henry Ford, and Thomas Edison. Orville lived here with his father and sister.

Woodland Cemetery and Arboretum

This site is a large "garden cemetery" founded in 1841; it includes the gravesites of Wilbur and Orville Wright and Paul Laurence Dunbar.

Wright State University Special Collections and Archives

The Wright Brothers Collection is housed at Wright State University and includes more than 6,000 items, including the Wrights' own personal and technical library and family papers.

Wright "B" Flyer

A fleet of look-alike Wright "B" Flyers, the Wright brothers' first production airplane, is housed at Dayton-Wright Brothers Airport in Miamisburg, Ohio, and offers visitors a thrilling ride.

Wright Company Factory

This facility was the first in the nation built to manufacture airplanes. It produced approximately 120 planes in 13 models. There are plans to open the facility to the public in the future.

Triumph of Flight

This dramatic monument and associated park and facsimile of the Wright Flyer III will honor the story of flight, from ancient people gazing at the stars to Neil Armstrong's footprint on the moon. The area is under construction.

For more information about National Aviation and to help plan your visit, see the area's official website (visitnaha .com) and the website of the National Park Service (nps.gov/avia/index.htm).

National Coal Heritage Area

State: West Virginia

Description: The coal mines of West Virginia helped power America's Industrial Revolution, but also transformed the state's traditional rural character, raised concerns over public safety, and precipitated sometimes violent conflicts between labor and industry; today, the mountains are wild again, offering world-class opportunities for outdoor recreation.

Sample Attractions:

- Coal Heritage Trail
- Exhibition Coal Mine
- West Virginia Mine Wars Museum
- New River Gorge National Park and Preserve

The Appalachian Mountains of southern West Virginia have produced some of the richest and most valuable bituminous coal the world has known, literally and figuratively fueling America's Industrial Revolution, starting in the second half of the 19th century and continuing to the present day.

Coal mining was a dangerous job, and there were sometimes violent clashes between labor and industry.

But the story of America's coal industry starts substantially earlier when English explorer John Peter Salley boated along the Coal River in Boone County and reported finding "a great plenty of coals." Thomas Jefferson also wrote about the coal in western Virginia in his *Notes on the State of Virginia* (West Virginia was established as a separate state in 1863.) However, the region's first industry was salt, used to preserve meat; salt brine was abundant along the Kanawha River and boiled to produce crystals. Wood fires fueled the furnaces for a number of years, but as the supply of wood dwindled, coal was used as a substitute and this led to many small coal mines in the area. Narrow-gauge railroads and small flatboats along rivers were used to transport the coal and by 1850, an estimated 250,000 tons of coal were produced annually.

However, the national and international coal movement didn't start to blossom until the mid-1800s when households and industry demanded coal oil for lamps; coal oil—oil distilled from coal—emitted little smoke or odor and this made it vastly superior to oil derived from animals. But the larger coal industry had to wait for development of the railroads to ship very large quantities of coal efficiently, and that began right after the Civil

War. However, attempts to build track in the Appalachian Mountains and their steep river valleys was especially challenging. The first of the three railroad companies to succeed in this endeavor was the Chesapeake and Ohio (C & O) Railroad, so named because it connected the East Coast (Chesapeake Bay) and the Midwest (Ohio River). Perhaps the greatest challenge in constructing the track was the "Great Bend," a long tunnel at Talcott; new-fangled steam-powered machinery was used and historians suggest this may have been the origin of the "John Henry" folk song that pitted the folk hero against a steam shovel in an epic digging contest. Shortly after, the Norfolk & Western (N & W) line was completed; the population of the little town of Bluefield along the track grew from 600 to more than 11,000 over the next twenty years, and Bramwell became the center of local banking, earning it the name "home of the millionaires." The Virginian was the last of the three railroads to be completed, and by the early 1900s, rail lines extended into all the West Virginia mines, connecting them to the Atlantic Ocean and the Great Lakes.

West Virginia's coal is traditionally considered the world's finest, in terms of both quality and quantity. The state led the nation in production from 1927 to 1973, and this coal heated homes and powered the boilers of the nation's trains, factories, fleets, and power plants. Coke is a processed fuel derived from coal and used extensively in the country's iron and steel industries. Coal provided jobs and homes for many people, some of them fleeing persecution, and made fortunes for industrialists. For many decades and continuing into the present day, coal has powered American industry, making the nation an industrial powerhouse and military force. This was "King Coal."

West Virginia's coal heritage had foundational impacts on the region's natural resources and economy, but its effects were profoundly social as well. The rural, agrarian character of the state was transformed by rapid population growth, construction of new "company" towns, introduction of great cultural diversity, concerns over public safety, and sometimes violent conflicts between labor and industry. West Virginia's population exploded from less than 100,000 in 1880 to nearly 450,000 in 1920, due almost entirely to the coal industry. Because of the rural character of West Virginia, new towns were constructed for the quickly growing number of workers and their families, but stores built by the company were often expensive and were considered by some to be exploitive, and there were little or no opportunities for spouses to work. Many freed slaves and European immigrants flocked to the state to work the mines and were sometimes discriminated against. Moreover, there was tension among these cultures (though it was often assuaged by the popular baseball teams and leagues that were an important activity for men). Coal mining on an industrial scale turned out to be dangerous; mines collapsed, coal dust created in the mines was prone to explosions, and workers exposed to coal dust developed lung disease. In 1925, a shocking 16 percent of all coal miners died on the job. And the inherent tension between miners and the coal companies was persistent and occasionally erupted into violence. The first labor strike occurred in 1880 and the formidable United Mine Workers of America

was formed in 1890. On several occasions over the next forty years, the West Virginia National Guard and US Army troops were needed to maintain order.

Things changed dramatically for the West Virginia coal industry beginning in the 1950s. Many economically inefficient mines closed and mechanization eliminated many mining jobs; large "loading machines" replaced many workers, but they also generated more coal dust, endangering the health of remaining workers. Many small mining towns were deserted. The railroads declined and consolidated in response to greater reliance on trucks to haul coal. Much coal extraction has shifted to surface mining using very large mechanized equipment, though this has dire environmental consequences. Coal is still an important industry in West Virginia, but it's no longer the nation's largest producer, and the King Coal period has diminished. Through efforts such as National Coal Heritage Area (National Coal), the state is telling its coal-driven history to its residents and visitors and building a strong heritage-based tourism industry around it. National Coal was established in 1996 and is managed by the National Coal Heritage Area Authority, a state agency overseen by an independent board. The NHA includes 13 counties in southern West Virginia that comprise 5,300 square miles.

Attractions

This large NHA includes a variety of natural and historical attractions. The Appalachian Mountain landscape invites scenic drives, wonderful hiking, great fishing, and exciting whitewater boating, all a part of West Virginia's "wild and wonderful" character.

Coal Heritage Trail is a grand 187-mile driving tour through much of West Virginia's coal country.

Historic towns, museums, and related sites tell the nationally important story of West Virginia's King Coal period. Consider starting your visit at the National Park Service's lovely and informative Canyon Rim Visitor Center in New River Gorge National Park and Preserve and/or the Thurmond Depot Visitor Center in the old C & O Railroad Station.

Coal Heritage Trail

This is a 187-mile grand driving tour through much of West Virginia's coal country. The drive takes visitors through coal towns, historic districts, and by company stores, railroad yards, and other features of West Virginia's coal heritage.

Bramwell

As noted earlier, Bramwell prospered as a banking and financial center of the early coal industry and was nicknamed "home of the millionaires." Pick up a brochure at the Bramwell Train Depot Visitor Center and follow its walking tour through the historic district.

Paint Creek Scenic Trail

This driving route takes visitors along beautiful Paint Creek where early labor strikes eventually led to the infamous Battle of Blair Mountain; miners fought (literally) for better living and working conditions.

The town of Bramwell prospered as a banking and financial center of the early coal industry and was nicknamed "home of the millionaires."

Paradoxically, the New River is one of the oldest rivers on the North American Continent.

Exhibition Coal Mine

The Exhibition Coal Mine in Beckley offers visitors a rare opportunity to ride a coal car through the dark passages of a vintage coal mine. The tours are conducted by veteran miners who recount stories of mining life. The town also includes several restored buildings associated with the region's coal heritage.

Beckley's Exhibition Coal Mine offers visitors a rare opportunity to ride a coal car through the dark passages of a vintage coal mine.

West Virginia Mine Wars Museum

The inherent tension between workers and coal companies occasionally boiled over into conflict and even bloodshed. This interesting museum tells the story, including the Paint Creek-Cabin strike of 1912-13, the 1920 Matewan Massacre, and the Battle of Blair Mountain.

New River Gorge National Park and Preserve

This is one of the country's newest national parks and preserves a rugged, whitewater river and its canyon. Paradoxically, the New River is one of the oldest rivers on the North American continent. The park is over 70,000 acres and offers wonderful scenery and great outdoor recreation opportunities.

Bluestone National Scenic River

Another unit of the National Park System, this area includes a 10.5-mile stretch of the river and much of the ancient and rugged gorge through which it flows. The area is ecologically diverse and offers great hiking.

Gauley River National Recreation Area

This unit of the National Park System protects 25 miles of the free-flowing and wild Gauley River. The Gauley is one of the most adventurous white-water boating experiences in the East.

For more information about National Coal and to help plan your visit, see the area's official website (coalheritage .org) and the website of the National Park Service (nps.gov/places/coal -national-heritage-area.htm).

Niagara Falls National Heritage Area

State: New York

Description: Niagara Falls is an eye-opening natural phenomenon and an international tourist destination; this NHA also helps celebrate the first state park in the nation, the American Conservation Movement, and the Underground Railroad.

Sample Attractions:
- Niagara Falls State Park (Niagara Reservation)
- Maid of the Mist
- Niagara Falls Underground Railroad Heritage Center
- Old Fort Niagara

Niagara Falls has a long-standing and well-deserved reputation as an international tourist attraction. The falls, along with the Niagara River, Niagara Gorge, and the Great Lakes, make up a powerhouse of a natural phenomenon. The falls are actually three water falls—the American Falls, Horseshoe Falls, and Bridal Veil Falls—that cluster along the route of the Niagara River that connects the United States with Canada; the three falls together are called "Niagara Falls." The vertical drop of the falls is 165 feet, which is impressive but not especially high compared to other waterfalls around the world. What's astonishing is the amount of water that flows over Niagara Falls—750,000 gallons per second during peak flow season! The Niagara River connects two of the Great Lakes— Lake Erie and Lake Ontario, and drains four of the Great Lakes that collectively contain 20 percent of the world's fresh water.

At the end of the last ice age about 12,000 years ago, the Niagara River flowed over a cliff known as the Niagara Escarpment. The water gradually eroded the underlying rock and the falls migrated south, creating the present-day nearly seven-mile Niagara Gorge. The Niagara River flows north for about 35 miles, flowing out of Lake Erie and into Lake Ontario and provided access into the interior of North America for Native Americans and European explorers; the river was a vital part of an extensive trade route that brought fur pelts from America's interior to Europe via the Great Lakes and St. Lawrence River.

Human presence in the region began over a thousand years ago with Native Americans; tribes included the Seneca and Tuscarora. It's uncertain who was the first European explorer to see the falls, but Native Americans told French explorer Samuel de Champlain about the falls as early as 1604. During the 19th century, Niagara Falls became a popular tourist destination. Visitors traveled by train and the Erie Canal, and the area became a honeymoon destination for many newlyweds. Popularity

American Falls is one of three major waterfalls at Niagara Falls National Heritage Area.

increased substantially in the first half of the 20th century with many travelers arriving by automobile.

The popularity of tourism at Niagara Falls is a cautionary tale about the potential for overdevelopment and seamy commercialism. In the late 19th and early 20th centuries, entrepreneurs lined both sides of the river. Water diversions from the river to power mills and hydroelectric power facilities were also developed and these, too, threatened the area's natural beauty. This unfortunate trend also gave rise to sensationalist daredevils who rode over the falls in barrels and crossed over the gorge on tightropes. However, America's great landscape architect, Frederick Law Olmsted, and similarly-minded others initiated the Free Niagara movement to control such inappropriate development and use. In 1885, the State of New York established the Niagara Reservation, the first state park in the nation, and Canada followed suit with

the Queen Victoria Park on its side of the river. Both countries began clearing away inappropriate tourist facilities and requiring water-powered factories to be located downstream from the falls. This new, more environmentally sensitive approach to tourism development helped fuel the American Conservation Movement of the late 19th and early 20th centuries.

The strategic location of the Niagara Falls region, at the junction of a major travel route between the United States and Canada, has meant the area has played an important role in several military conflicts, including the French and Indian War, American Revolution, and War of 1812. Another significant period of history in the region is its role in the Underground Railroad. Before and during the Civil War, many enslaved individuals escaped via a network of people and places that led through the Niagara area and into Canada and freedom. Niagara Falls was one of the most important transit points for the Underground Railroad along the US-Canadian border.

To celebrate the importance of Niagara Falls and its eventful history, Congress established Niagara Falls National Heritage Area (Niagara Falls) in 2008. The NHA stretches out along an approximately 13-mile section of the Niagara River "from the falls to the fort" as locals describe it, the fort referring to what is now called "Old Fort Niagara" (see below). The NHA is managed by a nonprofit organization with a board of directors representing stakeholders, including state and local towns and representatives of the Seneca and Tuscarora nations.

Attractions

This diverse NHA has an equally diverse array of visitor attractions; of course, the world-famous Niagara Falls heads the list—see it from the many observation points and consider getting an up-close and personal view from the sightseeing boat, Maid of the Mist. The area has historic sites, museums, parks, and lots of opportunities for outdoor recreation. Niagara Falls NHA established and operates the free Discover Niagara Shuttle bus system that serves the area and the Niagara Falls website has a useful Discover Niagara App (see below).

Niagara Falls State Park (Niagara Reservation)

The Niagara Reservation of the late 19th century (see above) has been transformed into Niagara Falls State Park, the oldest state park in the nation. Of course, the park's signature attraction is the namesake Niagara Falls and the park features the very best views. The park retains the original philosophy of famed landscape architect Frederick Law Olmsted, emphasizing the area's native vegetation and miles of walking paths through wooded areas and along the banks of the Niagara River. The park is a National Historic Landmark.

Niagara Falls Underground Railroad Heritage Center

This signature museum tells the story of the freedom seekers and abolitionists in Niagara Falls and encourages patrons to recognize the injustices of modern society that stem from slavery. The museum's permanent exhibit, "One More River to Cross," features Niagara's vital role as the last stop on the Underground Railroad before reaching Canada and freedom; the exhibit was given the Award of Excellence by the American Association for State and Local History. The museum also tells the story of "the waiters," a group of African American waiters at the up-scale Cataract House, who helped freedom seekers on the Underground Railroad escape into Canada.

Old Fort Niagara

This 18th-century fort at the mouth of the Niagara River features the original buildings where Native American, French, British, and American soldiers lived, worked, and fought from the 18th to the 20th centuries. The fort tells the story of how great empires struggled for control over North America; the fort was developed by the French (1726), captured by the British (1759), surrendered to the Americans after the Revolutionary War, and recaptured by the British (1813). The fort offers beautiful views, educational exhibits, and living history programs.

Old Fort Niagara at the mouth of the Niagara River offers living history programs.

Maid of the Mist

For more than 150 years, the Maid of the Mist tour boat has been taking visitors to the base of Horseshoe Falls (one of the three falls that make up Niagara Falls) to "explore the roar." This is a favorite attraction of

The Maid of the Mist tour boat takes visitors to the base of Horseshoe Falls, where they can "explore the roar."

Niagara Falls State Park and the tour begins at the Observation Tower. Visitors receive a souvenir rain poncho to protect them from the heavy mist.

Edward Dean Adams Power Plant/ Adams Plant Transformer House

The Adams Plant Transformer House was constructed in 1895 and is the only remaining structure that was part of the historic Edward Dean Adams Power Plant. The plant was the first large-scale alternating current electric generating plant in the world.

Discover Niagara Shuttle

This visitor-friendly shuttle bus service allows visitors to park their cars and experience the NHA's iconic landscape and thriving culture and communities along the Niagara River "from falls to fort." The shuttle bus serves a 14-mile route and 17 destinations with the convenience of a hop-on, hop-off program.

Outdoor Recreation

The Niagara Falls region offers lots of opportunities for outdoor recreation. Niagara Gorge offers hiking with great views down into the gorge and the river's impressive rapids. Biking is available at LaSalle Waterfront Park, Devil's Hole State Park, and Whirlpool State Park. And there are many fishing access areas along the lower Niagara River and Lake Ontario.

For more information about Niagara Falls and to help plan your visit, see the area's official website (discoverniagara .org) and the website of the National Park Service (nps.gov/places/niagara -falls-national-heritage-area.htm).

Niagara Gorge, upstream of the falls, offers a network of scenic hiking trails.

Northern Plains National Heritage Area

State: North Dakota

Description: This nationally important landscape is protected and interpreted by a large NHA that includes 80 miles of the Missouri River and celebrates the Native American presence, early American and immigrant settlers, arrival of railroad service, the rich farming and ranching history, the Lewis and Clark Expedition, the westward expansion of the nation, and today's many outdoor recreation opportunities.

Sample Attractions:

- Knife River Indian Village National Historic Site
- Lewis & Clark National Historic Trail
- North Dakota Heritage Center & State Museum
- Lake Sakakawea State Park

Northern Plains National Heritage Area (Northern Plains) was established by Congress in 2009 to celebrate the nationally important natural and cultural history associated with the Missouri River in central North Dakota. This NHA is a big landscape of 800 square miles that runs along 80 miles of the river and through five counties. The

Northern Plains Heritage Foundation is the coordinating body that partners with a number of public, private, and non-profit organizations. Modest funding from the National Park Service helps grassroots initiatives that protect local heritage and interpret it to residents and visitors. Important Northern Plains-associated stories include the historic Native American presence (and their membership in the community of today), the early fur trade, American settlers, the arrival of railroad service to the area and the immigrant settlers it brought, the building of the second transcontinental railroad, the area's rich farming and ranching heritage, and the remarkable Lewis and Clark expedition and the westward expansion of the nation. Other facets of Northern Plains include early anthropologists, naturalists, and painters such as George Catlin and Karl Bodmer, the military history associated with conflicts between settlers and Native Americans, and a striking landscape of grasslands, agricultural lands, and river bottoms filled with cottonwood trees. Today, this landscape offers a host of outdoor recreation opportunities.

The original inhabitants of the region traversed the landscape thousands of years ago, and later the Mandan, Hidatsa, and Arikara people settled in the area, using the fertile bottomlands of the Missouri River for agricultural purposes. The *Oceti Sakowin* (known as "The Great Sioux Nation" in the 19th century) also have strong ties to the region. The Lewis and Clark Expedition spent the winter of 1803-1804 here with help from the Mandan and Hidatsa people. This is where Lewis and Clark famously met Sakakawea (or *Sacagawea*), a young Native American woman who accompanied the expedition all the way to the Pacific Ocean and helped the party make contacts with other Native American tribes. Indigenous communities formed relationships with early European fur traders. George Catlin and Karl Bodmer were among the European scientists and artists who spent time in the area, studying and painting the Mandan people and their landscape, making the Mandan among the most fully documented indigenous groups in North America. Catlin went on to famously call for a "nation's park" to protect the symbiotic relationship between these native people and their environment.

As American and European settlers flowed onto the Northern Plains landscape, conflict between settlers and native people increased and ultimately precipitated the US Dakota Wars of the early 1860s. In 1883, the Northern Pacific Railroad completed construction of a permanent bridge over the Upper Missouri River at Bismarck (now called the Bismarck-Mandan Rail Bridge), an important element of the second transcontinental railroad. However, the federal government gave large areas of land to the Northern Pacific as an incentive to build this intercontinental track, and much of this land had previously been promised to Native American tribes through a series of treaties. The bridge at Bismarck is now known as an International Site of Conscience symbolizing the profound impacts of American expansion on Native Americans. Northern Plains encourages residents and visitors to the area to consider the multiple meanings of the bridge and to "foster understanding for the betterment of humanity."

Attractions

Northern Plains offers many attractions to both residents and visitors. State parks, museums, and historic sites showcase the important role of the Northern Plains and the Upper Missouri River in American history and westward expansion. Recreation areas provide lots of opportunities to hike, camp, and fish. The sometimes stark but dramatic landscape is a common denominator throughout the NHA.

Heritage River Landing

This facility in Bismarck is a good place to begin your visit, as it offers information about attractions throughout the NHA. An expansive outdoor patio overlooks the Missouri River and includes food and beverage service.

Knife River Indian Village National Historic Site

This unit of the National Park System allows visitors insights into the lives of Northern Plains Indians along the Upper Missouri River. Extended families of Hidatsa people lived in distinctive domed earthen lodges (*awadis*) traditionally built, owned, and maintained by women. Earth lodge people hunted bison and other game, but were also

Knife River Indian Village National Historic Site is a unit of the National Park System; extended families of Hidatsa people lived here in distinctive domed earthen lodges.

farmers living in villages along the Missouri River and its tributaries. The site was a major Native American trade center for hundreds of years prior to becoming an important marketplace for fur traders after 1750.

Lewis & Clark National Historic Trail

Lewis & Clark National Historic Trail is a unit of the National Park System that traces the outbound and inbound routes of the Voyage of Discovery for 4,900 miles and runs through 16 states and many tribal lands. Northern Plains partners with the Lewis & Clark Interpretive Center in Washburn, North Dakota. This area was once the center of culture and commerce on the Northern Plains. The Mandan and Hidatsa people lived in this area and mingled with explorers and traders and supported the Lewis & Clark Expedition. Nearby stands a full-size replica of Fort Mandan which illustrates what life was like in the two years of the Corps of Discovery.

North Country National Scenic Trail

The North Country National Scenic Trail is a unit of the National Park System; at approximately 4,600 miles, it's the longest of the national trails. The trail connects North Dakota and New Hampshire, traversing forests and farmlands, remote terrain and nearby communities. The western terminus of the trail is in Northern Plains at Lake Sakakawea State Park (see below). Consider a short hike along this nationally significant trail in Northern Plains.

Fort Stevenson State Park

Named after a nearby fort that served as a supply depot for other military posts in the Dakota Territory in the late 1860s, this state park is located on the north shore of Lake Sakakawea (see below). The original Fort Stevenson was flooded by the Lake Sakakawea reservoir. The park includes miles of trails, breathtaking views, and is known as the "Walleye Capital of North Dakota."

Lake Sakakawea State Park

This state park is located on the south shore of Lake Sakakawea, one of the largest reservoirs in the nation. The lake offers miles of shoreline and stunning views. Recreation activities include swimming, hiking, camping, boating, and fishing.

Double Ditch Indian Village State Historic Site

This site was once a large earth lodge village inhabited by Mandan Indians for nearly 300 years, but only circular depressions in the ground remain. Double Ditch was one of several villages simultaneously occupied near the mouth of the Heart River. It's estimated that 10,000 or more Mandans lived in this area and traded with early European-American explorers. The Mandans were supported by extensive farming and hunting, including bison.

North Dakota Heritage Center & State Museum

This large museum showcases and interprets North Dakota's rich history and heritage and has been called "the people's place." The museum includes four galleries, thousands of artifacts and specimens, high-tech displays, and interactive exhibits.

Constructed in 1864, Fort Rice was the first of a chain of forts that guarded transportation routes through the northern plains.

Fort Rice State Historic Site

Fort Rice was constructed in 1864 and was the first of a chain of forts that guarded transportation routes through the northern plains. Hostilities with the Oceti Sakowin developed when Euro-American settlers began to occupy this region of the Northern Plains. Life was hard in this and other forts, isolated by distance and a seasonally ice-bound transportation system. Little is left of the fort other than depressions in the ground and foundation lines.

Fort Abraham Lincoln State Park

This is North Dakota's oldest state park, established in 1907. The park includes a diverse and historic landscape along the Missouri and Heart Rivers. Visitors can tour reconstructed military buildings and visit the ancient village site and earth lodge homes of early Mandan people. Recreation opportunities include hiking, biking, horseback riding, and fishing.

Cross Ranch State Park

This state park is located along some of the last free-flowing and undeveloped stretches of the Missouri River. The views suggest the

Cross Ranch State Park is located along some of the last free-flowing and undeveloped stretches of the Missouri River.

dramatic landscape as it appeared to Native Americans who occupied this land centuries ago and to members of the Lewis & Clark Expedition as it made its way along the river. Recreation activities include hiking, camping, and fishing. The trail system accesses a 5,000-acre nature preserve with mixed grass prairie, river-bottom forests, and bison.

Camp Hancock State Historic Site

This site preserves part of the military installation established in 1872 to protect workers who were laying tracks for the Northern

Pacific Railroad. A log headquarters building still stands on the site. An interpretive museum houses local artifacts and offers information on local history.

For more information about Northern Plains and to help plan your visit, see the area's official website (northern plainsheritage.org) and the website of the National Park Service (nps.gov /places/northern-plains-national -heritage-area.htm).

Northern Rio Grande National Heritage Area

State: New Mexico

Description: This NHA of 10,000 square miles in north-central New Mexico celebrates its Native American history, the grand landscape of the Rio Grande del Norte, tall mountains, broad mesas, high desert, and its rich cultural heritage.

Sample Attractions:
- Taos Pueblo
- Palace of the Governors
- Bandelier National Monument
- Scenic Byways

Ancient Native Americans called the mountains and high deserts of northern New Mexico their home for thousands of years. And this is still home for their descendants, including Jicarilla Apache and eight northern Pueblo settlements. These native people were later joined by the descendants of Spanish colonists who settled in the area beginning in 1598. And American settlers joined this mix of cultures in the mid-19th century. This blending of cultures has given

the region a distinctive and attractive human presence that defines the region and that is celebrated in its history and contemporary culture, including its principal towns of Santa Fe, Taos, and Espanola. The natural landscape is also a vital component of this culture. The region takes its name from the historic river—the Rio Grande del Norte—that flows through it, but other landscape elements—mountains (reaching more than 13,000 feet), mesas, and high desert terrain—also help define the area. This varied terrain supports a wide range of vegetation: sagebrush, yucca, and piñon/juniper forests dominate on the plains; scrub oak and ponderosa pine grow at higher elevations, mixed conifers, especially Douglas fir and blue spruce grow on higher mountain slopes; and smaller shrubs and wildflowers occupy the highest elevations. This varied terrain supports a range of wildlife, including black bears, mountain lions, mule deer, mountain sheep, elk, coyotes, and prairie dogs. Occasional bison are seen on Pueblo lands. Two national forests (Santa Fe National Forest and Carson National Forest), two national monuments (Bandelier National Monument, a unit of the National Park System, and Rio Grande del Norte National Monument, nearly a million acres of land managed by the federal Bureau of Land Management), several state parks, and a host of other public lands and preserves offer a substantial degree of protection for the historic and natural resources of this region.

Northern Rio Grande National Heritage Area (Northern Rio Grande) was established in 2006 to assist local communities and residents in preserving their unique historical, cultural, and natural resources and to support a program of sustainable tourism based on the area's resources. This is a big landscape and the NHA covers more than 10,000 square miles of north-central New Mexico, from Interstate 40 in central New Mexico to the northern border with Colorado. The area is managed by the Northern Rio Grande National Heritage Area, Inc., a non-profit organization that works with the National Park Service, state and local communities, tribal groups, and others.

Taos Pueblo is a Native American settlement that is one of several such settlements established in the 13th and 14th centuries in the valleys of the Rio Grande River and its tributaries.

Attractions

Given the size of Northern Rio Grande and the richness of its natural and cultural resources, there's an abundance of visitor attractions and many ways to see and appreciate them. Here are some of the more outstanding attractions.

Palace of the Governors

Originally constructed in 1610 to house the first Spanish royal governor of New Mexico, the Palace of the Goverhors reflects the complex heritage of the American Southwest, and is the oldest public building constructed by European settlers in the continental United States. The architecture of the building has changed many times over its more than 400-year history. Located on the historic square of downtown Santa Fe, the building is a National Historic Landmark and houses the New Mexico History Museum.

Taos Pueblo

The Taos Pueblo is a Native American settlement that is one of several such settlements established in the late 13th and early 14th centuries in the valleys of the Rio Grande River and its tributaries. Taos Pueblo has

been continuously occupied and maintained since this time and has retained most of its traditional forms and functions. It's the largest of the pueblos and its archecture is distinctive, including two large community houses that rise to five stories. The pueblo is near Taos, and holds the status of a limited sovereign nation with the United States; it's also a World Heritage Site.

Pecos National Historical Park

A unit of the National Park System, Pecos National Historical Park lies in the piñon, juniper, and ponderosa pine forests of the Sangre de Cristo Mountains, not far from Santa Fe. Here, the remains of Indian pueblos are tangible evidence of the ancient people who once occupied this region. This park interprets the rich natural and cultural history of the Pecos Valley.

Puye Cliff Dwellings National Historical Landmark

Home to an estimated 1,500 Pueblo Indians who lived here from the 900s to 1580, this National Historical Landmark preserves

Rio Grande del Norte National Monument is a large area of high plains dotted by volcanic cones and steep canyons.

extensive cave and cliff dwellings. The inhabitants were the ancestors of the present-day Santa Clara Pueblo people who moved into the Rio Grande River Valley, just ten miles east of Puye Cliff Dwellings.

Mesa Prieta Petroglyphs

The volcanic and erosional history of the 36-square-mile Mesa Prieta ("dark mesa") created ideal conditions for petroglyphs: light brown boulders covered in a dark patina of "desert varnish." Shallow pecking on the desert varnish uncovers the lighter-colored rock underneath, creating images, or petroglyphs. Over 100,000 images are estimated to exist in the area representing three time periods: Archaic, Pueblo IV, and Historic. Other archeological features are found here as well, such as shrines, water control systems, check dams, ceramics, and ancient and historic trails. This suggests intense human occupation over the past several thousand years.

Rio Grande del Norte National Monument

This is a large area of high plains dotted by volcanic cones and steep canyons. It has attracted human activity since prehistoric times as evidenced by petroglyphs and prehistoric dwelling sites, as well as abandoned homesteading sites from the 1930s. It's an important area for wintering animals and offers a wide range of outdoor recreation. The area is administered by the federal Bureau of Land Management.

Bandelier National Monument

This unit of the National Park System protects over 33,000 acres of this beautiful canyon and mesa landscape and the vivid evidence of human occupation going back over 11,000 years. Petroglyphs, dwellings carved into soft rock cliffs, and standing masonry walls testify to this early culture that grew corn, beans, and squash and ate meat from deer, rabbits, and squirels. Occupants

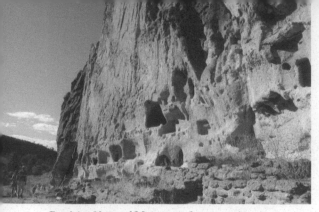
Bandelier National Monument features prehistoric dwellings carved into the area's soft rock.

eventually migrated to the present-day pueblos along the Rio Grande River.

Scenic Byways

Northern Rio Grande includes seven national and state scenic byways, a clear marker of the area's beauty and history. Enchanted Circle Scenic Byway is an 83-mile circle route that begins and ends in Taos and features stunning scenery that has been the backdrop for iconic western movies such as *Butch Cassidy and the Sundance Kid* and *Easy Rider*. The Turquoise Trail Scenic Byway is an approximately 50-mile drive that links Albuquerque and Santa Fe and features Sandia Crest and historic mining towns that now offer an array of arts and crafts, museums, and theaters. Puye Scenic Byway is only seven miles, but it travels through four of the state's seven life zones and delivers visitors to magical Puye Cliff Dwellings National Historical Landmark (described above). Santa Fe National Forest Scenic Byway starts at the Palace of the Governors in Santa Fe and loops 15 miles through evergreen and aspen forests to Santa Fe Ski Basin. Wild Rivers Backcountry Scenic Byway is a 13-mile loop road accessing the Rio Grande del Norte National Monument (described above). The High Road to Taos Scenic Byway takes visitors on a 105-mile adventure through an authentic remnant of Old Spain, traveling through Chimayo (known for its beautiful Santuario de Chimayo) and Ranchos de Taos (with its striking San Francis de Assisi Church); the drive connects Santa Fe with Taos. Legendary Route 66 Scenic Byway travels through much of Northern Rio Grande, capturing both the beauty of the landscape and the history of the "Mother Road."

Ghost Ranch National Natural Landmark

This strikingly beautiful 21,000-acre ranch about an hour's drive from Santa Fe was made famous by painter Georgia O'Keeffe who resided here on a part-time basis. People now come to the ranch from all over the world to paint, write poetry, ride horseback, and to rest and renew their spirits.

National Historic Trails

Three major National Historic Trails emerge from or terminate in the National Heritage Area. The El Camino Real de Tierra Adentro National Historic Trail is the original royal road connecting Mexico City to the northern frontier capital city of Santa Fe and served Spanish and Mexican trade. The Santa Fe National Historic Trail was opened in 1821 to facilitate trade between the United States and Mexico, from Missouri to the capital of Santa Fe. The Old Spanish National Historic Trail established trade between Santa Fe and northern New Mexico and the ranches in southern California at Los Angeles.

Rio Chama Wild and Scenic River

The Rio Chama is a major tributary of the Rio Grande; it flows through the Rio Chama

The Rio Chama Wild and Scenic River is a major tributary of the Rio Grande and flows through Rio Chama Canyon Wilderness Area.

Canyon Wilderness Area, a colorful sandstone canyon with walls that rise 1,500 feet above the river. Outdoor recreation activities include boating, camping, fishing, hiking/backpacking, and wildlife viewing.

For more information about Northern Rio Grande and to help plan your visit, see the area's official website (riogrand enha.org) and the website of the National Park Service (nps.gov/places /northern-rio-grande-national-heritage -area.htm).

Ohio and Erie Canalway National Heritage Area

State: Ohio

Description: Completed in 1832, the 308-mile Ohio and Erie Canal was an important manifestation of America's Industrial Revolution, linking the Ohio River with Lake Erie; today, the canal is a vital part of American history and offers hiking, biking, a series of canal towns, and sightseeing along its historic towpath.

Sample Attractions:
- Cuyahoga Valley National Park
- Cuyahoga Valley Scenic Railroad
- Ohio and Erie Canal America's Scenic Byway
- Canal Fulton

Canals are important manifestations of the nation's Industrial Revolution, large-scale manipulations of the landscape designed to advance commerce and the regional economy. And that's what happened in northeastern Ohio in the early 19th century. Ohio gained statehood in 1803, but it was sparsely populated and geographically isolated because of its poor accessibility to the rest of the nation and the sea. Agricultural products could serve only local markets and there was little capacity for manufacturing. Talk of a canal linking Lake Erie to the Ohio River (and on to the Mississippi River and New Orleans) can be traced as far back as George Washington and Thomas Jefferson, but the state of Ohio didn't act on this impulse until 1825 when construction began. The canal was completed in 1832 and totaled an impressive 308 miles (including several relatively short feeder canals connecting local communities) and 152 locks.

The canal proved a good investment as this region of Ohio flourished; in the 1840s, Ohio became the third most prosperous state in the union. The canal linked the Ohio River with Lake Erie, and this completed a network of water-based transportation routes that ran from New York City and the Atlantic Ocean to the Gulf of Mexico. New towns popped up along the canal and existing communities thrived, helping to fuel the nation's westward expansion. Moreover, the national economy expanded as well; raw materials and products from Ohio could be shipped to the East Coast region, supplying its cities and industries, and this diminished the need for trade with Europe. America's canals are sometimes called "routes of prosperity."

However, the nation's railroad system expanded rapidly in the second half of the 19th century, carrying freight and passengers faster and more economically than canal barges, and all of the country's canals rapidly declined. The Ohio and Erie Canal lost most of its transportation traffic, but its waters were used for power generation and industrial water supply. In 1913, Ohio experienced the Great Flood which destroyed much of the Ohio and Erie Canal's remaining operational capacity.

Today, the canal is still used for transportation, but this is generally limited to hiking, running, and bike riding along its historic towpath, canoeing the canal, riding the Cuyahoga Valley Scenic Railroad which parallels the canal, and driving the region's network of roads, some designated an America's Byway. In fact, much of the remaining Ohio and Erie Canal has been preserved thanks to grassroots organizations such as the Ohio and Erie Canalway Coalition and the Canalway Partners. Effective advocacy led to the area being designated the Ohio and Erie Canalway National Heritage Area (Ohio and Erie Canalway) in 1996. The NHA is managed by the Ohio and Erie Canalway Association that works with over 150 partner organizations that help preserve, celebrate, and tell the story of the canal and its contributions to both the local area and the nation. Moreover, the area contributes substantially to the region's landscape, culture, and recreational values.

Tracing the route of the remaining canal, Ohio and Erie Canalway is 110 miles long (connecting Cleveland and New Philadelphia), is generally 5-10 miles wide, and includes portions of five counties. The NHA and its partners are instrumental in taking a regional approach to managing the canal and Towpath Trail and maintaining the linkages among the canal's many towns and communities. Ohio and Erie Canalway is managed jointly by the original non-profit groups that contributed so much to its establishment. Key partners include Cleveland Metroparks, Cuyahoga Valley National Park, Cuyahoga Valley Scenic Railroad, Summit (County) Metro Parks, Stark County Park Districts, and Tuscarawas County Park Department.

Attractions

The 110 miles of the Ohio and Erie Canalway feature much of the diversity of the area's natural and cultural resources. Highlights include a national park and lots of other regional and local reserves, a very large and well-preserved historic site in the form of the canal, historic and charming towns on the banks of the canal, rides on a scenic train and canal boat, an America's Scenic Byway, and lots of outdoor recreation opportunities. There are several guidebooks that cover all or portions of the region. Enjoy!

Cuyahoga Valley National Park

Cuyahoga Valley National Park represents a new model for national parks in America. Cuyahoga Valley lies between the cities of Cleveland and Akron, Ohio, and includes urban and suburban lands. Moreover, its proximity to urban populations is an important part of the genesis of this national park—bringing national parks to large and diverse metropolitan areas. The park includes 33,000 acres strung out along 22 miles of the winding Cuyahoga River (*Ka-ih-ogh-ha* is Mohawk for "crooked river"); the park includes lush farmlands, rolling hills covered in forests, a historic river, an abundance of waterfalls, narrow ravines, important wildlife habitat, and wetlands. The Boston Store Visitor Center and the Canal Exploration Center include engaging exhibits and helpful staff. The park includes a lovely 20-mile section of the Ohio Erie Canal Towpath Trail, the path that mules walked as they pulled boats along the canal (see below).

Brandywine Falls is accessible by means of a short hike in Cuyahoga Valley National Park.

The Boston Store Visitor Center offers engaging exhibits and friendly staff.

Ohio Erie Canal Towpath Trail

Mules pulled boats along the Ohio and Erie Canal and much of this path has been converted into a walking and biking trail. The path follows the original trail as closely as possible and connects many communities over its 90 miles (it will ultimately extend to 101 miles). Visitor centers along the trail help interpret the history of the region. The trail can be accessed by more than 50 trailheads.

Cuyahoga Valley Scenic Railroad

This railroad operates on 25 miles of historic tracks and has regular service to the canal-era Village of Peninsula, Akron, and the Congressman Ralph Regula Canalway Center. This is a "Bike Aboard" train that makes it handy for people riding the Ohio and Erie Canal Towpath Trail. Special events include the "Grape Escape" wine tasting tour, "A Day with Thomas," and "The Polar Express."

The Cuyahoga Valley Scenic Railroad runs along 25 miles of historic tracks in Cuyahoga Valley National Park.

Ohio and Erie Canal America's Scenic Byway

America's Scenic Byways are designated by the US Secretary of Transportation because they connect key cultural, historic, recreational, and natural sites of interest along two-lane roads. This 110-mile route is a network of roads that connect 58 communities throughout Ohio and Erie Canalway; more than 600 blue and orange signs mark the route.

Canalway Samplers

The NHA website (see below) has engaged a number of community experts to put together several "Canalway Samplers"—short visits to the region that highlight lots of historic sites, tourist favorites, recreation activities, family friendly activities, and other attractions.

Consult the website and give these activities some serious consideration.

Outdoor Recreation

Ohio and Erie Canalway is lined with parks and outdoor recreation areas, including Cuyahoga Valley National Park, Cleveland Metroparks, Summit (County) Metro Parks, Stark County Park Districts, and Tuscarawas County Park Department. These offer many opportunities for hiking, biking, camping, birding, and fishing.

Historic Zoar Village

Founded in 1817 by a group of German Separatists who were fleeing religious persecution, Zoar Village thrived for 80 years and was one of the most successful communal settlements in American history. Several themed tours of the area are conducted.

Mules pulled narrow boats along the Ohio and Erie Canal.

Canal Fulton

This historic small town on the Ohio and Erie Canal grew and then declined with the fortunes of the canal. However, it has a new life as an attractive tourist destination that features the canal's history, and is a gathering place for cyclists, hikers, horseback riders, and birders. The town includes quaint shops lining Canal Street and rides on the St. Helena III, one of the few remaining working canal boats.

Richard Howe House

Richard Howe was the resident engineer for construction of the Ohio and Erie Canal. His home in Akron is a canal-era landmark and now serves as a visitor center to the canal. The house was constructed in 1836 and is a high-style federal structure. The house was restored to its original glory by the Ohio and Erie Canalway Coalition.

For more information about Ohio and Erie Canalway and to help plan your visit, see the area's official website (ohioanderiecanalway.com) and the website of the National Park Service (nps.gov/places/ohio-and-erie -canalway-national-heritage-area.htm).

Oil Region National Heritage Area

State: Pennsylvania

Description: As the name suggests, this NHA in northwestern Pennsylvania celebrates and interprets America's first commercial oil well and how oil helped shape the world's economy, society, politics, and daily life; today, this region has been transformed from its industrial focus to a land of attractive hills, rivers, and forests, and associated opportunities for outdoor recreation.

Sample Attractions:
- Drake Well Museum and Park
- Oil City Downtown Commercial Historic District
- Oil Creek State Park
- Allegheny Wild and Scenic River Water Trail

For many years, small deposits of oil were found in waterways and on the surface of the earth in northwestern Pennsylvania, leaking from seeps and oozing out of the ground. However, this oil couldn't be captured in an economical way—that is, not until Edwin Drake (also known incorrectly as "Colonel Drake") adapted the drilling techniques used for salt wells and applied them to oil. In 1859, Drake and a small crew of men drove a pipe into the ground at appropriately named Oil Creek near Titusville, Pennsylvania. When the pipe hit bedrock, Drake and his men inserted drilling equipment into the pipe and used a small steam engine to power the drill. At 69.5 feet below the surface, the drill hit a crevice in the rock and oil began to rise in the pipe; using a hand pump, the oil was collected in a bathtub. This relatively simple experiment gave birth to the petroleum industry which has shaped the economy, society, politics, and daily life of people around the world.

Postscript: Drake wasn't much of a businessman and he neglected to patent his drilling technique, ironically living his later years in poverty. In 1901, a Standard Oil executive paid to erect a large tomb in Titusville to honor Drake and his remains were moved there. In 1946 the Commonwealth of Pennsylvania built a replica of Drake's oil derrick and engine house at the original well site, which subsequently became part of the Drake Well Museum (see below).

Today, Oil Region National Heritage Area (Oil Region) celebrates the birth of the oil industry in the very place in northwestern Pennsylvania that is now known as the "valley that changed the world." More wells were drilled in Oil Creek and the surrounding area, leading to several oil boomtowns and the "black gold rush." The NHA includes all of Venango County and a portion of Crawford County, including Titusville, Hydetown Borough, and Oil Creek Township, and was established in 2004. It's administered by the Oil Region Alliance (ORA), a merger of four non-profit groups designed to preserve and promote the area. ORA has been successful in receiving grants to assist with local economic development, built recreational trails and amenities, assisted in the development of local businesses, and helped preserve and interpret the region's internationally important history and heritage.

Oil Region also features a "Victorian Region," clusters of handsome Victorian homes and other buildings in several towns scattered across the region's historic landscape. These homes were built in the late 19th century by the region's oil and lumber magnates. Good examples of these Victorian homes can be found in the communities of Titusville, Franklin, Oil City, Emlenton, and Pleasantville. Oil Region celebrates and promotes historic preservation through a House Plaque Program, a historic preservation awards program, and has rehabilitated numerous properties, including Tarbell House, Neilltown Church, Coal Oil Jonny House, and the Salvation Army Building in Oil City. Owners of historic properties are encouraged to participate in these programs to help recognize and maintain the region's cultural heritage.

In addition to the history associated with oil, the NHA includes a pleasing natural and cultural landscape that's marked by wooded hills and valleys, farms, a network of streams (including the Allegheny River, French Creek, and Oil Creek), scenic communities, and industrial landscapes, and draws residents and visitors for all these attractions.

Attractions

The diverse region included in Oil Region offers a wide array of attractions. Of course, the primary focus of the area is the world's first commercial oil well and all the foundational changes it brought to the world, but the region also features historic homes and buildings, the transformation of the region's landscape from an industrial focus to today's attractive hills, rivers, and forests, and associated opportunities for outdoor recreation.

Drake Well Museum and Park

Located on the banks of Oil Creek, this 240-acre site and large museum tell the story of the rise of the petroleum industry

Drake Well Museum and Park sits on the banks of Oil Creek and tells the story of the rise of the petroleum industry in Pennsylvania and around the world.

in Pennsylvania and around the world. The museum features a life-size replica of the world's first commercially successful oil well, operating oil field machinery, 12,000 square feet of interior exhibits, and large collections of artifacts and archives. There are also opportunities for hiking, biking, fly fishing, picnicking, and a neighboring 9,000-acre state park.

Oil City Downtown Commercial Historic District

Oil City started as a small Native American community in the 1600s and boomed as an oil town after the successful oil well developed by Drake in 1859. Oil City's downtown historic district, located at the confluence of the Allegheny River and Oil Creek, was added to the National Register of Historic Districts in 1997. The district includes 51 contributing buildings. This historic town housed companies such as Standard Oil, Pennzoil, and Quaker State Oil and is known as having a city vibe in a rural area.

Historic Pithole City

Historic Pithole City is a quintessential boomtown, vanishing nearly as quickly as it boomed. Oil was struck here in 1865 with several high-producing wells. Within a year, the town's population grew to 15,000. However, oil prices declined and the city hit hard times that included several fires. Population declined until 1877 when the Pithole City Borough Charter was revoked. The town site is now part of the Drake Well Museum and Park (see above) and features a visitor center.

Coal Oil Johnny House

The historic McClintock-Steele-Walitz House, better known as Coal Oil Johnny House, has been relocated adjacent to the Oil Creek and Titusville Railroad Rynd Farm Station. Former owner John Steele made considerable money from the oil wells on his property and famously went on a lavish spending spree in Philadelphia which earned him his nickname. The house is open to the public by appointment and for special events.

Tarbell House

Investigative journalist Ida Tarbell spent her teenage years in the family home in Titusville. She later wrote a serialized set of articles in *McClure's Magazine* (later published as a book) about John D. Rockefeller's Standard Oil Company that helped lead to the breakup of the company and implementation of America's first antitrust laws. The house is used for public functions.

Neilltown Church Building

Built in 1842, the Neilltown church is a Greek Revival building which can seat more than 100 people. ORA has completed

The NHA includes the family home of investigative journalist Ida Tarbell, who wrote a series of magazine articles about John D. Rockefeller's Standard Oil Company.

Oil Creek State Park is a manifestation of the ways in which the industrial landscapes of the oil boom period are being transformed back into forests and clean rivers.

extensive interior and exterior renovations. The property serves as a special events venue which can be rented; it's open for public tours by appointment.

Oil Creek State Park

Oil Creek State Park tells the story of the early petroleum industry by interpreting oil boomtowns, oil wells, and early transportation. The primary purpose of the park is to tell the story of the changing landscape, and the early petroleum industry's oil boom towns and oil well sites are in contrast to the reclaimed clean trout streams and forested

hillsides seen today throughout the park. Scenic Oil Creek carves a valley of deep hollows, steep hillsides, and wetlands, and is home to four waterfalls. The park offers a wide variety of environmental education and recreational programs. Through hands-on activities, guided walks, and evening programs, participants gain appreciation, understanding, and develop a sense of stewardship toward the region's natural and cultural resources.

Allegheny Wild and Scenic River Water Trail

Eighty-six miles of the historic and beautiful Allegheny River are included in the US Wild and Scenic River System; the Allegheny rebounded dramatically from a heavily used industrial past to become an inspiring example of successful restoration. ORA is working to upgrade access areas and interpretive materials along the river which offers great opportunities for boating and fishing.

Hiking Trails

The NHA encourages residents and visitors to be active and offers lots of hiking trails. The long-distance Erie to Pittsburgh Trail runs through the NHA. Oil Creek State Park Trail is a 9.7-mile paved trail that runs through the park along Oil Creek to Oil Creek Petroleum Center and includes the Drake Well Museum. The 5.8-mile Samuel Justus Trail runs along the Allegheny Wild and Scenic River and offers lots of history and scenic views. The Allegheny River Trail runs for approximately 27 miles along the river from Franklin to Emlenton at the southernmost tip of the ORNHA and includes two long tunnels where a flashlight is advised. Sandy Creek Trail intersects with the Allegheny River Trail at Belmar, providing 12 miles of additional hiking over seven bridges and through one tunnel in the heart of Oil Region's natural beauty.

> For more information about Oil Region and to help plan your visit, see the area's official website (oilregion.org) and the website of the National Park Service (nps.gov/oire/index.htm).

Rivers of Steel National Heritage Area

State: Pennsylvania

Description: An eight-county region in southwestern Pennsylvania tells a firsthand account of the rise of "Big Steel," the people who worked there, the landscape they lived in, and the culture they developed; today, the region has repurposed historic mills, cleaned up polluted areas, and developed a suite of outdoor recreation opportunities.

Sample Attractions:
• Carrie Blast Furnaces
• Bost Building
• Pump House
• Sightseeing Riverboat Cruise

The partner organizations in the Rivers of Steel National Heritage Area (Rivers of Steel) help preserve the industrial heritage of this eight-county region in southwestern Pennsylvania. And they do this well as reflected in their passionate descriptions of this cultural landscape. For example, the National Park Service (NPS) writes:

> From 1875 to 1980, southwestern Pennsylvania was the "Steel Making Capital of the World," producing steel for some of America's greatest icons such as the Brooklyn Bridge and the Empire State Building. During World Wars I and II, its steel workers carried the nation's defense on their backs, producing more steel, armor and armaments in a single year than entire countries. While many of the region's legendary mill sites have been dismantled, and decades have passed since the mills belched fire and smoke over Pittsburgh's skyline, the enormity of the region's steel-making contributions and its historical significance to the nation demand that its story be told and its sites be preserved.

In a similar manner, the Rivers of Steel Heritage Corporation, the non-profit that manages Rivers of Steel in cooperation with the NPS and other partner organizations, writes:

> Situated in southwestern Pennsylvania, the Rivers of Steel National Heritage Area reveals how one region, in a sustained and thunderous blast of innovation, ambition and fire, forever changed America and its place in the world. It is the story of the industrialists and the workers who pushed an infant industry to its ultimate limits and in doing so pushed the world into the Age of Steel.

So this NHA tells the story of an industry, the people who worked there, the landscape they lived in, and the culture they developed as they brought "Big Steel" to the world. It's the all-encompassing and interdisciplinary concept of "heritage" that epitomizes the system of National Heritage Areas that are located across the nation. NHAs are designated by Congress as places where natural, cultural, and historic resources combine to form distinctive, cohesive, and nationally important cultural landscapes.

Rivers of Steel was established in 1996 in response to the collapse of the American steel industry in the 1980s. This designation was preceded by a group of local citizens who were concerned about the destruction of shuttered steel mills and the region's disappearing culture. This movement— "a vision for the future, built on the past"—helped to ensure that some of the iconic steel plants were preserved and the stories of the workers and their accomplishments were told as a way to inspire future generations.

This National Heritage Area engages in "creative placemaking" by engaging arts-based initiatives to address the post-industrial communities of the region. Working with community partners, trails have been built along riverfronts and old railroad corridors that feature the natural resources of the region. Through public-private partnerships, Rivers of Steel supports conservation, heritage-based tourism, and outdoor recreation as a means of economic redevelopment. Rivers of Steel is strengthening the economic and cultural fabric of western Pennsylvania by fostering dynamic initiatives and transformative experiences. These initiatives rely on community partners and are encouraged by a grants program to communities administered by Rivers of Steel Heritage Corporation. Brownfields (polluted areas) have been redeveloped, main streets revitalized, river landings made accessible, recreational trails developed, and much more.

Attractions

Rivers of Steel includes a host of attractions that focus on the heritage of the region, including historic sites, exhibits, tours, and demonstrations. It also includes two units of the National Park System and several National Historic Landmarks.

Carrie Blast Furnaces

The remnants of this iconic steel plant are a vestige of Pittsburgh's 20th-century domination of the steel industry and are a National Historic Landmark. Allow two hours for the guided Industrial Tour that highlights the drama of the iron-making process while sharing stories of the plant's technology, as well as stories of its workers and their culture. The Iron Garden Walk is a botanist-led tour of the wild gardens and grounds of the blast furnaces site.

The remnants of the Carrie Blast Furnaces are a vestige of Pittsburgh's 20th-century domination of the steel industry; the site is a National Historic Landmark.

Bost Building

Built in 1892 as a hotel for the steelworkers' ward of Homestead, the Bost Building was

The Bost Building was constructed in 1892 as a hotel for steel workers and was at the center of the Homestead Lockout and Strike, an important period of American labor history; the building now serves as the visitor center for Rivers of Steel National Heritage Area.

at the center of the Homestead Lockout and Strike, a dramatic episode of American labor history. The building is a National Historic Landmark that now serves as the visitor center of Rivers of Steel. There are permanent exhibits on the 1892 Battle of Homestead and the US Steel Homestead Works, along with changing exhibits on places and issues associated with the region's steel heritage. Stop here to plan and start your visit and to purchase tickets for tours and the cruise on the *Explorer* riverboat.

Sightseeing Riverboat Cruise
PGH 101: An Introduction to Innovation is a 90-minute sightseeing tour of Pittsburg's three rivers on the 94-foot riverboat *Explorer*.

The city has been a leader in the Industrial Revolution and its periodic reinventions over the past 250 years, and this tour tells that story through the area's landscape, natural resources, and people.

Pump House
Just across the Monongahela River from the Carrie Blast Furnaces is the Pump House, once part of the US Steel Homestead Steel Works. This is a private facility, but the public is welcome to visit the grounds and enjoy the views of the river and the surroundings. Interpretive panels help visitors learn about the site. Private and group tours of the building are available by appointment. A large labyrinth has been constructed on the grounds that honors those who died during the 1892 Battle of Homestead; visitors are welcome to take a meditative walk.

W. A. Young & Sons Foundry & Machine Shop
This large shop was built in 1900 and produced parts for steamboats, coal mines, railroads, and

The W.A. Young & Sons Foundry and Machine Shop produced parts for steamboats, coal mines, and railroads.

Fort Necessity National Battlefield is a unit of the National Park System and commemorates the opening skirmish of the French and Indian War.

Friendship Hill National Historic Site, a unit of the National Park System, honors Albert Gallatin, longtime Secretary of the Treasury.

local businesses. Check the Rivers of Steel website (see below) for a schedule of tours of the building, a National Historic Landmark. The site hosts the annual Hammer-In Festival where blacksmith artists offer demonstrations and sell their handmade artworks.

Fort Necessity National Battlefield

This unit of the National Park System is also part of Rivers of Steel; the battle at Fort Necessity in the summer of 1754 was the opening skirmish of the French and Indian War. This war was a clash between British, French, and American Indian cultures and ended with the removal of French military power from North America.

Friendship Hill National Historic Site

This unit of the National Park System is also part of Rivers of Steel. Albert Gallatin is best remembered for his 13-year tenure as Secretary of the Treasury during the Jefferson and Madison administrations. In that time he reduced the national debt, purchased the Louisiana Territory, and funded the Lewis & Clark exploration. Gallatin's accomplishments and contributions are highlighted at Friendship Hill, his restored country estate.

> For more information about Rivers of Steel and to help plan your visit, see the area's official website (riversofsteel .com) and the website of the National Park Service (nps.gov/rist/index.htm).

Sacramento-San Joaquin Delta National Heritage Area

State: California

Description: California's extensive Sacramento-San Joaquin Delta is widely recognized for its fertile lands, the water it provides to help irrigate the farmlands of the state's Central Valley, the drinking water for millions of Californians, the immigrant communities it attracted, its recreational opportunities, and the ecological productivity of this estuary.

Sample Attractions:
- John Muir National Historic Site
- Big Break Regional Shoreline
- Locke Historic District
- Isleton Chinese and Japanese Commercial Districts

The significance of Sacramento-San Joaquin Delta National Heritage Area (Sacramento-San Joaquin Delta) is appropriately embodied in three concepts and associated slogans. The first is the Chinese Proverb, "When you drink water, consider the fountain." This reminds Californians that the Sacramento-San Joaquin Delta—the joining of the state's two largest rivers, the Sacramento and the San Joaquin—is the hub of the state's water supply, providing potable water to two-thirds of California's more than 30 million residents. It behooves the state to take good care of this "fountain," the largest estuary on the West Coast of the Americas, and the NHA is designed to help do this. The second slogan is "California's Cornucopia," signifying that the Delta's waters also irrigate millions of acres of fertile agricultural lands, feeding Californians and the greater United States and, in some cases, the world. This water must be used wisely, and Sacramento-San Joaquin Delta NHA also helps to address this issue. And the third slogan is "Delta as Place," reminding us that the Delta is even more than a fountain and cornucopia—it's a place, a great cultural landscape that has an important history and an especially diverse cultural heritage, and the NHA helps celebrate this distinctiveness.

Sacramento-San Joaquin Delta was established in 2019 and was the first NHA in California (though there will certainly be more in this powerhouse of a state). However, many groups in the state had been laying the groundwork for this NHA for the last decade or more. The idea emerged out of an earlier state initiative—"Delta Vision"—that attempted to address the inherent conflicts associated with withdrawing the Delta's water for drinking and agriculture versus leaving enough water to maintain the Delta's foundational ecosystem. The state's 2009 Delta Reform Act charged the Delta Protection Commission, a state agency, to develop a proposal to protect, enhance, and sustain the Delta's historical, cultural, recreational, and agricultural values, including a plan to establish state and federal designation of the Delta as a place of special significance. The commission completed a feasibility study for an NHA in 2012, but it took several years to work its way through Congress. Sacramento-San Joaquin Delta is managed by the Delta Protection Commission. NHA boundaries extend from Sacramento in the north, Stockton to the east, and along the Carquinez Strait to the west; this is an appropriately large area of more than 1,200 square miles. Though the NHA has only recently been established, a number of projects have been conducted, including studies of adaptive reuse of historic sites, a Delta branding and marketing campaign, a Delta sign program, recording of oral histories of residents, legacy plans for historic legacy communities, and plans for potential museums and other interpretive initiatives.

The natural productivity of the Delta's vast wetlands attracted Native Americans for thousands of years. It's thought that the population density of these people may have been the second highest in North America before European contact. Historic interest in the Delta began in the California Gold Rush period around the middle of the 19th century. Most miners traveled from San Francisco through the Delta to get to the gold fields to the east, and in the process the fertility of the Delta's soils was also discovered; this led to a massive reclamation project that converted much the area's vast marshes into one of the most productive agricultural regions in the world. Immigrants from many parts of the world flocked to California to help build the state's railroads, but many also helped build the Delta's network of levees. This led to a long history of Asian-American—Chinese, Japanese, and Filipino—presence in the Delta region. For example, the small town of Locke is the only community in the United States developed exclusively by and for Chinese immigrants. Large-scale water development projects were constructed in the 20th century to supply water for cities as far away as southern California and to help irrigate the state's great Central Valley agricultural region. The Delta is also important for its navigational value, a historic waterway between inland California and San Francisco Bay and the Pacific Ocean. More recently, the waters of the Delta are coveted for their recreational and ecological values as well. The ecology of the region has added a more contemporary layer of value to Delta NHA, focusing particularly on the area's wetlands, fish, and birds. The Delta is an estuary where saltwater from the Pacific Ocean mixes with freshwater from the mountains to create an especially rich biological area; withdrawals of water can upset the natural balance of the region.

Attractions

Sacramento-San Joaquin Delta includes lots of attractions for both residents and visitors. A primary objective of the NHA is to foster a program of economic development that's built on a foundation of heritage-based

John Muir National Historic Site was the home of this conservationist, known as "the father of the national parks."

tourism, encompassing ecotourism, agritourism, cultural tourism, and outdoor recreation.

John Muir National Historic Site

A young Scottish immigrant, John Muir ultimately found his way to the Sierra Nevada Mountains and spent much of his adult life working for the preservation of the area that became Yosemite National Park and other protected lands. He's generally acknowledged as the "father" of America's national parks. However, he spent a period of his life in Martinez, California, growing fruit, raising a family, and writing. A small historical unit of the National Park System, including his home, part of his ranch, and a 326-acre natural area, honors this period of his life.

Port Chicago Naval Magazine National Memorial

This unit of the National Park System commemorates World War II's worst homefront accident. Two Navy ships were loading ammunition on the night of July 17, 1944,

The Sacramento-San Joaquin River Delta offers extensive outdoor recreation opportunities.

Big Break Regional Shoreline is a great place for birding (northern mockingbird).

when they exploded, killing 320 Americans—many of them African American—in the horrific blast that woke residents in San Francisco's east bay communities. When African American sailors refused to work until conditions improved, the subsequent court martial of fifty sailors was a landmark event in the early Civil Rights Movement.

Historic Downtown Martinez

Established in 1849, Martinez is a traditional gateway to the Delta region. The downtown is surrounded by waterfront and open space preserves and has retained many of its historic buildings. It's popular with both residents and visitors.

Big Break Regional Shoreline

This large regional park in the town of Oakley is located directly on the Delta at a bay on the San Joaquin River. Popular recreational activities include birding, hiking, biking, swimming, boating, and fishing. Facilities include a visitor center, fishing pier, boat launch, and picnic area, and naturalist programs are offered.

Isleton Chinese and Japanese Commercial Districts

Historic Chinese and Japanese commercial districts are preserved in the town of Isleton. Asian laborers and farmers played important roles in the early railroad and agricultural industries of central California, and the residential and commercial Chinese and Japanese districts in Isleton have been preserved. The districts include residences, stores, schools, gambling halls, and gardens.

Grand Island Mansion

Walnut Grove is one of the earliest settlements on the Sacramento River Delta, established in 1850. Lewis W. Meyers, a wealthy resident, built Grand Island Mansion, a four-story, 24,000-square-foot, 58-room villa that evokes the glamour of the 1920s and now welcomes visitors.

The Locke Historic District was built in 1915 and is the most complete example of a rural, agricultural Chinese community in the United States.

Locke Historic District

The Locke Historic District, also known as the town of Locke, was built in 1915. It's the most complete example of a rural, agricultural Chinese community in the United States. Chinese immigrants worked in the agricultural industries in large numbers and many lived in enclaves built for their use. When the Chinese District in Walnut Grove was destroyed by fire in 1915, residents constructed a new village outside of town on land leased from the George Locke family. The town has a large array of buildings, including residences, schools, stores, a theater, church, boarding houses, restaurants, hotels, post office, dentist office, and a community garden. The district was designated a National Historic Landmark in 1990.

For more information about Sacramento-San Joaquin Delta and to help plan your visit, see the area's official website (delta.ca.gov/nha/) and the website of the National Park Service (nps.gov /places/sacramento-san-joaquin-delta -national-heritage-area.htm).

Sangre de Cristo National Heritage Area

State: Colorado

Description: This large NHA features the vast San Luis Valley that lies at the foot of the striking Sangre de Christo Mountains; the NHA celebrates the rich culture of the people who settled here and offers extensive opportunities for outdoor recreation.

Sample Attractions:

- Great Sand Dunes National Park and Preserve
- Los Caminos Antiguos Scenic and Historic Byway
- Cumbres & Toltec Scenic Railroad
- Culebra River Villages

This large geographic area in south central Colorado features the vast San Luis Valley that lies between the striking Sangre de Cristo Mountains on the east and the San Juan Mountains on the west, both subranges of the famous Rocky Mountains. Like the area it helps protect, Sangre de Cristo National Heritage Area (Sangre de Christo) is also vast—more than 3,000 square miles, larger than the state of Delaware. The jagged Sangre de Cristo ("Blood of Christ") Mountains, some over 14,000 feet, are named for their reddish glow which can occur at sunrise and sunset. The mountains define the eastern edge of the San Luis Valley, one of the largest and highest alpine valleys in North America. It's home to Colorado's oldest town, San Luis, established in 1851. The mix of Native American, Spanish, Mexican, Japanese, and European American people who have settled here offers visitors to the area a rich cultural heritage that's expressed in local religious, artistic, and architectural traditions.

Sangre de Christo was established in 2009 with the support of two of its longtime and high-profile residents, former US Senator and Secretary of Interior Ken Salazar and former US Representative John Salazar, both of whom were born in Alamosa, Colorado, and grew up in the area's farming community known as Los Rincones. The mission of the NHA is to preserve and promote the region's unique cultural landscape, including its natural environment, history, and culture. Four interpretive themes guide management of the NHA. The first addresses the area's natural environment, including its high desert valley and surrounding mountains. Here, mountains, wind, water, and sand dunes have developed unusual and biologically rich landscape features. The second theme honors the Native American presence in the area that has been traced back 11,000 years. Selected landscape features of the area are considered sacred by the descendants of these people. Third, the rich and diverse history and culture of the area has been complemented with more recent Spanish and Mexican influences. Moreover, after the United States annexed Mexico's northern territories in 1848, European-Americans settled in the region, adding to its diverse culture and heritage. And fourth, the area has given rise to a unique Hispano culture based on early Spanish and Mexican residents; this culture features local folklore, religion, and language. Sangre de Christo is managed by the Sangre de Christo Board of Directors in cooperation with its public, private, and non-profit partners.

Attractions

Sangre de Christo is large and diverse and includes a national park, three national wildlife refuges, a national forest, several state wildlife areas, the headwaters of the Rio Grande River, and more than twenty sites listed in the National Register of Historic Places. Plan on several days to sample this important cultural landscape. Here are a few places to start.

Great Sand Dunes National Park and Preserve

Yes, this striking national park has impressive sand dunes—more than 30 square miles of them, and at 750 feet high they're the tallest dunes in North America. Climb on them to your heart's content (but the going can be challenging). But this park has so much more. The dune fields are set against the often snow-covered Sangre de Cristo Mountains, making one of the most unusual and striking landscapes in the National Park System. The park also includes a portion of the mountains along with surrounding grasslands, streams, and wetlands.

Great Sand Dunes National Park and Preserve features dunes that rise more than 750 feet, the tallest in North America.

San Luis Valley National Wildlife Refuges Complex

This complex of three national wildlife refuges—Alamosa, Monte Vista, and Baca—helps preserve the important biological resources of the San Luis Valley. The refuges offer water and habitat to the area's wildlife, including many species that migrate through the area. Visitors can enjoy wildlife viewing and photography and regulated hunting and fishing.

Old Spanish National Historic Trail

There are 19 National Historic Trails in the United States. The Old Spanish Trail is a 2,700-mile route that connects Santa Fe, New Mexico, with Los Angeles, California, and travels through portions of six states, including Colorado and Sangre de Christo. Mexican trader Antonio Armijo led the first commercial caravan in 1829; later, several routes were explored and used. Find sites along this historic trail in Sangre de Christo using the website (see below).

Los Caminos Antiguos Scenic and Historic Byway

This 129-mile drive through the San Luis Valley connects many of the historic towns and other attractions. The tour is anchored at one end by Alamosa, the largest town in the valley, and on the other end by the beautiful southern San Juan Mountains where the native aspens turn a golden yellow in the fall.

Zapata Ranch and Falls

The non-profit group, the Nature Conservancy, owns the over 100,000-acre Zapata Ranch just west of Great Sand Dunes National Park and Preserve. The ranch includes rare wetlands, historic homesteads, a herd of 2,000 bison, and offers dramatic views of the park. While this is currently private property, limited public access is available, including tours of the area. Zapata Falls is a secluded 25-foot waterfall within a cave and forms a dramatic frozen cascade in winter; reach the site by an adventurous half-mile hike. Eventually, Zapata Ranch

Vast grasslands fill the San Luis Valley at the base of the Sangre de Christo Mountains.

Reaching Zapata Falls requires an adventurous half-mile hike.

will be incorporated into Great Sand Dunes National Park and Preserve.

Shrine of the Stations of the Cross

These evocative sculptures capturing the last hours of Christ's life were created for the parishioners of the Sangre de Cristo Parish in San Luis. The shrine is located on a mesa in the center of town and the bronze statues depicting the Stations of the Cross were created by local artist and resident Hubert Maestas.

Jack Dempsey Museum

Heavyweight boxing champion Jack Dempsey was born in the historic town of Manassa where a museum—located in the cabin where Dempsey was born—has been established in his honor. Many residents are inspired in their daily lives by Dempsey's hard-won success.

Fort Garland

This is a military outpost that operated in the valley from 1858 to 1883. Explore the fort by walking the parade grounds and touring five of the original adobe buildings. An exhibit features the role of the Army's African American "Buffalo Soldiers" who helped manage several national parks before there was a National Park Service.

Cumbres & Toltec Scenic Railroad

The Cumbres & Toltec Scenic Railroad is a National Historic Landmark that moves, an authentic steam-powered narrow-gauge railroad ride through the Rocky Mountains of Colorado and New Mexico, connecting Antonito, Colorado, and Chama, New Mexico. This railroad has steamed through history and across the Rocky Mountains since 1880, when tracks were laid across Cumbres Pass. The ride is especially scenic in the fall when the area's aspen trees turn a bright gold; make your reservations early.

The Sangre de Christo Parish Church includes a series of bronze statues depicting the Stations of the Cross.

Ride the historic Cumbres & Toltec Railroad through the Rocky Mountains of Colorado and New Mexico.

Founded in the mid-19th century, Capilla de Viejo San Acacio reflects its Hispano heritage.

Culebra River Villages

Since their establishment in 1851, the villages of the Rio Culebra (in Costilla County) and their associated cultural landscapes have been representative of early Hispano settlement in Colorado. The vernacular architecture of the villages incorporated hybridized styles characteristic of the outside influences introduced into the villages over time. The landscape and built environment of this area reflect the evolution of Hispano vernacular architecture and the associated cultural landscape in southern Colorado. The original settlers of the Culebra Villages brought with them a form of land settlement and irrigation that was based on principles of equity, shared scarcity, and cooperation in which water was viewed as a resource in place, rather than a commodity. These types of water systems are called *acequias* and they continue to be the lifeblood of residents in southern Costilla County; they not only provide the water for the farms on which 270 families depend, but they also serve as a conduit for community services and support.

Capilla de Viejo San Acacio

Founded in the mid-19th century, this church reflects the Hispano culture of the times and is generally considered the oldest non-Native American religious space in Colorado. Residents renamed their village San Acacio (named after the "miracle of San Acacio" when the town was spared from attack by Ute Indians as a result of prayers to San Acacio). The church has been stabilized and remodeled several times over the years, but still celebrates Sunday mass and the feast day of its namesake.

For more information about Sangre de Christo and to help plan your visit, see the area's official website (sangre heritage.org) and the website of the National Park Service (nps.gov/places /sangre-de-cristo-national-heritage -area.htm).

Santa Cruz Valley National Heritage Area

State: Arizona

Description: This large NHA in southern Arizona includes a lovely and diverse landscape that features the historic Santa Cruz River, great forests of iconic giant saguaros, open grasslands, deep canyons, and 9,000-foot mountain ranges covered in forest; the region's distinctive culture is influenced by Native Americans, descendants of Spanish explorers, and recent generations of American pioneers.

Sample Attractions:

- Tubac Presidio State Historic Park
- Arizona-Sonora Desert Museum
- Saguaro National Park
- Tumacacori National Historical Park

The Santa Cruz Valley in southern Arizona is a unique watershed with a combination of natural and cultural features that distinguishes it from the rest of the American Southwest. The Santa Cruz River rises in the state's southern grasslands and flows south into Mexico where it loops northward back into Arizona and eventually disappears into the desert north of Tucson. The surrounding landscape is exceptionally diverse, including cactus-covered desert, open grasslands, deep canyons, lush oases, and 9,000-foot mountain ranges covered in forest. The iconic giant saguaro cactus is found in this region, sometimes in dense forests. The scenic symbol of the Southwest, these remarkable plants are sometimes called the "Monarch of the Sonoran Desert" and the "Redwood of the Desert." Instantly recognizable, these large, graceful tree-like plants have upward-thrusting branches or arms that suggest human figures.

The area's human history is equally diverse and constitutes one of the country's longest-inhabited regions. An ancient Native American presence can be traced back 12,000 years and portions of the landscape have been continuously farmed over the last 4,000 years. The people who live here today represent several cultures, including Native Americans, descendants of Spanish ancestors who colonized the valley in the late 17th century, Mexican families who settled here before it was part of the United States, and recent generations of American pioneers searching for the American dream. This grand cultural landscape is one of the nation's most recent National Heritage Areas, established in 2019.

The large Santa Cruz Valley National Heritage Area (Santa Cruz Valley)—more than 3,000 square miles—is sometimes called the "Borderlands" and is managed by the non-profit Santa Cruz Valley Heritage Alliance in cooperation with the National Park Service and a host of other partners. The primary management objectives are to foster an effective working relationship with all levels of government, non-profit organizations, and the private sector to conserve the region's heritage while supporting compatible economic opportunities, increase heritage and nature-based tourism, develop heritage-based education programs, promote local foods, crafts, and other traditional products, restore riparian habitats, rehabilitate historic buildings, and improve the quality of life for residents by instilling a sense of place.

Attractions

The 3,300 square miles of Santa Cruz Valley includes an abundance of attractions for both residents and visitors. Here, you'll find well-preserved historic and archaeological resources; national, state and local parks; a cultural landscape that's historic, beautiful, and ecologically important; and outdoor recreation opportunities. The following are highly recommended.

Tubac Presidio State Historic Park

This is Arizona's first state park and it preserves and interprets the ruins of the oldest Spanish Presidio site in Arizona, San Ignacio de Tubac, established in 1752. Spanish troops were stationed here to protect settlers and to further explore the Southwest. The park also includes the state's second oldest territorial schoolhouse, the hand press used to print the first newspaper in Arizona, a visitor center, and an award-winning museum that presents 2,000 years of Santa Cruz Valley history.

Tubac Presidio State Historic Park includes a museum that houses 2,000 years of Santa Cruz Valley history.

These cottonwood trees signal the presence of a rare, perennial stream in the Patagonia-Sonoita Creek Preserve.

Catalina State Park

This is a large park—5,500 acres—located at the base of the Santa Catalina Mountains just outside Tucson. Its diverse landscape includes foothills, canyons, streams, and desert plants and wildlife, including nearly 5,000 majestic saguaros. Recreation activities include camping, hiking, biking, picnicking, birding, and horseback riding.

Patagonia-Sonoita Creek Preserve

This 873-acre site contains two miles of Sonoita Creek, a rare, permanently flowing stream. This riparian area and surrounding watershed offer a great deal of biological diversity, including a magnificent forest of rare Fremont cottonwoods and Goodding willows. It's a great place to hike and watch wildlife.

Arizona-Sonora Desert Museum

A nationally acclaimed tourist destination, this largely outdoor "fusion" museum includes a zoo, botanical garden, art gallery, natural history museum, aviaries, and aquarium. A desert loop trail is available for hiking and educational classes are offered.

Catalina State Park is over 5,000 acres and includes foothills, canyons, streams, and desert plants and animals.

Presidio San Agustin del Tucson Museum

This site is a re-creation of the Tucson Presidio built by the Spanish in 1775. The museum offers docent tours that describe life in the Santa Cruz Valley for early Native Americans, Presidio residents, and territorial period settlers. Visitors can walk along the original Presidio wall and experience a 150-year-old Sonoran row house.

Juan Bautista de Anza National Historic Trail

This is one of three units of the National Park System in the NHA. Juan Bautista de Anza led some 240 men, women, and children on an epic 1,200-mile journey in 1775-76 from Nogales, Arizona, to establish the first non-native settlement at San Francisco Bay.

San Xavier del Bac Mission

This National Historic Landmark, locally known as the White Dove of the Desert, is located in Tucson and is an active Catholic mission church. It's a historic site on the Juan Bautista de Anza National Historic Trail noted above. Father Kino founded the mission in 1692, explored the region, and worked with the indigenous Native American population.

Saguaro National Park

This a second unit of the National Park System in the NHA. The park is found in two sections, just to the east and west of Tucson. The park features extensive forests of the iconic and magnificent saguaro cactuses, often used as a symbol of the American Southwest. The park includes scenic drives and a network of hiking trails.

Tumacacori National Historical Park

Tumacacori sits at a cultural crossroads in the Santa Cruz Valley. Many cultures crossed paths in this place, including Native Americans (O'odham, Yaqui, and Apache), Europeans, Jesuit and Franciscan missionaries, American settlers and soldiers, and Mexican immigrants. This is the third unit of the National Park System in the NHA

Often called the "White Dove of the Desert," San Xavier del Bac Mission was founded by Father Kino in 1692; it remains an active Catholic mission church.

Saguaro National Park lies just outside Tucson and features great forests of the distinctive giant saguaro catcuses.

Tumacacori National Historical Park interprets the history and interactions of the many cultures that have inhabited this area.

and interprets the history and interactions among these diverse cultures.

Mission Garden

This agricultural site is a manifestation of greater Tucson's designation by the United Nations Educational, Scientific, and Cultural Organization (UNESCO) as the first "City of Gastronomy." Mission Garden is a re-creation of the Spanish walled garden that was part of Tucson's historic San Agustin Mission. The garden features heirloom Sonoran Desert-adapted fruit orchards and vegetable gardens, interpreting 4,000 years of agriculture in Tucson.

San Xavier Co-op Farm

The San Xavier Cooperative Association is committed to healthy farming practices and traditional crops to support cultural and environmental values and to advance community economic development. Its philosophy and practices are based on the way of

life of the Tohono O'odham people. Ancient crops such as teary beans and squash are grown, and visitors can purchase wild food products such as mesquite meal (ground from mesquite pods). Farm tours are offered.

Arizona State Museum and Arizona History Museum

Both of these state museums are located in Tucson at the University of Arizona. The former includes a repository of ancient Southwest artifacts, exhibitions, and an education and events center for Native American culture and arts. The latter interprets Arizona history from the Spanish colonial period through the territorial eras.

For more information about Santa Cruz Valley and to help plan your visit, see the area's official website (santacruz heritage.org) and the website of the National Park Service (nps.gov/places /santa-cruz-valley-national-heritage -area.htm).

Schuylkill River Greenways National Heritage Area

State: Pennsylvania

Description: The Schuylkill River watershed in southeastern Pennsylvania is one of America's most significant natural, cultural, historical, and industrial regions; it's nationally significant for the role that its people, places, and events played in the American, Industrial, and Environmental Revolutions.

Sample Attractions:
* Independence National Historical Park
* Valley Forge National Historical Park
* Hopewell Furnace National Historic Site
* Schuylkill River Trail

Schuylkill River Greenways National Heritage Area (Schuylkill River Greenways) celebrates the Schuylkill River watershed in southeastern Pennsylvania, one of America's most significant natural, cultural, historical, and industrial regions. In fact, it's both a National Heritage Area and Pennsylvania Heritage Area (designated by the State). Schuylkill (SKOO-kill) is a Dutch word meaning "hidden river." The five-county area (including Philadelphia) comprising the NHA is nationally significant for the role that its people, places, and events played in the American, Industrial, and Environmental Revolutions. It's home to more than three million people and, like all NHAs, its natural, cultural, historic, and recreational resources combine to form a cohesive, nationally distinctive landscape, one that's been shaped by both nature and humans.

Schuylkill River Greenways is managed by the non-profit Schulykill River Greenway Association in ways that feature and honor the three themes noted above, the American Revolution, the Industrial Revolution, and the Environmental Revolution (the latter often called the Conservation Movement), and the vital role that the Schuylkill River watershed played in each. The watershed was front and center in the American Revolution. Philadelphia was the official gathering place of those who crafted the revolutionary ideas of freedom, independence, and democracy. The ensuing battles with the British Army at Germantown, Paoli, Fort Mifflin, and Brandywine, were challenging for the American forces, but the subsequent difficult winter for General George Washington's troops at Valley Forge, camped on the bluffs overlooking the Schulkill River, allowed for regrouping

and much needed training and discipline; all these sites are in the Schulkill River watershed. Food and other supplies for the troops were provided from the local area. Following the Revolutionary War, the Constitutional Convention met in Philadelphia to fashion and sign the historic Constitution, and the city served as the nation's first capital.

The region defined by the present-day National Heritage Area was also a leader in the nation's Industrial Revolution. Abundant natural resources included iron, forests, limestone and granite, rich soils, and the country's largest supply of anthracite coal. The Schulkill and other streams provided a source of power and transportation. Coal and iron ore were combined to make steel in factories throughout the region. Immigrants—German and Welsh miners were followed by Scots, Irish, Italians, Slovaks, Lithuanians, Greeks and others—were attracted to the area in response to plentiful jobs, substantially enhancing the historic and present-day cultural diversity of the region. At the turn of the 20th century, Philadelphia was known as the "Workshop of the World." Transportation on the area's rivers was eventually replaced in the early 1800s by railroads. As railroads ultimately declined in importance and tracks were abandoned, these rights-of-way allowed for some sections to be used for the present-day 120-mile Schuylkill River Trail (described below).

Conservation of the environment is the third revolution that contributes to the distinctiveness of Schulkill Rivers Greenway. The Bartram family and John James Audubon were early residents of the area and helped lead the nation in appreciating and conserving its natural environment. John

Bartram is generally considered the nation's first true botanist, serving as Royal Botanist before the Revolutionary War, studying and propagating native plants. Bartram's son William is known for his travels through the wetlands of the Southeast, and for his subsequent book, *Travels*. Aububon also lived in the Schuylkill region (right next to the river!) where he explored the natural world and developed his fascination with birds and painting and published his enduring book, *The Birds of America.*

Part of the region's interest in the environment was more pragmatic and a manifestation of the pollution that was a byproduct of the Industrial Revolution, coal mining in particular. Coal mines in Schuylkill County had turned the river black from coal dust, and local communities used the river to discard industrial and household waste. Philadelphia, on the receiving end of this pollution carried by the Schuylkill River, began a large program of improving water quality, constructing modern water reclamation plants to help clean the region's drinking water. Open space was purchased by towns all along the river to control industrial development and filter water flow into the river; Philadelphia's 9,000-acre Fairmount Park is a nationally significant example. Settling ponds were developed along the river to trap and dispose of coal dust. The 1947 Schuylkill River Project was the first major environmental cleanup effort in the United States. As a marker of the success of these programs, the Schuylkill was designated the state's first Scenic River, and the area was designated a National Heritage Area in 2000. Schuylkill River Greenways administers a conservation grants program to communities and other organizations along the river.

Attractions

The size and diversity of Schuylkill River Greenways results in an extensive and wide-ranging set of visitor attractions and activities offered by public agencies, nonprofit groups, and private entities. Activities include visiting historic sites, art and cultural attractions, biking, birding, hiking, camping, cross-country skiing, driving and walking tours, festivals and fairs, fishing, horseback riding, boating, and picnicking. The following is a representative list of attractions, but only scratches the surface.

Independence National Historical Park

This important unit of the National Park System interprets the founding ideals of the nation and vital symbols of freedom and democracy, including Independence Hall and the Liberty Bell. The Declaration of Independence and the US Constitution were debated and signed inside Independence Hall, a World Heritage Site.

Valley Forge National Historical Park

Also a unit of the National Park System, this is the 1777-78 winter encampment of the Continental Army. This 3,500-acre site includes monuments, meadows, and woodlands and tells the story of the sacrifices of the soldiers during the severe winter conditions.

Hopewell Furnace National Historic Site

A third unit of the National Park System, this site is a manifestation of the early life and industry of the Industrial Revolution.

Valley Forge National Historical Park tells the story of the bitter winter encampment of the Continental Army in 1777–78.

Hopewell Furnace National Historic Site contributed to the American Industrial Revolution.

Hopewell is one of the many "iron plantations" that developed in the Schuylkill region in the late 18th and early 19th centuries.

Schuylkill River Trail

This long-distance trail has been constructed through the region's rural, agricultural, suburban, urban, and industrial landscapes and generally follows the Schuylkill River. Today, over 75 miles of paved and crushed stone trail are open to the public, much of it located on abandoned railroad beds. Ultimately, it will extend to 120 miles.

Circuit Trails

Greater Philadelphia boasts a regional network of hundreds of miles of multi-use trails, designed to ultimately extend to 750 miles. Bike Pottstown/Bike Schuylkill offer a free bike share program.

The Schuylkill River Trail follows the river for more than 75 miles and is a great resource for walkers and bikers.

Schuylkill River Water Trail

The Schuylkill River rises in the mountains near the tiny coal-region town of Tuscarora, Pennsylvania, and flows 137 miles on its way to the confluence with the Delaware River in Philadelphia. The river can be paddled most of this distance (there are several dams that must be portaged) and there are places where recreational motorboats can also be used. A local outfitter offers recreational/educational programing.

River of Revolutions Interpretive Center

Located in Pottstown, this visitor center includes a relief map of the region, displays and videos describing Schuylkill River Greenways, and a large wall map noting visitor sites, recreation opportunities, and other points of interest.

Tourist Destinations

The website for Schuylkill River Greenways (see below) notes several geographic locations where visitors can appreciate the history and diversity of the area. These include Coal Country, the Blue Mountains, Eastern Berks, Western Berks, Greater Reading,

Oley Valley, French and Pickering Valleys, Perkiomen Valley, Skippack Valley, and Philadelphia. See the website for descriptions of these areas.

For more information about Schuylkill River Greenways and to help plan your visit, see the area's official website (schuylkillriver.org) and the website of the National Park Service (nps.gov/places/schuylkill-river-national-heritage-area.htm).

Shenandoah Valley Battlefields National Historic District

State: Virginia

Description: The Shenandoah Valley was a strategic location during the Civil War, a natural route between the northern and southern states, and it was the location of many important battles; today we know the region for its Civil War history, but also for its biological diversity, agricultural productivity, surrounding mountains, and outdoor recreation opportunities.

Sample Attractions:
- Shenandoah National Park
- Driving Tours
- Museums
- Civil War Monuments

The Civil War was a wrenching period of American history that deeply divided the nation over the issues of slavery and the secession of many of the southern states from the United States of America. After Abraham Lincoln was elected president in 1860, seven slave states seceded to form the Confederate

States of America. War broke out in April 1861 when Confederate forces attacked Fort Sumter in South Carolina. An additional four slave states joined the Confederacy over the next two months. The majority of states remained loyal to the United States and were known as the Union. The war raged for four years, effectively ending on April 9, 1865, when Confederate General Robert E. Lee surrendered to Union General Ulysses S. Grant at the Battle of Appomattox Court House. The war left between 620,000 and 750,000 soldiers dead, the highest number of casualties of any American war; an unknown number of civilians also died. Life was severely disrupted in many locations and much of the industrial infrastructure of the southern states was destroyed.

Before the war, Virginia's Shenandoah Valley was a beautiful and peaceful place marked by productive agricultural lands and the surrounding Blue Ridge Mountains. However, the valley was also a geographically strategic location, a natural route between the northern and southern states. Moreover, the valley was known as the "Breadbasket of the Confederacy," signaling its importance in feeding Confederate troops. Consequently, it was the location of many important battles and related historic sites.

For example, Confederate General Thomas "Stonewall" Jackson led a campaign in the spring of 1862 that's considered a masterpiece of military maneuvering. Though substantially outnumbered and facing as many as three Union armies, Jackson marched his troops 350 miles over the course of a month and fought a series of battles in the Shenandoah Valley, inflicting more than 5,000 casualties, compared to 2,000 of his own army; he captured needed supplies as well. But more importantly, he deliberately kept nearly 60,000 Union soldiers occupied in the valley, troops that would have been available to join in the campaign to capture the Confederate capital of Richmond.

Other important military campaigns that were at least partially fought in the Shenandoah Valley include Confederate General Robert E. Lee's Gettysburg Campaign in 1863, marking the geographic "high tide" of the Confederacy, and Union General Phillip Sheridan's Shenandoah Campaign in 1864, driving Confederate troops from the Shenandoah Valley, and conducting "The Burning," setting fire to mills, barns, and public buildings, and destroying or carrying away forage, grain, and livestock. Important battles include First and Second battles of Kernstown, First, Second, and Third Winchester, Cross Keys, Port Republic, New Market, Fisher's Hill, and Cedar Creek. In total, the Shenandoah Valley saw more than 325 armed conflicts.

In 1992, the National Park Service conducted a study of the area, calling attention to the importance of the Shenandoah Valley's Civil War heritage. The study was stimulated by the threat to these historic sites by growing residential and commercial development of the region. In 1996, Congress established Shenandoah Valley Battlefields National Historic District (Shenandoah Valley Battlefields), a National Heritage Area, to conserve the Valley's historic importance—its Civil War battlefields and related historic sites such as courthouses and historic buildings, towns, museums, and cemeteries—and interpret that history to the region's residents and visitors

Cedar Creek & Belle Grove National Historical Park is a unit of the National Park System and tells the story of the Shenandoah Valley and the Civil War.

through a heritage-based tourism initiative. This management approach emphasizes a local community-based effort to protect the region. The non-profit Shenandoah Valley Battlefields Foundation was established by the Secretary of the Interior and guides management of the NHA. The foundation works with the National Park Service, the National Trust for Historic Preservation, and local communities and landowners to carry out its mission. The foundation acquires key battlefield properties and/or easements from willing sellers, assists local communities interested in developing land use plans to protect their battlefield landscapes, and works to ensure that federal, state, and local governments consider potential impacts of public projects on the valley's battlefields.

Of course, the Shenandoah Valley is also noted for its scenic beauty and natural resources, including its biological diversity, agricultural productivity, surrounding mountains, and outdoor recreation opportunities.

Attractions

The Shenandoah Valley includes a rich collection of historic sites that tell many stories of the Civil War; the region also features lovely scenic views and outdoor recreation opportunities. Shenandoah Valley Battlefields has developed a helpful visitor's guide (*Shenandoah at War: Visitors Guide to the Shenandoah Valley's Civil War Story*) that can be downloaded from the website (see below) and also publishes a magazine (*Shenandoah*).

Driving Tours

Shenandoah Valley Battlefields has developed a series of self-guided driving tours of battlefield and related historic sites that are helpful in learning about the Civil War era in a coordinated way. The tours are posted on the NHA website (see below).

Museums

Given its important Civil War heritage, it's not surprising that the region includes a number of interesting and informative museums. Good examples include the Shenandoah Valley Civil War Museum (Winchester), Berkeley County Museum (West Virginia), Hupp's Hill Cedar Creek Museum (Strasburg), Newtown History Center (Stephens City), Warren Rifles Confederate Museum (Front Royal), Virginia Museum of the Civil War (New Market), Rocktown History Museum (Dayton), VMI Museum (Lexington), Stonewall Brigade Museum (Verona), and the Civil War Orientation Center (Winchester).

Civil War Monuments

The Shenandoah Valley is dotted with dozens of Civil War Monuments that help tell the history of important events and people while interpreting the history of the area. The monuments at battlefields are also markers of hallowed ground where Americans struggled to help define the nation.

Stonewall Jackson's Headquarters

This National Historic Landmark was used as headquarters by Jackson during the winter of 1861-62. The house contains a large collection of Jackson memorabilia.

Civil War Trails

This large system of interpretive signs about the Civil War are posted throughout Virginia (as well as Maryland, North Carolina, Tennessee, and West Virginia). Nearly 100 are located in the Shenandoah Valley; many are found along routes 11 and 340.

Cedar Creek & Belle Grove National Historical Park

This unit of the National Park System tells the larger story of the Shenandoah Valley, including Native Americans, pioneer history, and the Civil War. The park encompasses the site of the Battle of Cedar Creek, a decisive Union victory.

Shenandoah National Park

This long and narrow national park of 200,000 acres runs along the spine of the Blue Ridge Mountains for more than 100 miles. Best known for its Skyline Drive, the park also features 500 miles of trails, including more

Shenandoah National Park runs along the spine of the Blue Ridge Mountains for more than 100 miles.

This historic home was once part of a 7,500-acre plantation; it's now a National Historic Landmark and offers educational programs to visitors.

than 100 miles of the Appalachian National Scenic Trail.

Belle Grove

This historic mansion was once part of a 7,500-acre plantation and now offers educational programs to visitors. It's a National Historic Landmark.

For more information about Shenandoah Valley Battlefields and to help plan your visit, see the area's official website (shenandoahatwar.org) and the website of the National Park Service (nps.gov/places/shenandoah-valley-battlefields-national-historic-district.htm).

Silos and Smokestacks National Heritage Area

State: Iowa

Description: This vast region of Iowa includes remnants of America's tallgrass prairie and still grows crops on the most fertile soil in the world; here, you'll find much of the history of American agriculture and the ways in which it's been revolutionized over the past several decades.

Sample Attractions:
- Living History Farms
- John Deere Tractor & Engine Museum
- Iowa's Dairy Center
- Effigy Mounds National Monument

Agriculture is at the heart of much of American history, culture, and economy, and Silos and Smokestacks National Heritage Area (Silos and Smokestacks) preserves and tells this story. This is a big mission in a big place. Appropriately, the NHA is located in Iowa, a state synonymous with agriculture, and focuses on 37 counties in the northeastern part of the state, an area encompassing a staggering 21,000 squares miles. This is the heart of America's tallgrass prairie and some of the most fertile soil in the world spread across rolling terrain that breaks into hills, valleys, and bluffs as it approaches the Mississippi River. Though some readers may not have visited them, the names of these agriculturally based Iowa cites in the NHA will probably be familiar: Des Moines, Cedar Rapids, Davenport, Waterloo, Dubuque, and Iowa City.

Like Iowa's soils, the history of American agriculture is deep and fertile. First, 10,000 years ago came the glaciers depositing the soil that is the foundation of all agriculture. Shortly after, Native Americans began to farm the valleys and improve wildlife habitat by periodically burning upland prairies. Then came waves of European immigrants in the 1850s from all corners of Europe, using the provisions of the distinctly democratic American Homestead Act to divide the land into 160-acre farms (a "quarter section" of a square mile) and "improve" it by building a home and growing crops. This was historically hard work that justly earned

American farmers their legendary reputation for toughness and persistence. Of course, farming has evolved—indeed, has been revolutionized—over the last century and a half as small farms have been consolidated into larger ones, markets for agricultural products have globalized, equipment has been industrialized, farming practices have been modernized, and science and technology have improved the productivity of seeds.

Silos and Smokestacks tells this story through a network of sites, programs, events, and partner organizations scattered across the landscape and organized into six themes. "The Fertile Land" emphasizes the gift of rich topsoil, the black gold that is the foundation of the region's legendary agricultural heritage.

"Farmers and Families" pays tribute to the people who adopted the challenging agricultural lifestyle, one that demands long hours of hard work. The original pioneers tilled a virgin land with nothing more than horse power; ultimately dependent on themselves and the weather, they're the archetype of the American farming family.

The multiple ways in which farming has evolved is explored in the theme, "The Changing Farm." Examples include consolidation of small into larger farms, new and bigger machines, and evolving consumer preferences. Paradoxically, many large farms have become specialized while many small family farms have diversified.

"Higher Yields: The Science and Technology of Agriculture" celebrates the remarkable advances in farming, including the steel plow, the tractor, agricultural universities and extension services, genetic engineering, and food processing and preservation.

Systems that produce, transform, and move farm products from field to table have been revolutionized from small-scale local enterprises into multi-billion-dollar, multi-national industries. Examples include John Deere, Quaker Oats, Archer-Daniels-Midland Company (ADM), Pioneer, Cargill, Amana, and Maytag, and this is the focus of the theme "From Farm to Factory: Agribusiness in Iowa."

While farmers are characteristically independent, they've joined together in effective ways when the need arises; fluctuating market prices and public policy that affects agriculture are examples of this common need. In these cases, groups such as the Grange and Farm Bureau have been effective in helping shape local, national, and international agricultural policy, and this theme is entitled "Organizing for Agriculture: Policies and Politics."

Silos and Smokestacks was established in 1996, though it was originally called America's Agricultural and Industrial Heritage Partnership and was under the auspices of the US Department of Agriculture. Shortly after this, it became like other NHAs, an affiliated area of the National Park Service. The NHA is administered by a non-profit organization that goes by the same name. Silos and Smokestacks works with more than 100 partner organizations that make up the heritage area, each telling a unique agriculturally related story and promoting heritage-based tourism in the region. Related activities include educational programs for schools, historic preservation, flood assessments, and supporting food security through heritage plants and breeding exchanges.

Attractions

This very large NHA includes an equally large and diverse set of attractions, including dairy farms, vineyards, museums, and tractor assembly plants. Of course, it also includes the iconic landscape of the Great Plains, the Mississippi River, and a network of farming communities. Here are just a few examples of Silos and Smokestacks' attractions.

Living History Farms

For more than 50 years, Living History Farms has been educating, entertaining, and connecting people to Midwestern rural life through hands-on, interactive experiences. The site includes three working farms and the historic 1876 town of Walnut Hill. This outdoor museum recreates the daily routines of 300 years of agricultural history.

John Deere Tractor & Engine Museum

The site of the first Deere factory is now part of an impressive museum featuring a collection of John Deere equipment, artifacts, and interactive exhibits. See the evolution of farming from "horse drawn to horsepower." Grip the handles of a simple steel plow and test your strength against real horsepower.

Amana Colonies

The Amana Colonies are a group of seven German-American settlements established in Iowa in the mid-1800s. They were inspired by religious beliefs and operated in a communal fashion. Now a National Historic Landmark, they invite several forms of tourism, including their historic agricultural way of life, a museum, restaurants, and shops.

Living History Farms includes three working farms that educate visitors about 300 years of Iowa agriculture.

Iowa's Dairy Center

This popular attraction tells the story of Iowa's dairy farms, including modern farming practices, caring for animals, and protecting the environment. See cows being milked at parlor and robotic facilities, visit the freestall barn where cows live, pet calves, and visit the Dairy Museum.

Effigy Mounds National Monument

The unit of the National Park System includes more than 200 Native American mounds, remnants of a prior civilization. The monument includes 14 miles of hiking trails that feature the mounds, wooded bluffs, tallgrass prairies, and scenic overlooks of the Upper Mississippi River Valley.

Scenic Byways

Since Silos and Smokestacks is so large, driving can be an ideal way to appreciate it. Several scenic byways meander through the area and the granddaddy is the Great River Road which lives up to its name: a 3,000-mile National Scenic Byway that follows the course of the Mississippi River from Minnesota to the Gulf of Mexico. Of course the section of road through Silos and Smokestacks is considerably shorter. There are also several state scenic byways including Historic Hills, Grant Road, Lincoln Highway Heritage, Iowa Valley, Driftless Area, River Bluffs, and Delaware Crossing.

Herbert Hoover National Historic Site

Born in West Branch, Iowa, and raised as an orphan, Herbert Hoover went on to be president of the United States. His childhood helped him learn the values of community, hard work, honesty, and usefulness to others. The site includes his birthplace cottage, schoolhouse, Friends Meetinghouse, and the Presidential Library and Museum.

National Mississippi River Museum and Aquarium

This museum, aquarium, and science center focuses on the Mississippi River and includes terrestrial and aquatic environments of this great American river and its watershed. The facility is an affiliate of the Smithsonian Institution.

Neal Smith Wildlife Refuge

A tallgrass prairie and oak savanna reconstruction project, this site offers scenic views of over 5,000 acres of tallgrass prairie and is home to herds of bison and elk, grassland birds, and numerous other species; it features the Prairie Learning and Visitor Center.

Indian Creek Nature Center

Explore miles of trails through lovingly restored prairie, woodland, and wetlands, and enjoy the area's innovative Amazing Space visitor center.

Iowa is bordered on the east by the Mississippi River, and the National Mississippi River Museum and Aquarium tells the story of this great American river.

Neal Smith Wildlife Refuge includes a restored tallgrass prairie and a resident herd of bison.

African American Museum of Iowa

This statewide museum traces Iowa's African American history from its origins in western Africa to the present, including slavery, the Civil War, the Underground Railroad, segregation, and the Civil Rights Movement.

Norman Borlaug Boyhood Home and Heritage Farm

The "Father of the Green Revolution," Dr. Borlaug developed revolutionary changes to agriculture through genetic engineering.

See his humble boyhood home, including farm buildings, fields, and his one-room schoolhouse.

For more information about Silos and Smokestacks and to help plan your visit, see the area's official website (silosandsmokestacks.org) and the website of the National Park Service (nps.gov/places/silos-and-smokestacks-national-heritage-area.htm).

South Carolina National Heritage Corridor

State: South Carolina

Description: In a stroke of brilliance, this NHA was created in the form of a broad 320-mile cross section of the state that runs from the Appalachian Mountains to the sea; its long history features the plantation era when rice and cotton were grown with the labor of slaves, and the Revolutionary and Civil Wars.

Sample Attractions:
- Chattooga National Wild and Scenic River
- Edisto River
- Historic Plantations
- Fort Sumter and Fort Moultrie National Historical Park

South Carolina is a geographically diverse state with a long, eventful history, making it an attractive and engaging region to live in and visit. The state is generally recognized as having three geographic features. The Blue Ridge region in the western part of the state is defined by the low mountains of the southern Appalachian Mountain Range.

At 3,560 feet, Sassafras Mountain is the highest. Most of this region is forested and marked by whitewater rivers flowing out of the mountains.

The Piedmont region lies directly east of the Blue Ridge and has considerably less topographic relief. Though the area was once agricultural, farming has diminished, and the region is now generally reforested in loblolly pine, the basis of the state's timber industry. The eastern extent of the Piedmont is defined by a fall line, a steep drop where rivers flow onto the Coastal Plain. These quickly flowing rivers were an important economic asset in the 19th century when they were used to generate the power needed to run textile and other mills.

The large Atlantic Coastal Plain extends from the Piedmont to the ocean and is generally flat. Historically, it has supported agricultural development, first by Native Americans and then more heavily for cotton and other crops associated with the plantation era of the state. The eastern extent of the region is marked by salt marshes, estuaries, natural harbors, and coastal islands; this area is a popular retirement and tourism destination.

The state's history begins with the very long presence by many tribes of Native Americans, estimated to be present for as long as 40,000 years. At the time of European arrival, Cherokee and Catawba were the primary tribes; they grew crops such as corn and beans, harvested oysters and fish, hunted deer, and gathered nuts and fruit. The Spanish and French were the first Europeans to attempt to settle the area, but they were generally unsuccessful. In 1670, English settlers arrived from Barbados at what they called Charles Towne with indentured servants and African American slaves. This would be the birthplace of the modern-day Carolinas and the beginning of the plantation system in the American South. Shortly after, the British claimed much of the southeastern region of the United States and it was then that the slave trade flourished, first with Native Americans and then with African and Caribbean people. Large plantations growing rice and later cotton developed in the Coastal Plain and Piedmont regions.

Much of the Revolutionary War was fought in South Carolina; the state was invaded by the British and there was conflict between patriots and loyalists. Of course, the state was also affected dramatically by the Civil War; South Carolina was the first state to secede from the Union. Confederates attacked the Union's Fort Sumter in Charleston Harbor in April of 1861, marking the beginning of the war, and much of the state's infrastructure, including its plantations, was destroyed. South Carolina is now a modern state with a diversified economy that includes agriculture (tobacco, poultry, cotton, dairy, rice, and swine), military bases, industry (textiles, paper, and automobiles), and tourism. The state has a long and complicated history with its struggle over race relations.

In 1996, Congress established the South Carolina National Heritage Corridor (South Carolina) to honor the diverse heritage of the state. In a stroke of brilliance, the NHA was created in the form of a broad 320-mile cross section of the state that runs from the Appalachian Mountains to the sea, encompassing 17 counties. South Carolina is managed by South Carolina National Heritage Corridor, Inc., a non-profit group that partners with the National Park Service and other governmental, private, and non-profit groups. The objectives of South Carolina are to help protect the natural and cultural resources of the state, to tell the story of South Carolina to its residents and visitors, and to help expand the state's heritage-based tourism industry in a sustainable manner.

Attractions

This large NHA celebrates the distinctive natural and cultural history of South Carolina by means of a grand cross section of the state. Travel through historic sites and natural areas, by car, on foot, or in a canoe to appreciate this state that is both historic and contemporary.

Chattooga National Wild and Scenic River

The Chattooga River begins in mountainous North Carolina and travels approximately 50 miles to Lake Tugaloo; throughout most of its course, it forms the border between South Carolina and Georgia. The river drops steeply, making it one of the most spectacular free-flowing rivers in the Southeast and is coveted by white-water boaters and anglers. The Chattooga was designated a national wild and scenic river in 1974.

Edisto River

The Edisto is the longest free-flowing blackwater river in the nation. The riverbanks showcase the remarkable forests of massive oaks draped in Spanish moss and the country's largest old-growth groves of tupelo-cypress trees, some more than a thousand years old. Adventurers can paddle the 250-mile length of the river; the 56-mile section

The Edisto River is the longest free-flowing blackwater river in the nation.

Magnolia Plantation and Gardens was founded by the Drayton family in 1676 and features a remarkable 464 acres of gardens.

known as Edisto Canoe and Kayak Trail runs between Colleton and Given's Ferry State Parks and is popular. The river runs through the 15,000-acre Francis Beidler Forest, a National Audubon Society sanctuary renown for birding. A 1.75-mile boardwalk shows off this pristine ecosystem that has been untouched for millennia.

Charles Pinckney National Historic Site

This unit of the National Park System tells the story of Charles Pickney, an author and signer of the US Constitution. Twenty-eight acres of his coastal plantation, Snee Farm, are preserved and his life of public service is documented. The history of slavery on South Carolina plantations is also addressed.

Historic Plantations

South Carolina includes several historic plantations; like all southern plantations, they tell the story of a way of life and a powerful economy, but this history is tempered with the inhumanity of slavery. Magnolia Plantation and Gardens was founded by the Drayton family in 1676 and is known for its

extensive and remarkable 464 acres of gardens; the site is on the National Register of Historic Places. Middleton Place Plantation includes museum houses, working stables, lush gardens, and agricultural fields. McLeod Plantation Historic Site includes a Georgian-style home that was constructed in the 1850s as part of a large, cotton-growing plantation. Touring this historic site offers tangible evidence of the pre-Civil War southern lifestyle and economy, but the site is also a place of conscience.

South Carolina State Botanical Gardens

The 295-acre site is described by its owners as "a refuge of life," conserving representative examples of the region's plants, animals, minerals, and associated culture.

Fort Sumter and Fort Moultrie National Historical Park

This unit of the National Park System tells the story of the important role that Charleston played in the American Revolution and the American Civil War. Fort Moultrie heroically fought off an initial attack by the

British Navy during the Revolutionary War and Fort Sumter was the focus of the first battle of the Civil War.

Jocassee Gorges Wilderness Area

The large Blue Ridge Escapement marks the sharp boundary between the Blue Ridge geographic region of the state and the lower Piedmont region. Here, the land slopes steeply and mountain streams have cut a series of dramatic gorges. *National Geographic* has named the gorges "one of the last great places on earth." The wilderness area offers lots of hiking.

Overmountain Victory National Historic Trail

This unit of the National Park System is a long-distance trail that stretches 330 miles through four states (Virginia, Tennessee, North and South Carolina) commemorating the American Revolution. The trail traces the route used by patriot militia during the pivotal Kings Mountain campaign of 1780. Follow the campaign by utilizing a Commemorative Motor Route which uses existing state highways marked with the distinctive trail logo, or enjoy 87 miles of walkable pathways.

> For more information about South Carolina and to help plan your visit, see the area's official website (scnhc.org) and the website of the National Park Service (nps.gov/places/south-carolina -national-heritage-corridor.htm).

South Park National Heritage Area

State: Colorado

Description: A lovely and historic basin surrounded by the high-elevation Rocky Mountains, South Park NHA celebrates its western frontier period, sprawling and diverse landscape, early mining days, historic ranching culture, and plentiful outdoor recreation opportunities.

Sample Attractions:

- Historic Towns of Fairplay and Alma
- Mosquito Range
- Lost Creek Scenic Area National Natural Landmark
- South Park City

First, the obvious question: Is South Park National Heritage Area (South Park) related to the popular and award-winning (but irreverent) animated TV show, *South Park?* Well, yes and no. The creators of the TV show are from Colorado and modeled the set after the (real) South Park region of the state; fans of the show will probably recognize some of the local buildings and the snowcapped mountains. But the real South Park region is a lovely and historic basin surrounded by mountains in central Colorado. South Park is a nearly 1,800-square-mile area that preserves the spirit of America's western frontier period, including its sprawling and diverse natural landscape, its early mining days, the historic ranching culture, and its modern tourism-oriented economy.

South Park is a vast and fertile grassland basin measuring approximately 50 miles long and 35 miles wide in the geographic center of Colorado. The floor of the basin is about 8,500 feet in elevation with surrounding mountains that rise to more than 14,000 feet. The natural landscape is varied and includes a vast valley, mountain peaks, the Middle and South Forks of the South Platte River and other streams (some of which disappear into the ground), canyons, interesting geologic formations, ancient bristlecone pine trees, expansive wetlands and fens, herds of elk, and the endangered lynx. Portions of two large wilderness areas are included in the NHA.

The South Park region has a long history of honoring its natural and cultural heritage. South Park was established in 2009 and is managed by the government of Park County, Colorado, in partnership with the South Park NHA Advisory Board and many other community organizations. The human history of the area began approximately 12,000 years ago with a Native American presence, particularly the Ute Tribe who used the area on a seasonal basis for hunting. Spanish and French explorers and trappers also used the area for its abundant natural resources. However, American settlers poured into the area in response to the Pikes Peak Gold Rush in 1859, and the area's ghost towns and mining camps are reminders of this colorful history. Rich deposits of other minerals such as silver, zinc, lead, molybdenum, uranium, rhodochrosite (the state mineral), and coal are also found in the area. Cattle ranching (some ranches raised sheep as well) sprung up as a way to feed the miners and prospered in response to the area's rich grasses with an unusually high amount of protein; several large ranches are still present, some of which offer hospitality services for hunters, anglers, and visitors who wish to sample the ranching

lifestyle. Railroad service was established in the latter part of the 19th century to carry ore for processing, cattle to market, and early tourists to and from the region. Today the area's remaining colorful western towns, such as Fairplay and Alma, are centers of tourism activity and offer appropriate visitor facilities and services.

Attractions

The large and diverse region of South Park offers lots of attractions for visitors. Driving tours of this lovely valley are popular with stops at the region's colorful western towns. More active vacations are also available that include hiking, climbing, fishing, hunting, camping, backpacking, and four-wheel driving. The following suggestions will get you started.

Fairplay

The town of Fairplay was established in 1859 at the junction of Beaver Creek and the South Platte River, and was a supply center for the nearby mining camps. (Local lore suggests that the town's unusual name is derived from a gunfight that followed appropriate "rules" of such events.) After the mines played out, the region turned to ranching and then tourism as its economic base. Among anglers, it's known as the Trout Fishing Capital of Colorado.

Alma

Northwest of Fairplay is the town of Alma which once served as the ore-processing center of the South Park region; it was settled in the mid-1800s. The commercial district served as an entertainment area for the surrounding region. Visit the town cemetery

The Mosquito Range includes five mountains that rise above 14,000 feet.

The historic town of Alma was settled in the mid-1800s and served as an entertainment area for the surrounding region.

for a glimpse into pioneer life. The Alma area attracts lots of hikers, bikers, and four-wheel-drive enthusiasts.

Mosquito Range

The Mosquito Mountains are an especially high range known for five mountains that rise above 14,000 feet, the magic number for those who wish to climb all the "fourteeners" in Colorado. The area was the ancestral hunting ground for the nomadic Ute people, but white settlers moved here during the Colorado mining boom of the 1850s, giving rise to the historic towns of Fairplay and Alma. The area is now a mecca for hiking and climbing.

Lost Creek Scenic Area National Natural Landmark

This interesting and strikingly beautiful area is part of the Pike National Forest and features unusual rock formations, including spires, pinnacles, narrow ridges, and steep, narrow gorges. Namesake Lost Creek

The region's Lost Creek Wilderness offers lots of hiking and backpacking.

disappears from the surface and reappears several times. This nearly 17,000-acre site is part of the large Lost Creek Wilderness and offers great hiking and backpacking.

Paris Mill

The Paris Mill is located in the Mosquito Mountain Range at an altitude of 11,000 feet and was constructed in 1895 to process ore from the Paris Mine. It operated sporadically until 1937 and was modified many times to increase its effectiveness and efficiency. Over the past decade, the mill is enjoying a phased renovation and is one of the few intact mills that represent this period of Colorado history.

Como Roundhouse, Railroad Depot, and Hotel Complex

A narrow-gauge railroad began service to Como, Colorado, in 1879; the town is primarily a ghost town now, though portions of it survive and have been renovated, and a few hundred people live in the historic town. The Como Roundhouse, a large stone structure built by Italian masons and used to turn locomotives around, is the most distinctive feature. The depot now serves as a museum

and the South Park Hotel is open for business. This collection of buildings and associated equipment are listed on the National Register of Historic Places.

Horseshoe Mountain

This nearly 14,000-foot mountain is in the Mosquito Range of the Rocky Mountains near the town of Leadville. From the east, this peak is a landmark and features a large, distinctive glacial cirque. The mountain offers a popular 7.3-mile hike with great views.

Nearly 14,000-foot Horseshoe Mountain features a distinctive glacial cirque.

This narrow gage railroad began service to Como in 1879 and is famous for the large stone Como Roundhouse.

Old Park County Courthouse

This distinctive public building was constructed in 1874, two years before Colorado achieved statehood. Located in the town of Fairplay, the building is constructed of locally sourced red sandstone and includes Italianate design features. The building is listed on the National Register of Historic Places.

Eleven Mile Canyon

This multi-use recreation area in the southeast corner of South Park includes a large reservoir (Lake George) and Eleven Mile Canyon below the dam. The lake offers outstanding fishing, boating, and camping while Eleven Mile Canyon offers hiking and backpacking along the South Platte River.

South Park City

This museum is a remarkable representation of a Colorado mining town in the last half of the 19th century. Forty-four authentic buildings are filled with over 60,000 artifacts of the times. Seven of the buildings are on their original sites and the others have been moved from abandoned camps and ghost towns in South Park.

For more information about South Park and to help plan your visit, see the area's official website (southparkheritage.org) and the website of the National Park Service (nps.gov/places/south-park-national-heritage-area.htm).

The outdoor museum of South Park City sits on the edge of the town of Fairplay; the museum is a facsimile of a historic Colorado mining town.

Susquehanna National Heritage Area

State: Pennsylvania

Description: The Susquehanna is one of the oldest rivers in the world, and at 444 miles, is the longest river in the eastern United States; it has a long and storied history that includes a transportation route for Native Americans and European-American settlers, the iron industry, the Revolutionary and Civil Wars, and the Underground Railroad; today, the river and surrounding lands are valued for their scenic beauty, as rich agricultural areas, and outdoor recreation opportunities.

Sample Attractions:
- Zimmerman Center for Heritage
- Captain John Smith Chesapeake National Historic Trail
- Susquehannock State Park
- Susquehanna River Water Trail

The Susquehanna River is one of the oldest rivers in the world, and at 444 miles, is the longest river in the eastern United States Its headwaters are in Cooperstown, New York, and the river flows generally south and east, through Pennsylvania and into the Chesapeake Bay in Maryland. The river's watershed is an impressive 27,500 square miles, drains nearly half the land area of Pennsylvania, and carries half the fresh water that flows into the Chesapeake Bay, the largest estuary in the United States. "Susquehanna" is derived from the Len'api (Native American) term meaning "Oyster River"; early Native Americans farmed oysters near the river's mouth and left shell middens at their villages. More recent Native Americans, the Susquehannock, were known by European-Americans, participated in early fur trading, and traveled the river in their large dugout canoes.

The river and surrounding lands in Pennsylvania were an important gateway to the American frontier during the 18th and 19th centuries. The river allowed for transportation and trade for indigenous people and European-American settlers. York, Pennsylvania, sits 10 miles west of the river and was the temporary site of the Continental Congress during the Revolutionary War; this is where the Articles of Confederation were signed. The region was at the center of 19th-century conflicts over slavery and served as a major route of the Underground Railroad; the Susquehanna defined a travel route north for escaping enslavement and, though crossing the river could be challenging, arriving in Pennsylvania usually meant safety. The region was also a strategic location during the Civil War.

The region is also known for the iron industry that thrived in the last half of the 19th century. Iron furnaces were established along the river in the vicinity of Columbia, Marietta, and Wrightsville; the area was known as "the Pittsburg of the East" and the river and associated canals were a key to its success, carrying raw materials to the furnaces and shipping resulting "pig iron" (large

bars of iron that resembled sows and smaller bars that resembled pigs) to Philadelphia and other locations. Technological advances near the end of the century made it difficult to compete and the region's iron industry faded into the pages of history books.

The river and surrounding landscape in southeastern Pennsylvania have a long-standing reputation for their scenic beauty, rich agriculture, and home for Amish communities and other Plain People. The region is often described as "a ribbon of scenic and historic landscapes and communities" and attracts both residents and visitors. The river offers outstanding opportunities for outdoor recreation, including boating, fishing, hiking, and wildlife viewing.

The Susquehanna is nationally known for two great natural phenomena: spawning shad and the Atlantic Flyway. Sometimes called "America's Founding Fish" and "poor man's salmon," shad migrate in the millions from the ocean to the Susquehanna where they swim upstream and spawn. Native Americans relied on them as part of their diet as did settlers and their descendants. The fish were harvested in baskets, nets, and weirs, and extreme competition among fishers led to violence, called "The Shad Wars." Eventually, dams constructed on the river and over-fishing led to the decline of the species.

The Atlantic Flyway is the other grand natural phenomenon of the region. This flyway is the route of migratory birds as they travel to southern locations in the fall and northern locations in the spring. On these remarkable journeys of as long as 3,000 miles, the birds need stopover points that offer rest and food, and the Susquehanna and adjacent lands are critical locations. The Conejohela Flats in the southern region of the Susquehanna is a good example of the type of sites that need to be protected.

A decade-long movement to establish a National Heritage Area in the region came to fruition in 2019 when legislation was passed by Congress and signed into law by the president creating Susquehanna National Heritage Area (Susquehanna). The area is managed by a non-profit organization of the same name that works with a host of partners including the Pennsylvania Department of Conservation and Natural Resources and the National Park Service's Chesapeake Bay Office and Captain John Smith Chesapeake National Historic Trail. Susquehanna includes the historic and scenic landscapes of York and Lancaster Counties in Pennsylvania. The area is also a Pennsylvania Heritage Area and includes the Susquehanna Riverlands Conservation Landscape, another state program.

Attractions

Susquehanna features the river, historic and vibrant river towns, historic sites, agricultural landscapes, and outdoor recreation opportunities. The NHA has developed websites, maps, guides, and interpretive exhibits to enhance the experience of visiting the area.

Zimmerman Center for Heritage

This historic riverfront home built in the mid-18th century serves as the offices for the NHA and as the official visitor contact station for the Captain John Smith Chesapeake National Historic Trail (see below). The center includes the Visions of the Susquehanna River Art Collection, Susquehannock Indian

The Zimmerman Center for Heritage is housed in a historic riverfront home.

artifacts, a put-in point for canoes and kayaks, exhibits of area history, and a trail to nearby Native Lands County Park. The home also hosts River Discovery Boat Tours during the summer season (see below) and an annual heritage lecture series and guided tours.

Captain John Smith Chesapeake National Historic Trail

This is the nation's first water-based National Historic Trail and explores the routes that Englishman John Smith took in the Chesapeake Bay and Susquehanna River regions between 1607 and 1609. The trail network is more than 3,000 miles and focuses on the natural environment Smith found and the 17th-century Indian cultures he encountered. Some of the land-based places he explored are accessible by car.

River Discovery Boat Tours

Susquehanna staff guide visitors on a 70-minute tour of the river that describes its rich natural and cultural history. Participants start their cruise at the Zimmerman Center and experience the joy of being on the water, hearing stories of river-related history, and viewing beautiful scenery and wildlife.

Columbia is one of several colorful riverside towns with historic buildings, parks, and local foods.

The Susquehanna River is one of the oldest in the world, and at 444 miles, is the longest river in the eastern United States.

Columbia Crossing River Trails Center

Located in Columbia River Park on the Susquehanna River, Columbia Crossing River Trails Center is managed by the NHA for the river town of Columbia as the primary visitor information center for exploring Susquehanna. The facility includes exhibits, programs, a power and paddle boat launch area, picnic pavilion, restrooms, and views of the historic Veterans Memorial Bridge. Canoe, kayak, and bike rentals are provided by a local outfitter. Columbia Crossing is also the southern trailhead for the 14-mile Northwest Lancaster County River Trail (see below).

Northwest Lancaster County River Trail

This 14-mile paved trail follows the route of the historic Pennsylvania Main Line Canal, tracing the Susquehanna River northwest from Columbia to Falmouth.

Susquehannock State Park

This 224-acre state park offers great views of the Susquehanna River and is a good

The river town of Wrightsville marks the northern terminus of the historic Susquehanna and Tidewater Canal.

location to learn the history of the Susquehannock. The park features several miles of trails and picnic facilities.

Historic Towns

Susquehanna is home to several colorful and historic river towns that offer parks, historic sites, exhibits, art galleries, and local foods. Favorite towns include Columbia (the site of Wright's Ferry, the first commercial river crossing), Marietta (the town's historic

A historic postcard shows the Susquehanna River and surrounding agricultural landscape.

district is listed on the National Register of Historic Places), and Wrightsville (the northern terminus of the historic Susquehanna and Tidewater Canal).

Susquehanna River Water Trail

This water-based trail follows the river for 400 miles, but the lower 53-mile section is managed by the NHA and is designated a National Recreation Trail. The trail passes through a great variety of natural and built landscapes and includes Conejohela Flats (with great birding in the spring and fall). There are more than 30 access points. The NHA has developed water trail maps and a guide.

For more information about Susquehanna and to help plan your visit, see the area's official website (susquehannaheritage .org) and the website of the National Park Service (nps.gov/places/susquehanna -national-heritage-area.htm).

Tennessee Civil War National Heritage Area

State: Tennessee

Description: Since Tennessee sits on the border between the North and South, attitudes toward slavery were deeply divided in Tennessee and many Civil War battles were fought in the state; today, this NHA tells this complex story and examines America's long-standing struggle with race relations and the meaning of freedom.

Sample Attractions:

- National Battlefields and Military Parks
- Museums
- Andrew Johnson National Historic Site
- Tennessee Civil War Trails and Driving Tours

Given the wide geographic scope and foundational importance of the Civil War, it's not unreasonable that it might take a whole state to adequately address its many dimensions. Of course, elements of the war are told in a number of National Heritage Areas across the country, but Tennessee has struggled with the tension over slavery and freedom more than most states. Many Civil War battles were fought in the state—second only to Virginia—the lives of many Tennesseans were lost in the war, and the post-Civil War Reconstruction period was overseen by President Andrew Johnson, a state resident. Those are just some of the reasons the entire state was designated as Tennessee Civil War National Heritage Area (Tennessee Civil War) by Congress in 1996. The NHA is managed by Middle Tennessee State University's Center for Historic Preservation. Tennessee Civil War has taken its mission to heart, preserving much of the physical evidence of the war and interpreting its broader context, including the period leading up to the war, the post-war period of Reconstruction, and the legacy of the war for all Americans as the nation continues its contemporary struggle with race relations and the meaning of freedom.

Since it sits on the border between the North and South, attitudes toward slavery were deeply divided in Tennessee. Part of this ambivalence was a function of the state's varying topography. In east Tennessee, mountains and valleys allowed for only small, family farms, and most residents condemned slavery. But in the western region of the state, the terrain is much flatter and lends itself more easily to plantations and slave labor, and it's estimated that there were more slaves living here than free residents. Though there was concern over slavery in some parts of the state, slaves were treated especially harshly. In the 1830s, some plantation owners developed a fear and mistrust of slaves based on a highly publicized slave rebellion in Virginia. In response, Tennessee didn't allow free blacks to enter and live in the state and a constitutional amendment took away the right of free black men to vote. An 1836 law severely punished anyone who encouraged resistance to slavery. In 1860, slaves made up a large percentage of the state's population, and slave trading in market towns like Nashville and Memphis was highly profitable. Nevertheless, the Underground Railroad operated in the eastern part of the state, and the Quaker presence here spoke out strongly against enslavement.

Perhaps the most defining quality of Tennessee Civil War and the many partners that manage the area is the comprehensive treatment of the war, from the deep divisions among Tennesseans in the decades preceding the war to the legacy of the war for all Americans. As noted above, the attitudes toward slavery were at least partially defined by the state's geography, economy, and religion.

Of course, the most obvious period of Civil War history is the war itself, the armed conflict between the 11 southern states that formed the Confederacy and the majority of states that remained loyal to the Union. Tennessee's pivotal location at the juncture of the North and South, and its western border along the strategic Mississippi River, led to the very high proportion of battles in the state. President Lincoln called Tennessee "the keystone of the Southern arch." Civil War battlefields are well represented in the state, both in number and importance. Historians count nearly 3,000 military engagements here, including the infamous battles at Shiloh, Stones River, Fort Donelson, Chickamauga/

Chattanooga, and Franklin. Tennessee fell quickly to Union forces and many free blacks and escaped slaves joined the Union forces; 20,000 African Americans from Tennessee fought for the Union. In the end, 64,333 Confederate soldiers and 58,521 Union soldiers perished in the state.

Of course, the war had other important consequences for Tennessee: the lives of residents were severely disrupted; farms, crops, and infrastructure were destroyed; women were left to manage farms and businesses; women also aided the war effort as nurses, weavers, and spies, and former slave women worked as cooks and laundresses for the Union Army. Cities grew as refugees and ex-slaves sought refuge from the war.

The war was followed by a decade-long period of Reconstruction in which efforts were made to rebuild the state's economic infrastructure. Tennessee was the first of the southern states to rejoin the Union. Freed slaves established communities and constructed churches, schools, and cemeteries. First Beale Street Baptist Church in Memphis is the state's oldest surviving African American church edifice, and Jubilee Hall of Fisk University in Nashville is the nation's first permanent building for the education of black citizens. Many black Tennesseans commemorated Emancipation Day with celebrations in communities across the state. However, the reality of the years after the war saw continuing discrimination against African Americans, including laws designed to limit their right to vote and violence against them by the Ku Klux Klan and others.

Of course, America continues its centuries-long struggle with race relations and defining freedom in a way that extends to everyone. Tennessee Civil War tells the story of the Civil War and the history that surrounds it; visiting this area is a good way to stimulate our thinking about freedom in our contemporary society. Perhaps this would be the best way to pay our respects to the thousands of soldiers who died here.

Attractions

Using an extensive network of historic sites, driving routes, and museums, the story of the Civil War is told from the historical perspectives of native Tennesseans, enslaved African Americans, and soldiers in both the Confederate and Union armies. This is a long and foundational story, so plan to spend time here.

National Battlefields and Military Parks

Several of the most well-known battlefields are units of the National Park System. For example, Shiloh National Military Park

Fort Donelson National Battlefield includes the Civil War Altar of Remembrance.

Stones River Battlefield was the site of one of the bloodiest conflicts of the Civil War.

Tennessee State Museum includes exhibits on the Civil War and its effects on the state.

is large and includes several units, some of them detached. Of course, this military park includes the important Shiloh Battlefield, but also the site of the Siege and Battle of Corinth and a US National Cemetery. The park is a National Historic Landmark and includes Shiloh Indian Mounds. The Union victory at Fort Donelson National Battlefield was celebrated by Brigadier General Ulysses S. Grant when he wrote, "Fort Donelson will hereafter be marked in Capitals on the maps of our United Country." Stones River Battlefield was one of the bloodiest conflicts of the Civil War, but led to important military and political gains for the Union. The battle to control the strategic city of Chattanooga, known as the "Gateway to the Deep South," was fought in two locations. The Confederates were victorious at nearby Chickamauga, but the battle at Chattanooga two months later was won by Union forces.

Museums

Tennessee Civil War includes several state, regional, and local museums that help interpret and illustrate the Civil War and related issues. For example, Tennessee State Museum opened in Nashville in 2018 and presents a comprehensive story of the state, including, of course, exhibits on the Civil War and its effects. The Heritage Center of Murfreesboro and Rutherford County tells engaging stories about the area with a special emphasis on Murfreesboro as a Civil War Battlefield and key federal occupation base. The Museum of East Tennessee History is located in the historic district of Knoxville and tells the story of the Civil War as it affected this important region of the state.

Andrew Johnson National Historic Site

Andrew Johnson, a Tennessee native, was president of the United States immediately after the Civil War and helped guide the

The town of Greenville features the home of President Andrew Johnson, who helped guide the post–Civil War period of Reconstruction.

There's a large monument to Georgia soldiers at Chickamauga & Chattanooga National Military Park.

period of Reconstruction. His disagreements with Congress led to foundational arguments over the Constitution. This site is a unit of the National Park System in Greenville and includes a visitor center and his tailer shop, the Homestead (his home before and after his presidency) and the national cemetery where he was buried (wrapped in an American flag and with a copy of the US Constitution).

Tennessee Civil War Trails and Driving Tours

Civil War sites throughout the state are marked and interpreted by 250 historic markers that can be connected to form a network of Civil War Trails. This program is accompanied by a statewide driving tour (found online at: tnvacation.com) that features the markers and connects with other Civil War-related states. Tennessee Civil War has also developed a number of special interest driving tours that focus on the Civil War and related topics; these tours are found on the NHA's website (see below).

For more information about Tennessee Civil War and to help plan your visit, see the area's official website (tncivilwar .org) and the website of the National Park Service (nps.gov/places/tennessee -civil-war-national-heritage-area.htm).

The Last Green Valley National Heritage Corridor

States: Connecticut and Massachusetts

Description: This island of green tucked into the great urban corridor that connects Washington, DC, and Boston is the heart of this rural NHA; the area includes forests and farmlands and a string of 35 historic and attractive towns.

Sample Attractions:

- Old Sturbridge Village
- Route 169 National Scenic Byway
- Farms/Farmers' Markets
- Museums and Historic Sites

Perhaps the very best name among all the national heritage areas, The Last Green Valley National Heritage Corridor (The Last Green Valley) is an alluring reference to the island of green in the great urban corridor that connects Washington, DC, and Boston. But the valley is both green (for all the right reasons that you might expect) and black—a nod to the unusually dark night skies this region enjoys. In fact, this "blank spot on the map" is one of the things that has brought attention to the region that's the focus of the NHA. See for yourself: Google a large-scale photo of the northeastern United States at night and you'll see it—an expanse of black that covers the northeastern corner of

Connecticut and south-central Massachusetts. Of course, green and black go together in this context, don't they? They're two sides of the same coin, a function of the remarkably rural and undeveloped character of this place. In the words of those who live here, it's "green by day and dark by night." It's also well known as a rural island in the midst of the most urbanized region in the nation and only an hour's drive from three of New England's four largest urban areas.

This is a large area of geography—1,100 square miles—defined by the Quinebaug and Shetucket River systems and the hills that surround them; these rolling hills in the southern part of the Corridor become more rugged in the north. The NHA includes a string of 35 historic towns, but forests and farmlands make up 84 percent of the area. The Last Green Valley was established by Congress in 1994 and is managed by the non-profit group The Last Green Valley, Inc., but the area is really a grand partnership of organizations—public, private, and non-profit. The Last Green Valley grew out of a process that started in the 1980s when the region began to experience the inevitable pressures of economic development. Citizens' groups responded with a call to action, and the National Park Service prepared a study and report in 1988 that led to creation of an initial Quinebaug and Shetucket Rivers Valley National Heritage Corridor in 1994. The NHA was expanded in 1999 through addition of several communities in Massachusetts and was renamed The Last Green Valley.

All places are affected by both nature and culture. Plate tectonics and the region's last glacial period of approximately 15,000 years ago laid the foundation for human

In the fall, The Last Green Valley turns to bright reds, yellows, and oranges.

occupation beginning 10,000 years ago. Native Americans lived here for thousands of years, and certainly left their imprint on the landscape. Over the last 300 years, European-Americans have altered the landscape more substantially. Forests were cut for timber and fuel, animals were hunted and trapped for furs and food, and intensive agriculture began to dominate the landscape. The region supplied goods and men for the Revolutionary War, while the Industrial Revolution brought water-powered mills that mass produced textiles and other consumer goods. Railroads were built to carry products to the expanding markets outside the region. But much of this industrial-scale development diminished as textile production moved out of New England and railroads were replaced by roads. Specialized agriculture (e.g., orchards, vineyards, pick-your-own businesses, farmers' markets) and a growing tourism industry now mark much of the region's economic base, and The Last Green Valley is designed to protect the attractive and appealing cultural landscape that's the foundation of the area's 21st-century future. And this is a gift to both residents and visitors.

Attractions

The Last Green Valley offers a wide array of attractions. Of course, the cultural landscape itself is the main attraction—a lovely land of rolling hills, clean waters, deep forests, progressive farms, historic towns, and a rural small-town lifestyle. Here's a sampling of some of the specific places and activities that make residents proud and draw so many visitors.

Museums and Historic Sites

The Last Green Valley is a historic landscape that's been shaped by humans over the last 10,000 years, but mostly over the last 300. The 35 towns in the NHA all offer interesting stories about this history. For example, Windham is known as the "Thread City" for its role in textile production and this story is told at the town's Mill Museum. Revolutionary War history is featured at Lebanon's Historical Society Museum and the Turnbull House & Wadsworth Stables. The Preston Historical Society has renovated the Long Society Meeting House, one of only a few of its kind left in New England. These are only examples of The Last Green Valley's 278 properties and historic districts on the National Register of Historic Places and its five National Historic Landmarks.

Old Sturbridge Village

Old Sturbridge Village is a 200-acre living-history museum that most people consider a "must-see" attraction. The museum depicts life in an early 19th-century rural New England village, featuring costumed historians, forty antique buildings, water-powered mills, and a working farm. Interactive facilities include carriage rides and a short river cruise.

A grand living-history museum, Old Sturbridge Village recreates life in an early 19th-century rural New England village.

Agriculture in The Last Green Valley has continued to evolve and now features specialized agriculture that lends itself to farmers' markets and pick-your-own opportunities.

Route 169 National Scenic Byway

Route 169 runs through much of the Connecticut section of The Last Green Valley and offers a 32-mile journey along what some say is the prettiest road in New England. This is storybook New England. The National Scenic Byway runs through a string of historic towns and features the scenic character of the landscape, including its rolling hills, historic towns, churches, stone walls, farms, forests, colonial village centers, farm stores, and industrial-era mill villages. Drive this road and you'll be convinced that the journey is often as important as the destination.

Farms/Farmers' Markets

Local farms and farmers' markets offers dozens of opportunities to find (and even pick) your own fresh produce and other products. Items include strawberries, heirloom vegetables, pumpkins, fresh milk, maple sugar, homestead cheese, honey, Christmas trees, free-range turkeys, wine, apples, and lots more.

Walking/Hiking

The Last Green Valley includes many state parks and other lands that offer lots of opportunities for walking and hiking that range from short nature trails to long-distance hikes. The "glamour" hike is the Air Line State Park Trail that follows the old railroad line for 55 miles. The Summit Trail to Mount Waddaquaduck is a popular two-mile trek that offers expansive views from the top. Go to the NHA's website (see below) for an on-line directory of hiking trails. Most of the region's 35 historic towns are best

Air Line State Park Trail follows an abandoned railroad bed for 55 miles of hiking and biking.

seen on foot, including the town greens. The Last Green Valley's "Spring Outdoors" and "Walktober" encourage residents and visitors to see the region on foot during these striking wildflower and fall foliage seasons.

Boating

The NHA's Quinebaug and Shetucket Rivers help to define The Last Green Valley, and these and other rivers and lakes offer great paddling adventures. The Quinebaug River National Recreation Water Trail features 45 miles of paddling, while the Shetucket River National Recreation Water Trail offers 20 miles and the Willimantic River National Recreation Water Trail offers another 22 miles. The NHA's website (see below) includes a paddle guide and other good references for these and other trips.

Festivals

Working with its partner organizations, The Last Green Valley region and its towns offer a number of festivals throughout the year that celebrate the region. Prominent examples include Spring Outdoors and Walktober (see above). Other examples include Harvest Tour (featuring local farms, orchards, vintners, brewers, and restaurants), South Woodstock's Woodstock Fair, Lapsley Orchard's Fall Harvest Festival, and Brooklyn's Fair. See The Last Green Valley website (see below) for these and more events.

Ranger Talks

It's unusual for NHAs to have rangers (much like all national parks do), but The Last Green Valley has a chief ranger on staff and a core of volunteer rangers to help cover the area. Rangers present programs to residents and visitors, much like national park rangers lead nature walks and campfire talks. Topics vary widely and include the forests of the area, how to avoid light pollution, the return of bald eagles, identifying flora and fauna, and infamous characters of the area. See the schedule of programs on The Last Green Valley website (see below).

For more information about The Last Green Valley and to help plan your visit, see the area's official website (thelast greenvalley.org) and the website of the National Park Service (nps.gov/qush /index.htm).

Upper Housatonic Valley National Heritage Area

States: Connecticut and Massachusetts
Description: This bistate NHA honors the lovely and historic Housatonic River and its surrounding valley; the area is known as a cradle of American culture, and for its rich deposits of iron, many 19th-century country estates, contributions to the Revolutionary War and democracy, and traditional New England towns.
Sample Attractions:
• Berkshire Museum
• Norman Rockwell Museum
• Historic Towns/Town Centers
• Performing Arts Heritage Trail

This multifaceted NHA in northwestern Connecticut and western Massachusetts is defined by the watershed of the Upper Housatonic River and the region's well-defined contributions to the natural and cultural history of New England and the

nation. It's been described as a singular geographic area that has an especially strong sense of place. It's a large NHA, particularly by eastern standards, including 60 miles of the Housatonic River, encompassing nearly 1,000 square miles, and including nearly 30 towns. The area is known for its scenic landscape that includes the river valley, the rolling hills of the Berkshires in Massachusetts and the Litchfield Hills of Connecticut, and traditional New England towns. Upper Housatonic Valley National Heritage Area (Upper Housatonic Valley) was established in 2006 and is managed by a non-profit group of the same name, though the group is generally called Housatonic Heritage. This group has many public, private, and non-profit partners that help administer the area.

Several themes define the distinctive character and features of Upper Housatonic Valley. First, the region has served as a cradle of American culture, nurturing and shaping enduring expressions of literature, art, architecture, music, dance, and theater. For example, Herman Melville wrote *Moby Dick* while living at Arrowhead in Pittsfield and Nathaniel Hawthorne wrote House of Seven Gables at Stockbridge. Other important authors associated with the area include Oliver Wendell Holmes, Sr., Henry Wadsworth Longfellow, Edith Wharton, and James Thurber. There are a number of prominent artists whose work is exhibited in local studios and museums; the most well-known is Norman Rockwell. These artists contributed to the reputation of the region as an area where humans can live in harmony with nature. The area is also known for its music and theater; examples include Tanglewood (summer home of the Boston Symphony

Orchestra) and the Berkshire Theater Festival (see attractions below).

A second theme is "cradle of industry." Much land in the NHA was cleared for agricultural use and the area's rich deposits of iron ore led to a landscape dotted with regional forges and furnaces that manufactured tools and armaments. Many trees were cut to fuel these furnaces and this forest clearing continued later for pulp and papermaking; by 1850, seventy-five percent of the area was deforested.

Third, historic events have helped shape the distinctive cultural landscape of the NHA. For example, in the late 19th century, wealthy entrepreneurs from New York built many country estates throughout the region, many of which still stand and some of which have been incorporated into public parks and forests such as October Mountain State Forest and Beartown State Forest, both in Connecticut, and Dennis Hill, Kent Falls, Macedonia Brook, Mohawk Mountain, and Campbell Falls in Connecticut.

A fourth theme of the region is its contributions to the Revolutionary War effort. The Sheffield Declaration drafted in 1773 at Colonel John Ashley's home in the region was an early document that enumerated grievances against the British. Militias from Ethan Allen's original home in northwest Connecticut joined Vermont's Green Mountain Boys in their decisive capture of Fort Ticonderoga in 1775. The region is sometimes referred to as "the arsenal of the revolution," as its iron forges purportedly produced nearly 80 percent of George Washington's canon.

A fifth theme addresses the development of democracy. Written in 1780, the Massachusetts State Constitution declared that all men are created "free and equal" and this was used by Sheffield black slave Elizabeth Freeman to successfully argue in court for her freedom. Massachusetts became the first state to abolish slavery in 1783. W. E. B. Du Bois was born in Great Barrington, Massachusetts, in 1868 and became an accomplished intellectual and writer, the first African American to earn a doctoral degree and a founder of the National Association for the Advancement of Colored People (NAACP).

Though not official, a sixth theme might be a long period of restoring and celebrating this important cultural landscape. Stockbridge, Massachusetts, originated the movement for community beautification when it established the nation's first village improvement society, the Laurel Hill Association, in 1853. More recently, much of the area's forests have been allowed to regenerate (the area is now 75 percent forested), the water quality of the Housatonic River is being restored, and historic sites have been preserved, all of which are important components of Housatonic Heritage and Upper Housatonic Valley.

Attractions

This large, bi-state NHA has lots to offer both residents and visitors. It's a large cultural landscape with dozens of historic villages and museums that tell much of the story of historic New England and the nation. But it's also a pleasing natural landscape organized around the lovely Upper Housatonic River and its surrounding hills, farms, and forests. Housatonic Heritage and its partners have established a series of themed routes

The Berkshire Museum was established as a "window on the world" for rural Berkshire County residents.

Norman Rockwell's painting *No Swimming* is one of his many illustrations of idealized American culture; explore this American icon at the Norman Rockwell Museum in Stockbridge.

that help guide visitors through the area in an informed way.

Berkshire Museum

The Berkshire Museum was established in the early 1900s as a "window on the world" for rural Berkshire County residents. This eclectic collection of nearly 40,000 objects ranges from local mineral specimens to Asian decorative arts.

Norman Rockwell Museum

Rockwell was a famous American painter and illustrator who celebrated idealized images of American culture. He's known most widely for cover illustrations for the popular 20th-century magazine, *The Saturday Evening Post*. He lived in Stockbridge for the last 25 years of his life, using this place and its people as subjects of his art. The Norman Rockwell Museum is located here.

Appalachian Trail

The iconic "AT" is a unit of the National Park System and runs 2,180 miles along the Appalachian Mountains. The trail was conceived in 1921 and completed in 1937. Look for the white blazes on trees and walk a few miles along the portion of the trail in this NHA.

Mount Greylock

At 3,489 feet, Mount Greylock is the highest point in Massachusetts. A road leads

Mount Greylock, served by trails and a road, is the highest point in Massachusetts and offers great views of the surrounding countryside.

Hancock Shaker Village, an open-air museum, interprets the life and work of this famous communitarian sect.

to its summit and a nearly 100-foot tower where there are expansive views that include portions of five states. The Mount Greylock State Reserve was created in 1898 and includes a network of hiking trails.

Beckley Furnace State Park

The Beckley Furnace Industrial Monument is a state-owned historic site that is the best preserved iron furnace in the region. The furnace produced "pig iron" that was used to manufacture guns, anchors, cannonballs, and train wheels. The furnace sits on the bank of the Blackberry River in North Canaan, Connecticut, and is part of a small state park.

Hancock Shaker Village

Western Massachusetts and upper New York State welcomed Shakers, one of 19th-century America's best-known communitarian sects. The Hancock (Massachusetts) Shaker Village is an open-air museum and interprets Shaker culture. The original village was organized in 1790 and was active until 1960. This National Register of Historic Places site includes 20 historic buildings, the most famous of which are the Round Stone Barn constructed in 1826 and the 1830 Brick Building that served as dormitory housing for more than 100 brothers and sisters.

Historic Towns/Town Centers

The NHA includes many historic buildings, the earliest of which date to 1734 when English settlement of the area began. Historic town centers include meetinghouses, commons, homes, and public buildings, more than 50 of which are on the National Register of Historic Places. Some historic homes now serve as museums, including Bidwell House (1750), Colonel John Ashley House (1735), and Gay-Hoyt House (1775). There are also three historic covered bridges in the region. The Berkshire 18th Century Trail, a route through the Berkshires, connects six historic homes.

Crane and Company Old Stone Mill Rag Room

The Crane Company manufactured paper beginning in 1801 and obtained a monopoly contract with the US government to provide paper for the nation's currency, which it still holds today. The Rag Room was built in 1844 and is the only remaining building; it's listed on the National Register of Historic Places and now serves as a museum.

Arrowhead (Herman Melville House)

This property was the home of author Herman Melville in the middle part of the 19th century. It was here that he wrote his most famous book, Moby-Dick. The building is now owned by the Berkshire County Historical Society and is a museum; the building is on the National Register of Historic Places. The NHA's Melville Trail leads visitors to other sites important to Melville and his writing.

The Mount

Edith Wharton was a novelist, short story writer, and designer in the late 19th and early 20th centuries. She was the first woman to win the Pulitzer Prize in Literature. She and her husband built their summer house, The Mount, on 113 acres. The entire estate, including the main house, stables, formal gardens, and sculpted landscape, is considered a work of art.

Housatonic River

This historic river runs the length of the NHA and is a great paddling adventure and includes both flat water and white water sections. Paddlers will enjoy the lovely forested surroundings and a string of historic villages. *A Paddling Guide to the Housatonic River in Berkshire County* will help plan your trip.

Great Falls punctuates the lovely Upper Housatonic River.

Walking/Hiking and Biking

Hiking and biking are pleasant ways to experience the beauty and history of this NHA. Several biking routes through this inspiring landscape, including the 45-mile HouBike Trail, are described in downloadable material on the Upper Housatonic Valley website. Hiking is also popular; a good place to start planning your adventure is the downloadable Northwest Connecticut and Litchfield Hills Hiking Trail Map on the NHA website. And don't forget to take a least a few steps on the famous Appalachian Trail (see above).

Tanglewood's Concert Hall is located in Berkshire County, Massachusetts, and is the summer home of the Boston Symphony Orchestra.

Walking is the best way to see and appreciate the NHA's many historic towns and greens.

Performing Arts Heritage Trail
This route through the NHA (described on the Upper Housatonic Valley website) links many of the region's performing arts sites, venues, and festivals. Examples include the Mahaiwe Performing Arts Center, Tanglewood, Berkshire Theatre Festival, Infinity Music Hall, and Shakespeare & Company.

African American Heritage Trail
This route through NHA towns honors African Americans who advanced the cause of freedom and African American identity. Examples include the boyhood homesite of W. E. B. Du Bois, the Colonel Ashley Home where Elizabeth "Mum Bett" Freeman was enslaved, and the Samuel Harrison House, the home of the 54th Massachusetts Regiment chaplain who protested discriminatory pay practices for African Americans.

Native American Heritage Trail
This route through the NHA invites visitors to view the region through a Native American lens. Mohican Indians were scattered across the region prior to European-American settlement. Unfortunately, these people were dispossessed of their land and were ultimately removed from the area. However, their descendants hope that this trail will contribute "mending the hoop" by reestablishing the importance of the area to their history and culture. Important sites include Stockbridge's Indiantown, Bidwell House and Grounds (where there's a walking tour of Native land and way of life), Kampoosa Bog (an archeological site), and Skatekook (an early land agreement).

For more information about Upper Housatonic Valley and to help plan your visit, see the area's official website (housatonicheritage.org) and the website of the National Park Service (nps .gov/places/upper-housatonic-valley -national-heritage-area.htm).

Wheeling National Heritage Area
State: West Virginia
Description: Wheeling is a historic city on the banks of the Ohio River and in the foothills of the Appalachian Mountains; it's known for early access to major transportation routes that stimulated industry, its modern transformation to a center of advanced communications technology, health, and education, and its preservation and reuse of historic buildings.

Sample Attractions:
- Victorian Old Town
- Wheeling Artisan Center
- Wheeling Island Historic District
- Historic Walking Tours

Wheeling is a small, historic town on the western side of West Virginia's panhandle that projects north from the main body of the state. The city sits on the shores of the Ohio River and in the foothills of the Appalachian Mountains. Part of the city includes a large island (Wheeling Island) in the Ohio River. Wheeling is part of the tri-state area, commonly called the "Ohio Valley."

The historic prominence of the city is related largely to its location on major transportation routes. Of course, the Ohio River was an important commercial route that carried people and freight over a wide geographic area. Wheeling was also served by the National Road, the nation's first major road constructed by the federal government. The road ran 620 miles, connecting the Potomac and Ohio Rivers, was constructed in the first half of the 19th century, and was the route for thousands of settlers heading west. The Baltimore and Ohio (B&O) Railroad reached Wheeling in 1853, connecting it to Pennsylvania, Maryland, and the Northeast.

The happy confluence of these three major transportation routes—river, road, and rail—favored industrial development of the city by making it easy to import raw materials and export finished products. By the late 19th century, Wheeling had developed into the state's largest industrial center. Nicknamed "Nail City" (a local sports team still uses this moniker), Wheeling's mills fashioned sheets of pig iron that were cut into nails as well as worked into other products including boiler plates, stoves, barrel rings, and decorative ironwork. Tobacco, glass, and steel were also produced on an industrial scale. Wheeling also played an important role in the American labor movement; it was one of the only cities in the country to refuse an Andrew Carnegie gift of a free library because of Carnegie's poor labor record. Some residents grew prosperous from industry and commerce and built fine houses, many of them on Wheeling Island (see below).

However, as happened in many other industrial cities, the Great Depression and changes in industry led to the city's decline in the middle of the 20th century. The city evolved by restoring and protecting its architectural and industrial heritage as the foundation of its active and successful program of tourism. The city has also modernized as a center of advanced communications technology, health, and education. Establishment of Wheeling National Heritage Area (Wheeling) was a major step forward in developing the city's heritage-based tourism economy. The NHA is managed by Wheeling Heritage, a non-profit group that works with many partner organizations, including the National Park Service. The mission of Wheeling Heritage is to be a catalyst for revitalization of the city, preserving its heritage, collaborating with partners, investing in the downtown and riverfront areas, and engaging citizens in this work.

Wheeling Heritage is a powerhouse organization. Wheeling Heritage Media is a subsidiary and creates a variety of multi-media experiences to tell Wheeling's story, both past and present. Weelunk (derived from a Native

American word) is an online magazine that encourages conservation and keeps readers in touch with important happenings in the city. Wheeling Heritage made key investments in the former Wheeling Stamp Company building, a project that was recognized by the National Trust for Historic Preservation. It also partnered in the revitalization of the landmark Capitol Theatre (home to Jamboree USA and the Wheeling Symphony), built the award-winning riverfront amphitheater, Heritage Point, and developed the Artisan Center, a renovated industrial building with a three-story atrium in the heart of downtown (see below). Wheeling Heritage also spearheaded a grassroots restoration of Mt. Wood Cemetery, West Virginia's oldest extant cemetery. Wheeling Heritage Trail and interpretive signage and historic markers around the city help visitors and outdoor enthusiasts learn about the city's past and present. It has developed a suite of programs to train and encourage entrepreneurship among city residents. Other projects and programs the organization works on include public art, city planning, business management, grants programs, historic tax credits, and architectural design guidelines and assistance.

Attractions

Wheeling is a relatively small NHA, but it includes a host of attractions that interpret its rich history and that take advantage of its attractive setting. Examples include historic homes and buildings, the Ohio River, art centers, museums, parks, and walking trails and tours. It's comforting to know that Wheeling is known as "the friendly city."

Wheeling Island Historic District includes hundreds of buildings, most of them residences built from the mid-19th century to the early 20th century.

Victorian Old Town

North Main Street runs along a high bluff above the Ohio River and features nearly seventy 19th-century Victorian-era residences. This area constitutes the North Wheeling Historic District and helps ensure the preservation and architectural integrity of these buildings.

Wheeling Artisan Center

The Wheeling Artisan Center showcases the work of local artists, with a special emphasis on West Virginia and Appalachian influences. The center is housed in a dramatic, six-million dollar renovation of three downtown historic buildings that are now joined as one, and includes a three-story atrium. The building includes a restaurant, the "Made in Wheeling" exhibit, event space, and the offices of Wheeling Heritage.

Wheeling Island Historic District

Listed on the National Register of Historic Places, this historic area includes hundreds of buildings, most of them residences constructed in the mid-to-late 19th century and early 20th century. There are also public buildings, a church, two bridges, Wheeling Island Baseball Park, Belle Island Park, and the Wheeling Suspension Bridge (see below).

Wheeling Heritage Port

Opened in 2002, Wheeling Heritage Port connects the city of Wheeling to the Ohio River. The port includes parks, river access, an amphitheater, an entry plaza, a river-edge walkway, mooring facilities, and pathways that connect downtown with the water's edge.

Capitol Theatre

Wheeling's historic Capitol Theatre opened in 1928 and was a state-of-the-art performance space, costing a million dollars and

The Wheeling Custom House was built in 1863 but was later renamed West Virginia Independence Hall.

seating 3,000 patrons. The theatre is now home to the Wheeling Symphony Orchestra.

West Virginia Independence Hall

West Virginia became the 35th state in 1863; but six years before this, construction began

The small historic city of Wheeling, West Virginia, sits on the banks of the Ohio River.

on the Wheeling Custom House, headquarters for federal offices in the Western District of Virginia. The building was the setting for great public debates, including the role of slavery in the new state (which opposed slavery). This grand building was renamed West Virginia Independence Hall and has been fully restored and features a museum on the first floor and self-guided tours.

Wheeling Suspension Bridge

This historic bridge was completed in 1849 and was the largest suspension bridge in the world for a few years. It spans the main channel of the Ohio River and connects Wheeling with Wheeling Island. The bridge, a National Historic Landmark, currently doesn't carry motorized vehicles and makes a scenic and exciting walk or bike ride.

Wheeling Heritage Trails

Taking advantage of Wheeling's railroad heritage, the city has established the Wheeling Heritage Trail, a network of 18 miles of paved trails that were once railroad tracks. The trail runs along the Ohio River and throughout the city.

Historic Walking Tours

Wheeling Heritage has developed seven self-guiding walking tours that showcase multiple dimensions of the city's Heritage. The tours focus on historic churches, North Wheeling, Warwood, Civil War, National Road, South Wheeling, and the Schmulbach Brewery Complex. Tour brochures can be downloaded from Wheeling Heritage's website (see below).

Wheeling's Oglelbay Park offers outdoor recreation to residents and visitors.

Wheeling Park

This is Wheeling's first public park, established in 1925. The park is over 400 acres and features a golf course, lake, pools, tennis, ice skating, playground, and picnicking.

The Museums of Oglebay Institute

The Mansion and Glass Museums interpret Wheeling's history from pioneer times through the Victorian Era. The Glass Museum includes 3,000 examples of Wheeling glass and offers glass-making demonstrations and workshops. The museum complex includes Wymer's General Store & Sinclair Pharmacy.

For more information about Wheeling and to help plan your visit, see the area's official website (wheeling heritage.org) and the website of the National Park Service (nps.gov/places /wheeling-national-heritage-area.htm).

Yuma Crossing National Heritage Area

State: Arizona

Description: Located at a historic crossing of the 1,400-mile Colorado River, this NHA includes important elements of the region's natural and cultural history; water from the river irrigates lands that grow much of the winter fresh vegetables for the nation and the area has been a cultural crossroads for Native Americans, Spanish explorers, Hispanic Americans, and Anglo-Americans, and this is reflected in the NHA's rich and diverse culture.

Sample Attractions:

- Colorado River State Historic Park
- Yuma Territorial Prison State Historic Park
- Yuma Historic Downtown Entertainment District
- Juan Bautista de Anza National Historic Trail

Yuma Crossing is deeply embedded in the history, culture, environment, and economy of the American Southwest. In fact, it's often called the "Gateway to the Great Southwest." As the name suggests, there is a historic crossing here of the 1,400-mile Colorado River. This legendary river drains much of the American Southwest, carved the Grand Canyon, and now provides water and power for millions of people in the seven southwestern states. For prehistoric people and even well into historic times, crossing this wild river was treacherous. But the two massive granite outcroppings at Yuma narrowed the river, offering the only reasonable crossing for many miles along the lower reaches of this great river that runs generally north/ south and divides Arizona and California. And the rest, as they say, is history.

And speaking of history, Yuma Crossing National Heritage Area (Yuma Crossing) is a grand celebration of the past—and present—of this important and interesting region. In prehistoric times, the crossing drew the interest of the Patayan and Quechan Native Americans. Recorded history began with the arrival of Spanish explorer Hernando de Alarcon in 1540 as part of Francisco Vasquez de Coronado's exploration of the Southwest. Later, the Spanish used the crossing as part of what was sometimes called the Sonora Road to access what is now California. In the middle of the 19th century, many California gold rushers crossed the river here to reach the foothills of California's Sierra Nevada Mountains. A pivoting railroad bridge was constructed in 1877, and the Ocean-to-Ocean Bridge was built in 1915 as part of Interstate Highway 80. Yuma is the oldest city established on the Colorado River. The greater Yuma community solicited designation of the area as a national heritage area in the late 1990s, and the NHA was established in 2000. Much of the area is on the National Register of Historic Places and is a National Historic Landmark.

As it has been for centuries, the river and its water are the focal point of much of the NHA. Throughout the 20th century, the Colorado River was transformed by a series of large dams and reservoirs to store and conserve precious water, generate electricity, control flooding, benefit navigation, and irrigate surrounding lands. The largest and most widely known dams and reservoirs are the Hoover Dam and associated Lake Mead and the Glen Canyon Dam and associated Lake

Powell, both well upstream of Yuma. This coordinated program of water development and management was the vision of President Theodore Roosevelt and was carried out by the federal Bureau of Reclamation. Perhaps nowhere has water for irrigation been more evident than in the Yuma region. These once arid lands benefit from a large-scale and sophisticated irrigation system that now provides an astounding 95 percent of winter fresh vegetables for the nation, a multi-billion-dollar industry conducted on 90,000 acres. If you eat a salad in the winter, it was probably grown in Yuma. In fact, the Lower Colorado River is often referred to as "America's Nile," referencing the way its dams and reservoirs have created a globally significant fertile valley, and the Yuma region is known as "Winter Vegetable Capital."

But this system of dams and reservoirs has a downside as well, lowering river levels in the Yuma region and making adjacent soils highly saline. Consequently, native vegetation along the river died and was replaced by monocultures of more sterile and less aesthetic salt cedar, and this dense vegetation cut off access to the river from the city of Yuma. This problem is now being successfully addressed through leadership of this NHA, along with partner organizations, including the Quechan Indian Tribe, City of Yuma, Arizona Fish and Game, Bureau of Reclamation, and Bureau of Land Management. Almost 500 acres of natural wetlands have been restored through planting of nearly 200,000 indigenous trees (cottonwoods, mesquite and willows) and native grasses.

One of Yuma Crossing's most important themes is the area's heritage as a cultural crossroads, featuring the intersection

Railroad and automobile bridges constructed at Yuma continued the long tradition of carrying people and freight across the Colorado River.

of Native American, Hispanic-American, Anglo-American, and African American residents as manifested in the area's architecture, art, music, food, and folkways. As noted above, these cultures have all played an important role in the history of the Yuma region, play active roles in the management of the NHA, and are reflected in the rich mix of cultures represented in Yuma's downtown entertainment district.

Yuma Crossing is managed by the non-profit Yuma Crossing National Heritage Area Corporation, an 11-member board of directors that's especially diverse. Its goals include environmental conservation, historic restoration and preservation, public education, and economic development. The NHA encompasses seven square miles in Yuma, Arizona, and this historic cultural landscape features the commanding presence of the Lower Colorado River with a backdrop of Castle Dome and the Chocolate Mountains of Arizona and California. Given environmental effects of climate change, including hotter and drier weather, along with steadily increasing demand for Colorado River water,

Yuma Crossing will have to be creative to find a long-term sustainable future for the region. But as the NHA confidently states,

> Yuma's residents have embraced a confluence of Native American, Hispanic, Black, and Anglo cultures while building a strong economic foundation of agriculture, the military, and tourism. A rich legacy of historic, cultural, and natural scenic resources only strengthens that future.

Attractions

Yuma Crossing offers a host of visitor attractions that include historic sites, parks, museums, and recreation activities that include birding, hiking, biking, kayaking, and sightseeing. Important attractions include the following.

Colorado River State Historic Park

This state park is located on a portion of the grounds of the old US Army Quartermaster Depot (QMD) established in 1864. The QMD served as a storage yard and a military supply center for fourteen military posts in the Southwest, maintaining a six months' supply of ammunition, clothing, and food at all times. It's also home to Yuma Crossing Discovery Center and features "must see" things to do in Yuma Crossing, exhibits, movie theater, and local arts gallery.

Yuma Territorial Prison State Historic Park

The Yuma Territorial Prison opened in 1876, and though it developed a reputation for its harsh conditions, it had modern conveniences

The guard tower at Yuma Territorial Prison State Park opened in 1876.

of electricity, running water, and flush toilets. When it closed in 1907, some called it the Country Club on the Colorado. The park sits on a bluff overlooking the Colorado River. Snap your own mugshot using the original mirror that created a simultaneous front and side profile in one photo.

Fort Yuma

Fort Yuma was constructed on the California side of the river in 1858 to provide protection to travelers crossing the Colorado River to reach the goldfields of California. It's now part of the Fort Yuma Indian Reservation and several historic buildings have been preserved or reconstructed.

Yuma Historic Downtown Entertainment District

Main Street and Madison Avenue define the central area of downtown Yuma where you'll find restaurants, bars, shops, galleries and more. The area is highly walkable.

Yuma's Historic Downtown Entertainment District is highly walkable.

Juan Bautista de Anza National Historic Trail

Juan Bautista de Anza National Historic Trail is a unit of the National Park System and traces the 1,200-mile journey to establish the first non-Native settlement at San Francisco Bay in 1775-76. Yuma Crossing overlooks Camps 39-42 of this historic journey.

East and West Wetlands

Ecological restoration of these areas that lie directly across the river from one another began in 2002 and has triggered a huge increase in the number and diversity of wildlife, especially birds. The wetlands include several trails and paths to walk or cycle. There are also playgrounds, picnic spots, trails, disc golf, and access to the river for fishing, swimming, and floating the river. Delightful Centennial Beach was developed to help celebrate Yuma's one hundredth anniversary.

Local Parks and Trails

Contiguous local parks and trails along the Colorado River offer visitors three miles of outdoor recreation opportunities. Walk or bike these trails and dip your toes in the Colorado River at lovely Gateway Park.

For more information about Yuma Crossing and to help plan your visit, see the area's official website (yumaheritage.com) and the National Park Service website (nps.gov/places/yuma-crossing-national-heritage-area.htm).

BIBLIOGRAPHY

Barrett, B. 2003. Roots for the National Heritage Family Tree. *The George Wright Forum* 20(2), 41-49.

Barrett, B. 2005. National Heritage Areas: Places on the Land, Places in the Mind. *The George Wright Forum* (20), 14-15.

Barrett, B. 2013. National Heritage Areas: Evaluating Past Practices as a Foundation for the Future. *Proceedings of the Faros Conference on Landsape and Greenway Planning.* 4(1), Article 66.

Barrett, B. and N. Mitchell. 2003. Stewardship of Heritage Areas. *The George Wright Forum.* 20(2), 5-7.

Barrett, B. and N. Mitchell. 2016. Parks in Partnership. *A Thinking Person's Guide to America's National Parks.* New York: Brazziler, pp. 205-216.

Barrett, B. and E. Mahoney 2016. National Heritage Areas: Learning from 30 Years of Working to Scale. *The George Wright Forum* 33(2), pp. 163-174.

Barton, A. 2016. From Parks to Partnerships: National Heritage Areas and the Path to Collaborative Participation in the National Park Service's First 100 Years. *Natural Resources Journal (*56), 23-56.

Brown, J., N. Mitchell, and M. Beresford, eds. 2005. *The Protected Landscape Approach: Linking Nature, Culture and Community.* Gland, Switzerland: IUCN, World Commission on Protected Areas.

Bodurow, C. 2003. A Vehicle for Conserving and Interpreting Our Recent Industrial Heritage. *The George Wright Forum* 20(2), 68-88.

Eugster, G. 2003. Evolution of the Heritage Areas Movement. *The George Wright Forum* 20(2), 50-59.

Gates, L. and N. Morgan. Report from the Field: The Whole Is So Much More than the Sum of Its Parts. *The George Wright Forum* 20(2), 60-67.

Keiter, R. 2013. *To Conserve Unimpaired: The Evolution of the National Park Idea.* Washington, DC: Island Press.

Laven, D., N. Mitchell, and D. Wang. Eds. 2005. Examining Conservation Practice at the Landscape Scale. *The George Wright Forum,* 22(1), pp 5-9.

Laven, D., D. Krymkowski, C. Ventriss, R. Manning, and N. Mitchell. 2010. From Partnerships to Networks: New Approaches for Measuring US National Heritage Area Effectiveness. *Evaluation Review* (34), 271-298.

Laven, D., R. Manning, C. Ventriss, and N. Mitchell. 2010. Evaluating National Heritage Areas: Theory, Methods, and Application. *Environmental Management* (46), 195-212

Longstreth, R., ed. 2008. *Cultural Landscapes: Balancing Nature and Heritage in Preservation Practice.* Minneapolis and London: University of Minnesota Press.

Manning, R., R. Diamant, N. Mitchell, and D. Harmon. 2016. *A Thinking Person's Guide to America's National Parks*. New York; Brazziler.

Minteer, B. and R. Manning. eds. 2003. *Reconstructing Conservation: Finding Common Ground*. Washington, DC: Island Press.

Mitchell, B. 2003. International Models of Protected Landscapes. *The George Wright Forum* 20(2), 33-40.

National Parks Second Century Commission. 2009. *Advancing the National Park Idea*. Washington, DC: National Parks Conservation Association.

National Park Service Advisory Board. 2006. *Charting a Future for National Heritage Areas*. US National Park Service.

National Park Service. 2014. *A Call to Action: Preparing for a Second Century of Stewardship and Engagement*. Washington, DC: National Park Service.

Phillips, A. 2003. Turning Ideas on Their Head: The New Paradigm of Protected Areas. *The George Wright Forum* 20(2), 8-32.

Runte, A. 2010. *National Parks: The American Experience (Fourth edition)*. Boulder, CO: Taylor Trade Publishing.

Sellars, R. 1997. *Preserving Nature in the National Parks: A History*. New Haven, CT: Yale University Press.

Taylor, K., A. St. Clair, and N. Mitchell. ed. 2015. *Conserving Cultural Landscapes: Challenges and New Directions*. New York: Routledge.

Vincent, C. and L. Comay. 2014. Heritage Areas: Background, Proposals, and Current Issues. Washington, DC: Congressional Research Service.

nps.gov/heritageareas

nationalheritageareas.us

livinglandscapeobserver.net

ACKNOWLEDGMENTS

I'm thankful to many people for their help in preparing this guidebook. Elizabeth Vehmeyer, National Park Service Program Coordinator for National Heritage Areas, and staff member, Katie Durcan, were helpful in introducing me to key staff members at all of the National Heritage Areas and in reviewing this book's introductory material. Former National Park Service Program Coordinators for National Heritage Areas Brenda Barrett and Martha Raymond were also helpful in reviewing Part I of this book. All of these National Park Service staff have done a great deal to help advance the innovative concept and practice of National Heritage Areas. Staff members at all 54 National Heritage Areas were especially helpful in reviewing the chapters I prepared on their National Heritage Areas, adding their insights and correcting any errors and misinterpretations on my part. Because of their careful reviews, I feel much more confident about these chapters and so should readers. Thanks to Sara Capen, head of the Alliance of National Heritage Areas, for help in contacting staff at all the National Heritage Areas. I appreciate my colleague, Dr. Nora Mitchell, founding director of the National Park Service's Conservation Study Institute (now Stewardship Institute), for introducing me to National Heritage Areas and their innovative approach to conservation, and to my former doctoral student, Dr. Daniel Laven, for conducting such a progressive review of the effectiveness of National Heritage Areas. And thanks to Amy Lyons, Acquisitions Editor at Globe Pequot, for her interest in this guidebook and granting me the leeway to prepare it in the way that I thought was most effective; thanks as well to Kristen Mellitt, Production Editor, for her editorial assistance. As always, thanks to my wife and frequent coauthor, Martha, for her good advice and kind assistance.

Although Native Americans were poorly treated during much of American history, they are honored today in many US national heritage areas (Knife River Indian Villages, Northern Plains National Heritage Area).

ABOUT THE AUTHOR

Robert Manning is Steven Rubenstein Professor (Emeritus) at the University of Vermont where he taught the history, philosophy, and management of national parks and related areas. He is the founding Director of the Park Studies Laboratory which conducts a long-term program of research for the US National Park Service and other agencies and organizations. He's written a half dozen scholarly books on the national parks, as well as several popular books, including *A Thinking Person's Guide to America's National Parks* and *Walks of a Lifetime in America's National Parks.*

The author conducting field research at Capitol Reef National Park (Mormon Pioneer National Heritage Area)